Écart & Différance

Écart & Différance:

Merleau-Ponty and Derrida on Seeing and Writing

Edited by
M. C. Dillon

HUMANITIES PRESS
NEW JERSEY

First published in 1997 by
Humanities Press International, Inc.,
165 First Avenue, Atlantic Highlands, New Jersey 07716.

This collection © 1997 by Humanities Press International, Inc.,

Library of Congress Cataloging-in-Publication Data
Écart & différance : Merleau-Ponty and Derrida on seeing and writing /
   edited by M. C. Dillon
      p.   cm.
   Includes bibliographical references and index.
   ISBN 0–391–03989–X.—ISBN 0–391–03990–3 (pbk.)
   1. Difference (Philosophy) 2. Merleau-Ponty, Maurice, 1908–1961.
   3. Derrida, Jacques. 4. Postmodernism. 5. Deconstruction.
   I. Dillon, M. C. (Martin C.), 1938–.
   B809.9.E23 1996
   149'.9—dc20   96–16192
                                                  CIP

Printed in the United States of America

10 9 8 7 6 5 4 3 2 1

This book is dedicated to

George Alfred Schrader, Jr.

gentleman, teacher, scholar,
exemplary human being

Contents

PART II: EXPANSIONS

Preface

How is *écart* to be thought or experienced? What does *différance* signify? What do the resonances and differences between them portend? I have pondered these questions for more than a decade, and attempted to consolidate my thinking in the essay I have written to introduce this volume.

I have also solicited efforts from other scholars I respect—creative and independent thinkers who know the work of Merleau-Ponty and Derrida, but whose perspectives necessarily diverge from my own—inviting them to contribute to a volume devoted to the theme of *écart* and *différance*. The results are collected here, in essays written specifically for this book, and published for the first time here.

The project that culminated in the present manuscript was prompted by an invitation to organize a session for the 18th annual meeting of the International Association for Philosophy and Literature held at Duquesne University, 13–16 May 1993, which was focused on the theme of "Visibility and Expressivity." I decided on the title, "Écart & Différance: Seeing and Writing in Merleau-Ponty and Derrida," presented an early version of the essay that appears as the Introduction to this volume, and Bernard Flynn, Robert Vallier, David Ferris, and Glen Mazis delivered papers that developed into the essays appearing herein. It became apparent during the session that the subject matter warranted further exploration, although I was still unaware of the full extent of its fecundity and centrality to contemporary debate.

I then scoured my files in search of scholars known to me personally or by reputation upon whom I could depend to generate a diverse range of perspectives and a broad scope of topical foci. I wanted to find thinkers who would represent prevailing viewpoints in the general problematic, and others who would expand that theme into such specific areas as metaphysics and time, literature and art, and politics and economics. The structure of the book set forth in the table of contents reflects this approach. Once again, the results of my solicitation were encouraging: well over half of the scholars I approached expressed a willingness to interrupt their own projects to write on the subject of *écart* and *différance*, and

to do so within a relatively short period of time. I offered my essay as a position paper to which the contributors could respond—
or not—as they saw fit.

Given the diversity, experience, and merit of the contributors to
this collection, it may not be unwarranted to suggest that the cu-
mulative result of this project is to provide a representative sampling
of the best thinking in this generation of North American scholars
on an issue whose importance to contemporary philosophy may
be equaled by a handful of others but is surpassed by none.

This volume makes no claim to have covered the subject matter
in a comprehensive way; there are other voices still to be heard.
The intent is to open discourse, not to undertake an ill-conceived
attempt to bring it to closure. The questions concerning how to
think difference and identity, alterity and ipseity, separation and
relation, fission and fusion, alienation and community, and so forth
both simplify and compound as thinking progresses: one sees patterns emerge, but these patterns, in turn, suggest further lines of
inquiry. This collection does not address itself directly to questions that emerge in the philosophy of science, gender studies, value
theory, multiculturalism, and other areas of research. It does, however, purport to open lines of thought which do have direct relevance to these questions. This book wants to evoke its own
surpassing.

The terms *écart* and *différance* are discrete; their relevance is
unbounded by traditional disciplines because they function both
to define the limits of these disciplines and, at the same time, to
invoke the breaching of any such delimitation. I cannot demonstrate this claim here, but I can elucidate it by offering a caricalog
indicating the directions taken by the scholars assembled here in
response to the themes of *écart* and *différance*.

Caricalog

M. C. Dillon argues that continental philosophy since Heidegger has searched for thought capable of thinking beyond the ontological difference, the difference between Being and beings. Surveying the field, one finds two leading contenders: Merleau-Ponty's *écart* and Derrida's *différance*. Both terms designate a non-coincidence of thought with itself and a parallel divergence of thought with its object. This isomorphism of function, however, is not an isomorphism of content: *écart* and *différance* are different ways of thinking non-coincidence and divergence, and the differences between them are philosophically consequential. For Merleau-Ponty, *écart* names a de-centering modeled on perceptual presence, and for Derrida, *différance* names an original repetition modeled on arche-writing which denies the possibility of perceptual presence. These differences mark points of philosophical irreconcilability, the implications of which are set forth in this essay.

Thomas W. Busch finds in Derrida's theory and practice of deconstruction a "grammatological reduction" at work which is "even more radical" than Husserl's phenomenological reduction and "has the effect of decontextualizing difference, of retiring signs from their specific functions in order to discover . . . their common decontextualized nature." This separates his thought from Merleau-Ponty's, for whom meaning cannot be separated from the "practices . . . possibilities, latencies, and pregnancies of the phenomenal situation." Under Busch's analysis, the difference between these two thinkers may be seen to reside in the manner in which they regard the phenomenon: "Merleau-Ponty places faith in the phenomenon, while Derrida views it with suspicion."

David S. Ferris presents a clear and cogent defense against the charge of semiological reductionism, arguing that "in any reflection on language, the difference between language and things can never be an issue . . . precisely because things have no determining role to play in either our understanding of language or how it represents, which is to say, they have no determining role in how we decide to understand perception." As Ferris reads Merleau-Ponty, the figure of the chiasm refers to an *écart* within language between a sign and its meaning, not a divergence between language and things.

Dorothea Olkowski proposes less to pit Merleau-Ponty and Derrida against one another than to delimit "the process by which each assesses language," and to identify the purposes, methods, and effects of the two philosophical approaches. To this end, she analyzes the ways in which Merleau-Ponty and Derrida address Husserl and Saussure, marking their points of appropriation and recoil and the underlying reasons. Here she takes a fresh look at such issues as: diacriticality, eidetic grammar, diachronic versus synchronic approaches to language and the related problem of accounting for change, the agon of privilege between spoken and written languages, and the relations of language to power and institutionalization. She concludes that although "it is true that Merleau-Ponty maintains an ontology of expressive acts, while Derrida establishes the role of inscription as the very creation of actors, the articulations of *écart* and *différance* remain very close to one another. . . . Merleau-Ponty's *auteur* theory of expression is less an ontology of a subject than it is a world ontology [whereas Derrida's] *différance* proclaims itself as writing . . . to trace out the possibility of an ethics of thought that is . . . sensitive to the always and ever originating functioning of thought as differentiation."

Patrick Burke raises a question which "can never be asked" by Derrida, hence "is forever absent" from Derridian discourse. This is the question of self-reference applied to the notion of *différance* in its functional role as transcendental condition for the possibility of differentiation. One cannot ask who or what differs, because "the question of *différance* already presupposes . . . the play of *différance* as the 'constitutive source' of all questioning." Yet, Burke argues, the question is a legitimate one, despite the fact that it is impossible to answer it without appealing to some notion of presence. He goes on to show that Merleau-Ponty does address the question, that his answer does indeed invoke an understanding of presence, but that the understanding of presence invoked excludes the thesis of absolute self-coincidence Derrida takes to be definitive of presence. Presence for Merleau-Ponty incorporates a fission, dehiscence, or *écart* within the flesh of the world that allows for the self-reference of reversibility, a mode of self-differentiation which allows the flesh to question itself. The flesh of the world is present to itself in a mode of interrogation which allows it to relate to itself without coinciding with itself. Thus, the question precluded by the play of *différance* is essential to the auto-interrogation definitive of the non-coincidental presence of flesh to itself named by *écart*.

Leonard Lawlor acknowledges the similarities between Merleau-Ponty and Derrida, but focuses his essay on "the deep difference between them." He provides textual evidence from a wide range of texts from both authors—concentrating on Merleau-Ponty's later works and Derrida's earlier ones—to show that the difference between them "lies in the fact that Merleau-Ponty... interrogates the element of being, while Derrida... interrogates the element of writing. The difference between being and writing unfolds into the difference between a sort of positivity in Merleau-Ponty... understood in terms of content... and a sort of negativity in Derrida... understood in terms of form." This difference "brings about" a further, structural, difference between the circularity of flesh in Merleau-Ponty and the supplementarity of *différance* in Derrida, which sheds light on their differing uses of the term, *écart*: "For Merleau-Ponty, *écart* is a difference based in continuity, while for Derrida, *écart* is a difference based in discontinuity." Lawlor's essay takes the opposition between Merleau-Ponty and Derrida to have an ethical portent centering on the question of alterity, but leaves this thought to be developed in further work.

G. B. Madison engages Derridian *différance* from the standpoint of a careful and revivifying reading of Merleau-Ponty, and argues that the insights of the deconstruction of the metaphysics of presence can be retained without lapsing into the relativism of postmodern semiological reductionism, on the one hand, or the absolutism of "metaphysical referentialist-representationalism," on the other. Following a crisp vindication of "the existential subject"—"writing does not simply write itself... even deconstruction presupposes a subject who writes deconstructively"—Madison elaborates a notion of truth as "creative adequation" based on Merleau-Ponty's reference to "*le mouvement rétrograde du vrai*." Truth so conceived is not reified in "some kind of stagnant in-itself to be 'referred' to by transparent word-signs," but is rather *made* in a reflective reprise: "Strictly speaking, reality, like truth, is *not*; it becomes, it transpires, *elle s'écrit*, and the locus of its most eloquent... inscription is the human seeing/writing subject."

Joseph Margolis argues that the themes of *écart* and *différance* "are, finally, no more than two quintessentially... French versions of the never-ending effort to dismantle the Cartesian confidence that lies at the base of modern Western philosophy [and yet] they are great extravagances." They are extravagant in that they exceed the properly discursive domain of philosophy in the attempt to pursue "what is unsayable in the inclusive milieu of what can be said." Their pursuits differ, however: whereas Derrida "proceeds deconstructively to expose the fatuousness of every attempt . . . to fix the originary *différance* . . . Merleau-Ponty invents an *ur*-phenomenology by which to limn the 'genesis' of the phenomenological competence of the originating subjectivity which 'first' constitutes the intelligibility of the experienced world." Under Margolis's analysis, Merleau-Ponty abandons the realm of philosophy for that of myth in his attempt to recover in a cognitive way, through the notion of dehiscent flesh, "the *noncognitive* ground of the cognitive, the forestructuring preparation *of* cognition itself." Although Derrida does have a philosophical doctrine, which Margolis sees adumbrated in the assertion *"il n'y a pas de hors texte,"* and although deconstruction is "an ingenious adjunctive strategy" that serves the purpose of that doctrine, "deconstruction is not philosophy and cannot be." Deconstruction is a "parasitic strategy" which returns us to the problematic of *différance* but does not attempt to use the term to answer philosophical questions about the nature of what is. To function in that way, *différance* would have had to be "a word [or] a concept."

Shaun Gallagher raises the question of the reality of time in the traditional metaphysical form that the question takes in the philosophy of McTaggart, follows the question through a series of interpretations of *différance* and *écart*, and concludes with an assertion of the "pre-intentional reality of time" in which "reality" no longer functions as it does in traditional metaphysics. "Time transcends consciousness, not in the direction of the objective world. It transcends consciousness in the direction of the pre-intentional/corporeal dimension." In the course of his comprehensive and remarkably lucid treatment of key texts in Derrida, Merleau-Ponty, and contemporary critical literature, Gallagher presents fresh, convincing, and incisive reinterpretations of both *écart* and *différance*.

Dennis T. O'Connor takes his discourse on *écart* and *différance* to its authentic and "remarkably untidy" site, the abyss: a "work site . . . fearful in its dimensionalities." O'Connor devotes his thinking primarily to the dimension of time and specifically to the understanding of history set forth by Husserl in his essay "On the Origin of Geometry," which establishes a point of contact between Merleau-Ponty and Derrida, both of whom comment extensively on it. Seeking a link between Merleau-Ponty's treatment of "The Body as Expression and Speech," on the one hand, and his discussion of "The Cogito" and "Temporality," on the other, O'Connor finds Merleau-Ponty discovering "fundamental obscurity" at the point at which living flesh seeks to understand itself through its objectifications, that is, through its history, through the *écart* which is the temporal self-differentiation of flesh. It is this development of the Husserlian problematic that brings Merleau-Ponty into proximity with Derrida, who addresses it in his seminal *Introduction* to Husserl's essay and arrives at the same abyssal work site, at the "precarious openness of a question: the question of the origin of being as history," which can no more be ignored than it can be answered.

Glen A. Mazis brings together the *personae*, the nobodies, to be found in the texts of Merleau-Ponty, Derrida, and Joyce, and finds them embarked on odysseys which resonate with and illumine each other as they wander toward the non-origins from which they departed. "Bloom, the archetypal Jewish wanderer, revealed in passing after 700 pages of *Ulysses* text to not really be Jewish, is he Merleau-Ponty? Is the Jewish Derrida a Stephen Dedalus, the one who writes, but can't write a book, who gives a theory of the impossibility of language being its birth, yet lives circling within language's charms—a wanderer and a writer who tricks us into believing he has given an odyssey?" Mazis's responses to these auto-interrogations reveal startling affinities and congruences that mere happenstance could not convincingly explain, and that Derrida's own reflections on Molly's "yes" in "Ulysses Gramophone" cannot explain away. This essay projects the questions of *écart* and *différance* into a context that exceeds the philosophy and literature whence they emerged.

Robert Vallier provides a concise reading of a text mentioned in several of the essays contained herein, Derrida's *Memoirs of the Blind*, which is crucial to the project at hand because it is the sole work in which Derrida has thematically addressed the philosophy of Merleau-Ponty. In that text, Derrida proposes a re-reading of the later Merleau-Ponty, notably *The Visible and the Invisible*, and Vallier develops this venture by paying close attention to such crucial working notes as the two having to do with the *punctum caecum*, or blind point, on the retina, which is an invisible that makes vision possible. "The *punctum caecum*, that anatomical mark of blindness within the physiology of the body, by virtue of its being bodily, constitutes [an] irremediable absence. . . . It is the body that is the *point* of view, and therefore, the body that is blind." Vallier's reflections on the invisibility of the point of view lead him to a provocative juxtaposition of Merleau-Ponty and Derrida on the issue of "the logic of the self-portrait," the attempt of the artist to draw what he cannot see, his own point of view.

Hugh J. Silverman elucidates the notions of *écart* and *différance* by deploying them in an essay which interprets the postmodern as interrupting the unity conceived by the modern as constitutive of identity. The modern incorporates within itself "breaks, ruptures, fissures between the presentable and the unpresentable," between the visible presentation and the invisible which is represented, but seeks to overcome these differences in a movement of totalization. The postmodern, "inscribed in the modern" but differing from it, indefinitely defers totalization by marking the interruptions intrinsic to identity, by "cultivating the difference-to-oneself... that constitutes identity." Silverman illustrates the postmodern interruption with concrete examples drawn from painting, architecture, politics, and culture at large.

Bernard Flynn describes the affinity between *écart* and *différance* as deriving from a shared rejection of any "ultimate grounding in the notion of a constituting subject," but points (1) to a consequential divergence concentrated on Derrida's attempt to think beyond "our insertion into the *there is* of the world" with his "infrastructure" of *différance* and (2) to Merleau-Ponty's use of *écart* to signify the impossibility of any such "next step." Flynn then shows that one important consequence of this divergence lies in the political domain, where Derrida contends that "any positive characterization" of European identity is impossible because it would be totalizing (under the headings of singularity, universality, exemplarity), but Merleau-Ponty allows for historically contingent, hence non-totalized, descriptions of "our insertion into the *there is*," taken here as the "flesh of history."

Wilhelm Wurzer takes up Derrida's notion of capital, views it through *écart*, and finds a divergence within the divergence designated by the term itself. Derrida, freeing the term from Marxian delimitation, sees capital, "the other heading of presence," as "deidentified," as "gathering itself in the difference with itself," as pure divergence. When regarded from the standpoint of Merleau-Ponty, however, capital takes on the appearance of "wild being," thereby silently diverging from postmodern textuality.

Acknowledgments

Many of the papers appearing here were presented at meetings of the Merleau-Ponty Circle and the International Association for Philosophy and Literature. Thanks are due to the members of those organizations for thoughts that enrich this work and for the collegiality that sustains all efforts of this kind.

Among the names that do not appear in the table of contents are others whose contributions to this book, albeit indirect, were indispensable in bringing it into existence.

Jeanne Constable and Melanie Yaworski shuffled manuscripts through the mail, orchestrated the correspondence, smiled through the telephones, caught the blunders before they became embarrassments, operated the machinery of production, and worked as long as was required to get the job done well.

Cindy Kaufman-Nixon, Editorial Manager at Humanities Press, in the role of benign shepherd, guided the manuscript and its editor through darkness into light. Keith Ashfield, President of Humanities Press, supported the project from its inception and graciously agreed to make the manuscript available to a wider audience by printing it in paperback as well as hardcover. Terry Mares, the Production Editor, moved the manuscript along briskly with the ease of a practiced professional. William Zeisel, the Copy Editor, found the flaws, large and small, and polished them out. And Milt Silver's discerning eye saw the things that the rest of us missed.

Hugh Silverman provided encouragement, counsel, and able assistance throughout.

Tom Blake once again exercised his wizardry to bring order out of chaos in the cyberspace where this book has passed through cycles of virtual incarnations.

Wesley Rehberg, in a gesture of grace, made time in a life devoted to ministering to the needs of others to compile the indexes. He did this onerous but important work with the acuity that follows from genuine understanding.

Yuk-Yiu Ip, Kai Lundgren-Williams, Elizabeth Morrison, Michael Motta, Deborah O'Connell-Brown, Mary Pernal, Paul Rector, Carolin Woolson, Isaac Ruedin, Raymond Simon, Joseph Tomaras, Taze Yanick, Jenita Young, and Tim Young contributed to the development and refinement of the manuscript.

The chairs of the Department of Philosophy at Binghamton University during the time this volume was being assembled, Stephen David Ross and Anthony Preus, promoted the endeavor with contributions which were not only administrative but also intellectual and moral in nature.

Binghamton University and The Foundation of the State University of New York provided generous grants in support of travel and administration.

Introduction:
Écart & Différance

M. C. Dillon

How are we to think difference, differentiation, alterity, otherness?

1

Difference must be thought in relation to identity. Identity and difference are correlates, terms which define themselves by opposing each other: a thing can differ from other things only by retaining its own identity; a thing can differ from itself in one way only by retaining its identity in another. Indeed, the classical formulation of the principle of identity as A = A requires numerical differentiation in order to assert essential identity.

Heidegger thought difference in relation to identity. In Heidegger's thinking, the principle of identity cannot be dissociated from the "ontological difference," the difference between Being and beings.

> The principle [Satz] appears at first in the form of a fundamental principle [Grundsatz], that is, of the ground of beings. This principle in the sense of a statement has in the meantime become a principle bearing the characteristics of a spring that departs from Being as the ground of beings, and thus springs into the abyss [Abgrund]. But this abyss is neither empty nothingness [das leere Nichts] nor murky confusion, but rather: appropriation [das Er-eignis]. In appropriation vibrates the essence [das Wesen] of what speaks as language, which at one time was called the house of Being. "Principle of identity" means now: a spring demanded by the essence of identity [das Wesen der Identität] because it needs that spring if the *belonging* together of man and Being is to attain the essential light [Wesenslicht] of appropriation.[1]

The passage appears toward the end of Heidegger's essay "The Principle of Identity." It summarizes a line of thought which will have to be traced and interpreted if we are to understand the bearing of the thought upon the question at hand.

Heidegger argues that the principle of identity asserts the "unity with itself," or self-identity of beings, which is a necessary condition

1

for science.[2] He also states that the "whole of Western European thinking" rests on the principle of identity insofar as this thinking is predicated on the assumption of the unity of Being as such.[3] Then he goes on to interpret identity as "the Same [τὸ αὐτό, *das Selbe*]" as that term appears in Parmenides's fragment: "For the same perceiving (thinking) as well as being" (Heidegger's translation).[4]

This assertion of the sameness of thinking and Being provokes Heidegger to query the meaning of "Sameness" and to venture the interpretation that Sameness means "belonging together [*Zusammengehörigkeit*]." Belonging together, in turn, can be interpreted as either (a) synthesis, necessary connection, or as (b) a belonging, not to be *represented* as the unity of *togetherness* but rather to be *experienced* as "the *belonging* together of man and Being [*Mensch und Sein*]" (*Identity and Difference*, hereafter I&D, 31/94). The first interpretation (a) presupposes that the two are separate or different and must be brought together. Heidegger indicates a preference for the second (b), which regards the relationship between humanity and Being as definitive of what humanity essentially is. As I interpret this distinction, Heidegger is asserting an ontological priority of the relationship of belonging over at least one of the relata, humanity.[5]

Actually, for Heidegger, the relationship turns out to be prior to both relata, both Being and humanity. Heidegger proposes to think Being "according to its original meaning" as presence (*Anwesen*), and then asserts that "it is man . . . alone who lets Being arrive as presence [*An-wesen*]" (I&D 31/95). Heidegger then names the relationship, the belonging to each other of humanity and Being, as appropriation (*Ereignis*).[6]

Granting ontological priorityx to appropriation constitutes a spring, a leap away from the traditional representations of humanity as subject separate from Being as the ground of beings. In traditional metaphysics, the separation of humanity and Being constitutes an abyss, a disconnection between humanity and its ground, which thinking tries to restore through dialectical or synthetic representation. But Heidegger, interpreting the principle of identity as asserting a Sameness or belonging together of humanity and Being, displaces the abyss with appropriation, and posits this relationship as prior to the representation of humanity and Being as separate from each other.[7]

Identity is, thus, a sameness that is not an equivalence. Appropriation is the origin of identity in the metaphysical sense expressed in the principle that A = A, but that understanding is errant:

Er-eignis subtends the ontological bifurcation of identity and difference, but the bifurcation obscures its source.[8] Being as presence is not identical to the thinking of humanity, but the two belong together in the primal relationship of appropriation.

This brings us to the penultimate sentence of the opening passage.

> In appropriation vibrates the essence of what speaks as language, which at one time was called the house of Being.[9]

The essence/being (*Wesen*) of language vibrates (*schwingt*) in appropriation, in the relationship between Being as presence and the thinking of humanity that underlies the bifurcation of identity and difference.

This thought marks a turning point or crisis in the development of contemporary continental philosophy. The terms of the triad, presence—humanity—language, and the triad itself, have been reconceived as thinkers following Heidegger have sought to develop his thinking beyond the bifurcations or oppositions constitutive of traditional metaphysics.[10]

2

Derrida, whom I take to be the key figure in the development of postmodern thought, took his departure from Heidegger by rejecting the conception of ontological difference in favor of the nonconcept of *différance*. He rejected Heidegger's ontological difference because he believed it to be grounded in the conception of Being as presence, which betrayed itself under deconstruction to be founded upon the very "onto-theo-logical constitution of metaphysics" which Heidegger had brought to light in an essay he wrote just before "The Principle of Identity." Derrida's own position is closer to an earlier Heideggerian thought, expressed twenty-two years before the essay just considered, that "it is in words and language that things first come into being and are."[11] This standpoint, the standpoint of semiological reductionism,[12] sets Derrida at a distance from Heidegger's later thought that the *Wesen* from which language springs belongs within the domain of appropriation.

Merleau-Ponty also departed from Heidegger's ontological difference, but took a different direction. Whereas Heidegger took voɛìv in Parmenides's fragment about the essential relationship between humanity and Being to designate thinking, Merleau-Ponty effectively understood that relationship according to an older meaning of voɛìv: perception. The privilege accorded to thought by Heidegger conferred privileges upon language as the vehicle of thought. Merleau-

Ponty departed from Heidegger by regarding perception as the domain in which the presence of Being is primordially manifest, and by conceiving the privileges of thought and language as deriving from perception. Merleau-Ponty designates the differentiation of the beings of Being reflected in thought and language as *écart*.[13]

Presence is one of the hinges on which the debate between Merleau-Ponty and Derrida swings. Derrida consistently interprets presence, in all its philosophical instantiations from οὐσία to *Anwesen*, as tacitly asserting a double coincidence or double identity: the coincidence of thought with itself coinciding with the coincidence of thought and its object. He correctly[14] identifies this thought of presence as underlying Husserl's phenomenological "principle of principles": the simultaneous presence of thought to itself and to its object rules out the possibility of error in cognition. The postmodern rejection of presence—which leads to its repudiation of foundationalism of all stripes—presupposes that Derrida is correct in identifying all accounts of presence as tacitly embodying Husserl's thesis of double coincidence.

In my judgment, this presupposition errs. We have just seen Heidegger arguing that identity cannot be conceived as strict coincidence, and that "Being arrives as presence" in the context of appropriation, which subtends the identity-difference opposition. And, as shall become quickly apparent, Merleau-Ponty conceives presence in terms of perceptual experience that incorporates the dehiscence named as *écart*. I shall return to the question of presence—whether it necessarily incorporates the absolute coincidence of Being and thinking definitive of Transcendental Subjectivity as divinity—in the concluding phases of my argument.

There is a functional isomorphism between Merleau-Ponty's notion of *écart* and Derrida's notion of *différance*: both terms designate a non-coincidence of thought with itself and a parallel divergence of thought with its object. This isomorphism of function, however, is not an isomorphism of content: *écart* and *différance* are different ways of thinking non-coincidence and divergence, and the differences between them are philosophically consequential. For Merleau-Ponty, *écart* names an ek-stasis or de-centering modeled on perceptual presence, and for Derrida, *différance* names an original repetition modeled on archi-writing which denies the possibility of perceptual presence. Although these differences themselves admit of a certain rapprochement, they mark a point of philosophical irreconcilability: Merleau-Ponty explicitly repudiates the semiological reduction which is the founding premise of Derrida's thought.

The divergence of thought with itself and its object named by *écart* and *différance* operates both within and across seeing and writing. Merleau-Ponty's thesis of the ek-stasis of vision holds that, although there is a narcissism implicit in all perceptual modes, this reference to itself implicit in vision is at the same time a dehiscence within vision: perceptual themes refer to perceptual horizons, both of which are extended in space-time, but this self-reference is possible only on the basis of the discontinuity introduced by the defining edge or limit of the perceptual theme which separates it from its horizon.

For Derrida, the *différance* at work in perception is far more radical: there is an absolute bar between the significance of the seen and its referent, the indefinitely deferred transcendental signified. All perception is mediated by the play of signifiers and reaches consciousness after a process of subterranean toil that remains forevermore unconscious. For a $trace_2$ to appear, it is essential that it efface beyond retrieval the $trace_1$ it traces or represents.[15] This has the consequence of denying to perceptual objects any meaning beyond that conferred by signifiers. Language betokens the loss of the object. This thesis—the thesis of semiological reductionism—appropriated by Derrida from Lacan's semiological reading of Freud, sets Derrida fundamentally at odds with Merleau-Ponty, for whom the *sens* or meaning of the perceived world remained to the last "the always presupposed foundation of all rationality, all value, and all existence."[16]

The divergent ways in which Merleau-Ponty and Derrida construe the difference within vision portend further divergencies in their accounts of language and the relationship of seeing and writing.

Both Merleau-Ponty and Derrida follow Saussure in contending that the reference of signifiers to each other within language—infra-referentiality—is a condition for signifying: we must be able to discriminate signifiers from one another, and then organize them functionally; in other words, language depends on both semantic differentiation and syntactic organization, and both of these depend on infra-referentiality.

Merleau-Ponty and Derrida disagree, however, on the nature of infra-referentiality. Derrida adopts a radical version of diacriticality: semantic identity depends on a pure play of differences without positive terms—thus departing from Heidegger's assertion of the inseparability of identity and difference. For Derrida, it is not their different appearances nor the difference in the manner in which they present themselves that make the written or spoken tokens

differentiable; it is, rather, their differences that give them separate identities. Merleau-Ponty regards diacriticality under the general heading of reversibility: the sounds of the notes make the melody,
but the melody confers upon the notes their tonal resonance. The
analogy is apt because Merleau-Ponty conceived languages as ways
of singing the world, intonations of being, cognitive-emotional responses to the world. These originating gestures, being responses,
admit of degrees of appropriateness, hence are not absolutely arbitrary (as Derrida conceives them).

Infra-referentiality for Derrida is finally reducible to the play of
differences in a process of substitution that takes place entirely
within the chain of signifiers. Infra-referentiality for Merleau-Ponty
is inconceivable apart from extra-referentiality, that is, apart from
the demand of the perceptual world to be sung and to be sung in
an appropriate manner. In his view, language is ultimately meaningful because it is allusive to itself *and* its world-context. For
Derrida, the world-context is a transcendental projection of language and only that.

Seeing and writing are intertwined for both thinkers, but they
regard this chiasm in irreconcilably different ways. For Derrida
seeing reduces to reading as the seen reduces to text, whereas for
Merleau-Ponty the reading of a text is derived from a primordial
vision of the world, in the sense that any interpretation or understanding is a kind of perception,[17] that is, a gestalting that is founded
upon the authochthonous organization of the world we witness in
perception.

Derrida and Merleau-Ponty agree that vision is an encounter with
meaning, and that the limit of vision is not sheer meaninglessness
but that kind of temporary absence of meaning designated by the
quest of questionability: it is impossible to see nothing where nothingness designates sheer absence or void, but all seeing is de-centered
toward a meaning that remains always still-to-be-grasped. This ultimate deferral of determination is core doctrine for both Derrida,
where it (with differing) defines the thesis of *différance*, and for
Merleau-Ponty, where it defines the thesis of ambiguity. We see
meaning unfolding toward determinacy, but the question of the
nature and provenance of that meaning remains.

For Derrida, there is no meaning apart from signification and no
signification apart from signifiers. It is idle speculation to look for
meaning *avant la lettre* because we know ahead of time that all we
can find is meaning represented through that speculation. This is
the semiological reduction at work. Within the reduction there can

be no reversibility of seeing and writing, or, to state the same point differently, there can only be a reversibility of reading and writing: for Derrida, the chiasm is a crossing of signifiers, a play of substitution, finally a double crossing in which the infra-referential play crosses itself out, obscuring itself in feigning a reference beyond which it defers absolutely.

For Merleau-Ponty, "the chiasm is . . . an exchange between me and the world. . . ."[18] "As there is a reversibility of the seeing and the visible, and as at the point where the two metamorphoses cross what we call perception is born, so also there is a reversibility of speech and what it signifies . . ." (*The Visible and the Invisible*, hereafter VI 154).[19] What does speech signify? The *sens* of the world. The pressing question here is whether that domain of meaning includes significance not derived from language. Merleau-Ponty's answer is clearly affirmative, a clear "yes," but a "yes, but. . . ."

"There is a world of silence, the perceived world, at least, is an order where there are non-language significations—yes, non-language significations. . . ." (VI 171)

Yes, there is meaning at the pre-linguistic level of perception. That much is clear, but. . . .

"Yes, non-language significations, but they are not for all that *positive*."[20]

These "non-language significations" are not positive: Does this mean that they are purely diacritical in the Derridian sense described earlier? I think not. In the following sentence, Merleau-Ponty writes that "there is for example no absolute flux of singular *Erlebnisse*." I take this to be a reference to Husserlian *Erlebnisse* which are characterized by a coincidence of consciousness and object, hence to be an affirmation of the *écart*, the ek-stasis of perception, the opacity or transcendence of the object.

I will return to this point shortly, but first I want to conclude the sequence of thought that led to it. The issue at hand is seeing and writing. I have argued that both Derrida and Merleau-Ponty conceive the divergence of seeing and writing chiasmatically, but that they use the figure of the chiasm in irreconcilably different ways. For Derrida, the chiasm operates exclusively within the domain of infra-referentiality, within the domain of signifiers: it cannot cross the bar between signifier and signified. For Merleau-Ponty, the chiasm is necessarily both infra-referential and extra-referential: the reference of signifiers to themselves which is necessary to establish meaning semantically and syntactically can take place only because signifiers draw upon the silent domain of pre-linguistic perceptual meaning, or "non-language significance."[21]

3

There are many locutions that are not correct in this twilight of postmodern modernism, and "pre-linguistic meaning" is one of them. If *il n'y a pas de hors-texte*, then all we have to do is re-write the world to correct its mistakes and injustices. All we have to do is re-possess the language that seems insidiously to have possessed us.... And that has to be done by fiat of political power rather than by appeal to truth, since any appeal to truth is nullified by denying access to any domain of meaning beyond that created by language. I think it is madness to displace the quest for truth by the autocracy of political rectitude, but that is a diatribe I shall defer.

What is wrong with saying that the world is full of meaning that language seeks to articulate? The words "pre-linguistic meaning" seem to have magic powers to awaken ghouls in souls otherwise untroubled when they open their eyes and see the world. This phrase, however, causes specters to rise from the graves of philosophical history, to haunt the minds of the quick. Naive realism. Natural attitude. Protocol statements. Pure qualia. Immediate impressions. Scientific reductionism. Onto-theology. Pure objectivity. *Deus sive natura*. Picture theory of language. And, driving them all, the phallocentric, phonocentric, ethnocentric, metaphysical Mephistopheles of the Western world: presence. Well, then, exorcism is in order. The demon to be purged is that of positivism.

Positivism sought to identify elements of perceptual experience that could not have been tainted by the active powers of imagination to introduce relations not obtaining in the real world, that is, the world in itself, prior to perception, which is the cause or origin of perception. Thus, positivism was motivated by the quest to achieve certainty by banishing all possible sources of error, the same quest that motivated Descartes's notion of simple natures and Locke's doctrine of primary qualities. One twentieth-century version of this quest led to the sense data theory underpinning positivism. The sense datum was conceived as a logical simple, incapable of analysis due to its simplicity or elementarity. It was held to be the building block of knowledge of the "external world" because (a) it could not have been created by mind, hence functioned as an access to transcendent reality, and (b) it could not have been distorted by mind, hence was free from the possibility of error. If one could trace a knowledge claim back to origins in sense data and defend the logic of combination which assembled the complex proposition articulating the assertion from its simple elements, one could rest assured in its certainty. There was, indeed, an appeal to presence here in the thesis that the immediacy of the apprehension of sense data guaranteed their incorrigibility. This thesis is the positivist version of Husserl's principle of principles: both ground themselves on the thesis of the coincidence of cognition with its object.

To purge the demon of positivism from Merleau-Ponty's conception of presence, one need only point to the following.

1. Merleau-Ponty explicitly repudiates the notion of sense data or qualia as logical simples, and asserts that the most basic structure of perceptual presence, the gestalt, the figure-upon-ground, is irreducibly complex.

2. Merleau-Ponty explicitly repudiates the Cartesian quest for certainty which drives the positivist notion of incorrigibility and the Husserlian notion of apodicticity, and asserts that what presents itself in perceptual experience is intrinsically ambiguous, multi-determinable—and would be so even for the divine intelligence that tacitly functions as the paradigm of determinacy in all variations of Cartesian epistemology.

3. Finally, to return to the central issue here, Merleau-Ponty explicitly repudiates the doctrine of identity, or coincidence of knowledge and object that could be realized only through divine intellect, and asserts a model of finite cognition structured around the notions of reversibility and intertwining in which presence presupposes depresentation or *écart*.[22]

As I have sought to show above, Merleau-Ponty is not the only philosopher to think presence as dehiscence and divergence, but he is the one who concerns us now. Here are the obligatory quotations from the Working Notes of *The Visible and the Invisible*.

We have to pass from the thing ... as identity, to the thing ... as difference, i.e. as transcendence, i.e. as always "behind," beyond, far-off ... the present itself is not an absolute coincidence without transcendence; even the *Urerlebnis* involves not total coincidence, but partial coincidence, because it has horizons and would not be without them—the present, also, is ungraspable from close-up, in the forceps of attention, it is an encompassing. (VI 195; *Le Visible at l'invisible*, hereafter VI-F 249)

Speaking of the *Selbsterscheinung* in Husserl, Merleau-Ponty says that this notion of "auto-apparition [or] apparition that is pure apparition . . . presupposes the idea of the for itself and in the end cannot explain transcendence," and directs himself to

> look in a completely different direction: the for itself itself as an incontestable, but derived, characteristic: it is the culmination of separation [*écart*] in *differentiation*—Self-presence is presence to a differentiated world—The perceptual separation [*écart*] as making up the "view" such as it is implicated in the reflex, for example—and enclosing being for itself by means of language as differentiation. To be conscious = to have a figure on a ground—one cannot go back any further." (VI 191; VI-F, 244–45)

The perceptual world which presents itself presents itself through the *écart* of the figure-ground divergence: it is non-self-coincident in space-time, hence always ambiguous, incomplete, etc.

We are of this world, flesh of its flesh, one of its differentiations, one manner in which it folds back on itself and senses itself. As such, we do not coincide either with the world (since in folding back on itself it does not coincide with itself) or with ourselves (since we, too, are de-centered in space-time). We are in touch with ourselves, but this reflexivity is not self-coincidence (since it presupposes a difference between the reflecting and the reflected), but neither is it total self-alienation[23] (since there is a reversibility of touching-touched and thinking-thought). This de-centered presence to oneself and world, or self-presence mediated by worldly flesh, is what Merleau-Ponty seeks to articulate in the figure of the chiasm. Chiasm, for Merleau-Ponty, is unthinkable apart from presence; chiasm, for Derrida, is also unthinkable apart from presence: the difference is that Derrida must think presence as that which is necessarily excluded from self-reference, as the absolute other that *différance* needs in order to be *pure* diacriticality.

Merleau-Ponty conceives language as the flesh of the world articulating itself in the flesh of the word. Once again, the governing figure is the chiasm, the reversibility of flesh of the world with flesh of the word (which, given its sensible vehicle, is also flesh of the world, a perceptible). World needs word to articulate and present itself, word also needs world to articulate and present itself, but this reversibility of world and word is asymmetrical: world comes first; there is a "passage from the perceptual meaning to the language meaning" (VI 176; VI-F 230); the perceptual world is a present origin, but the process of origination is not a self-coincident Absolute bringing himself into being by incanting his own name; it is dehiscence, self-mediation, *écart*, things differentiating themselves before our eyes.

4

What can be said to disabuse the words "pre-linguistic meaning" of their ghoulish portent? How might I reassure those who recoil from the term that nothing is lost in distinguishing reading from seeing, hearing, smelling . . . the whole synesthetic sphere?

The great truth of transcendental thought is that habitual[24] forms are deeply sedimented in both cultures and individuals, that the a priori nature of these habits increases with degree of latency (i.e., their potency to structure our lives is proportional to their taken-for-grantedness), that the life-sustaining nature of habituality is such that our ability to deal appropriately with the world is affected by our ability to interpret and judge with the fluid ease of trained proficiency. The faster we see something *as* something to be treated in a given way, the sooner we can dispense with it. The larger the segment of life we can put on automatic, the larger the segment we free for deliberate thought and aesthetic interrogation.

Habituality, however, is a mixed blessing: the more we overlook in automatic modes of response, the more we overlook; the more facile our judgments, the greater our proclivity for prejudice; the more efficient we are in manipulating the environment, the greater our capacity to reduce it to standing reserve (*Bestand*). Given that habituality lends itself as much to violence and brutalization of consciousness as it does to benign forms of efficiency, there is need for suspicion, wary hyper-reflexivity, the self-monitoring of doubt—and conceptual modes enabling retrieval.

Imagine the text you are now reading transformed into a language whose signs were foreign to you, Pali or ancient Sumerian, perhaps. We who read English easily see through these signs to their meanings, but our seeing is arrested by the signifiers of languages to which we have not habituated ourselves. There is a difference in mode of seeing. Or hearing, for that matter. But just as we can strip a word of significance by repeating it aloud over and over again, so can we attend to the visual aspects of our written language by taking up calligraphy or designing a new font with a bit-mapping program. We can retrieve the perceptual experience from the *habitus* of hearing through the words spoken to their discursive meaning (which is somewhat different from listening), retrieve the pre-linguistic meaning of the written sign by viewing it aesthetically rather than as discourse.

This is an instance of the difference I want to mark with the phrase "pre-linguistic meaning." I am quite willing to acknowledge the relativity of this distinction; indeed, I am eager to distance this thought from all claims to purity: the notions of pure sensa, sheer qualia, protocol experience, and the like are philosophically bankrupt abstractions which correspond to nothing in the perceptual domain.

What I am designating as retrieval differs from the methodology of the phenomenological reduction in the acknowledgment that there is no *terminus ad quem*—which is just another way of saying that the reduction cannot be carried to completion—the retrieval precludes the very notion of that kind of finality: as Levinas demonstrates (with very different intent), there is no way to exhaust the perceptual significance of another person's face, but there are ways of countering the effects of habituation.

The instance of retrieval I am about to describe took place in a flash, although it will take a while to read this paragraph. I passed the open door of a colleague's office and glanced in. The colleague is someone I had met first in writings which aroused my ire, and subsequently as an antagonist in campus politics. The sight of her face had become irritating to me. Through her open door, I caught a glimpse of a loving gesture directed toward an elderly man, a movement radiating unfeigned affection and solicitude, a soothing murmur in a language I do not speak. I took the man to be her father. I see the woman differently now: her face doesn't irritate me any more. (I also take a more generous view of her political motives.)

The example is far from decisive; any such example can be more or less readily accommodated within the conceptual scheme I am arguing against. (I saw the man *as* father, etc.) But. Just as there were perceptually grounded reasons for seeing my colleague's face as I initially did, there were other, deeper and more powerful, perceptually grounded forces that gave rise to the change of aspect, the gestalt shift. What I saw changed my vision of her face. Something beneath language occasioned a shift in the signifiers operative in my vision of this woman.

Given that there are paradigms operative in habitual modes of perception, there is also a presence, counter-balancing *habitus*, which accounts for the construction and adoption of the paradigm in the first place, and which accounts for such mundane satoris as the one described above. There is nothing to be lost in an attempt to retrieve a quality of experience that has been obscured by an a priori, and much to be gained.

I am arguing for a difference that is strictly inexplicable if all meaning is generated by signifiers. I am not arguing for a hard-edged line of demarcation between the linguistic and the pre-linguistic. I am contending that there is a continuum of human experience from the perceptual to the linguistic which is bounded by the impossibility of purity at either end: no purely linguistic experience (because there must be a perceived token or sign as vehicle of meaning); no purely perceptual experience (because everything we experience appears within a world horizon infused with symbolism). Within that continuum, however, there are relative differences of differing magnitudes, and those differences account for the origin of change in the ways we see things and talk or write about them.

"Pre-linguistic meaning" refers to the differential between that which is closer to the flesh of the world (the word seen in Pali rather than seen through in English, the face revealed in a moment of humanity rather than concealed by a *habitus*) and that which is closer to the flesh of language, which, as an outgrowth of the flesh of the world, is a dehiscence within it. Dogs live in a pre-linguistic world (as do we), but dogs also live in a world permeated by symbolism. Dogs talk, but they do not talk as we talk. Their speech is more poetic, in that they sing the world rather more than say it, but we can still communicate with them (not as well as we communicate with each other, perhaps, but it is hard to lie to a dog and nearly impossible for a dog to lie to us). My point here is that a relative difference is, for all that, still a difference—which is why I use "pre-linguistic" rather than "non-linguistic."[25]

It is, I think, this difference (or these differences) that Merleau-Ponty sought to explicate under the heading of *écart*, but which is banished from experience by the bar between signifier and signified which drives the Derridian non-concept of *différance*. The bar bars access to the perceptual domain, the bar transforms the continuum into a rigid line of demarcation generating a dualism of language and its other, conscious significance and unconscious processes of *frayage* (path-breaking or *Bahnung*), etc.

Heidegger, I think, saw the logic operative in these two models. Recall his words quoted in the opening passage.

> [The principle of identity] has... become a principle bearing the characteristics of a spring that departs from Being as the ground of beings, and thus springs into the abyss.

When the togetherness of humanity and Being is represented as a synthesis of two disjunct realms, thinking and Being (or language and its other), the spring from one to the other springs into the abyss of empty nothingness (sheer diacriticality, difference without identity, difference without positive term), groundlessness, total absence of foundations, etc.

When the relation between humanity and Being is experienced as a belonging that is prior to the polarizing disjunction of the two, the abyss is transformed into appropriation as the domain from which language speaks.

This abyss is neither empty nothingness nor murky confusion, but rather appropriation. In appropriation vibrates the essence of what speaks as language. . . .

The difference between the logic of the abyssal bar and the logic of appropriation is the difference between *différance* and *écart*. It is, I think, a momentous difference.

Notes

1. Martin Heidegger, "The Principle of Identity," in *Identity and Difference*, bilingual edition, trans. Joan Stambaugh (New York: Harper & Row, 1969), p. 39/104. Translation modified. Subsequently cited as I&D with page numbers in English separated from page numbers in German with a slash. "Der Satz der Identität," in *Identität und Differenz* (Pfüllingen: Neske, 1957).
2. "As a law of thought, the principle is valid only insofar as it is a principle of Being that reads: To every being as such there belongs identity, the unity with itself. . . . If science could not be sure in advance of the identity of its object in each case, it could not be what it is" (I&D 26/88–89).
3. "What the principle of identity, heard in its fundamental key, states is exactly what the whole of Western European thinking has in mind—and that is: the unity of identity forms a basic characteristic in the Being of beings" (I&D 26/89).
4. τὸ γὰρ αὐτὸ νοεῖν ἐστιν τὲ καὶ εἶναι. "Das Selbe nämlich ist Vernehmen (Denken) sowohl als auch Sein" (I&D 27/90).
5. "Man *is* essentially this relationship of responding to Being, and he is only this." (Der Mensch *ist* eigentlich dieser Bezug der Entsprechen, und er ist nur dies.) (I&D 31/94).
6. "Man and Being are appropriated to each other. They belong to each other." (Mensch und Sein sind einander übereignet. Sie gehören einander.) (I&D 31–32/95).
7. "Appropriation is that realm, vibrating within itself, through which man and Being reach each other in their essence, achieve their es-

sence, by losing those qualities with which metaphysics has endowed them." (Das Er-eignis ist der in sich schwingende Bereich, durch den Mensch und Sein einander in ihrem Wesen erreichen, ihr Wesendes gewinnen, indem sie jene Bestimmungen verlieren, die ihnen die Metaphysik geliehen hat.) (I&D 36/102, translation modified).

8. "What does appropriation have to do with identity? Answer: Nothing. Identity, on the other hand, has much, perhaps everything, to do with appropriation." (Was hat das Ereignis mit der Identität zu tun? Antwort: Nichts. Dagegen hat die Identität vieles, wenn nicht alles mit dem Ereignis zu tun.) (I&D 38/102).

    "Being belongs with thinking to an identity whose essence stems from that letting belong together which we call appropriation. The essence of identity is a property of appropriation." (Sein gehört mit dem Denken in eine Identität, deren Wesen aus jenem Zusammengehörenlassen stammt, das wir das Ereignis nennen. Das Wesen der Identität ist ein Eigentum des Er-eignisses.) (I&D 39/103, translation modified).

    The obscurity I mention has to do with the metaphysical framework (*Ge-stell*) of technology, which has become the manner in which Being speaks to us today.

9. "Im Er-eignis schwingt das Wesen dessen, was als Sprache spricht, die einmal das Haus des Seins genannt wurde." (I&D 39/104, translation modified).

10. This discourse, properly speaking, belongs in the domain of metaphysics. It may or may not also belong in the domain of onto-theology. This point is now the focus of philosophical controversy: whether the logic of general terms which range over particular disciplines is or is not onto-theologic. I contend that ontology, the logic of things, need not coincide with theology, the logic of divinity; it depends upon whether one thinks of things as created things which are bound by some necessity to a design attributed to divine creation, and one need not think of things in that way. Indeed, I would assert that we could begin to think of things in that way only after thinking of things in another way, that the conception of a being as a divinity is parasitic upon—logically derivative from—thinking of beings as things that remain more or less the same over time. (Children learn to re-identify objects over lapses in time or moments of disappearance long before the notion of a creator god can be made meaningful. The former can be detected before the emergence of coherent speech, the latter might reasonably be assumed to presuppose fairly sophisticated linguistic skills.)

11. Martin Heidegger, *An Introduction to Metaphysics*, trans. Ralph Manheim (New York: Doubleday, 1961), p. 11. *Einführung in die Metaphysik* was written in 1935 and published (Tübingen: Niemeyer) in 1953. "Der Satz der Identität" was written in 1957 and published in *Identität und Differenz* that same year.

12. "Semiological reductionism" is my term for the thesis, permeating postmodern thought if not definitive of it, that all worldly experience is mediated by language or signifiers of some kind, in such a way that worldly meaning is reducible in principle to the significance imparted to the world through systems of signs. It is the contemporary version of nominalism.

13. *Écart* can be rendered in English as divergence or difference. Merleau-Ponty also uses the terms fission and dehiscence to designate this incipient differentiation which resides within the plenum of experience. His thinking on this point resonates harmonically with Heidegger's: the binary opposition of identity and difference is subtended by a domain—appropriation, perception—in which these terms intertwine. Language allows us to separate these two aspects of a primal intertwining, but also generates the possibility of misrepresenting them as mutually exclusive.

14. Husserl does not in fact adhere consistently to his own principle. In the temporal dimension of presence, for example, Husserl argues that the now moment definitive of presence both coincides with itself in full lucidity and diverges from itself in modes of primal retention and protention. See M. C. Dillon, *Semiological Reductionism: A Critique of the Deconstructionist Movement in Postmodern Thought* (Albany: SUNY Press, 1995), Chapter 1, where the issue of presence is treated at length.

15. I use the subscripts to designate the difference between traces named in Derrida's well-known doctrine of "the trace$_2$ of the erasure of the trace$_1$."

16. Maurice Merleau-Ponty, "The Primacy of Perception and Its Philosophical Consequences," trans. James M. Edie, in *The Primacy of Perception*, ed. James M. Edie (Evanston: Northwestern University Press, 1964), p.13. The essay in which this passage appears was written in 1946, but the thought expressed resonates throughout Merleau-Ponty's last writings.

17. As the Greek νοεῖν reflects a perceptual basis for thought.

18. Maurice Merleau-Ponty, *The Visible and the Invisible*, ed. Claude Lefort, trans. Alphonso Lingis (Evanston: Northwestern University Press, 1968), p. 215. Subsequently cited as VI. *Le Visible et l'invisible*, ed. Claude Lefort (Paris: Gallimard, 1964), p. 268. Subsequently cited as VI-F.

19. "Il y a une réversibilité de la parole et de ce qu'elle signifie..." (VI-F 202).

20. "Il y a le monde du silence, le monde perçu, du moins, est un ordre où il y a des significations non langagières, mais elles ne sont pas pour autant positives..." (VI-F 225).

21. "Just as my body sees only because it is a part of the visible in which it opens forth, the sense upon which the arrangement of sounds opens reflects back upon that arrangement" (VI 153–54).

"Comme mon corps ne voit que parce qu'il fait partie du visible où il éclôt, le sens sur lequel ouvre l'arrangement des sons se répercute sur lui" (VI-F 201).

22. This paragraph attempts to summarize a historical analysis of perceptual givenness that is more fully elaborated in Part One of *Merleau-Ponty's Ontology* (Bloomington: Indiana University Press, 1988), pp. 9–81.

23. As Sartre, for example, thought it was. See his account of the "third ontological dimension of the body" in *Being and Nothingness*. Also, see M. C. Dillon, "Sartre on the Phenomenal Body and Merleau-Ponty's Critique," *Journal of the British Society for Phenomenology*, Vol. 5: 2 (1974), pp. 144–58.

24. The term "habitual" may strike some as provocative. It resurrects the Humean problem of accounting for the genesis of habit, and resurrects the Kantian arguments based on the transcendental function of categories: without a prior conception of X, how could one ever recognize an X as an instance of Xness? The answer I would propose—which could not be proffered by Hume, because, in the crucial case of causality, he sought an empirical (hence contingent) basis for the notion of *necessary* connection—is that one learns to identify and categorize things because they present themselves in perception as differentiated, as having perceptual meanings or identities, and as bearing striking resemblance to other things which present themselves in similar ways. Once one forsakes the quest for apodicticity, the contingency of habitual categories of thought can be accepted as a correlate of human finitude.

    Merleau-Ponty has addressed the issue of induction versus eidetic intuition in his essay "Phenomenology and the Sciences of Man" (in *The Primacy of Perception*). Derrida challenges the standpoint set forth there in his *Introduction to Husserl's "Origin of Geometry"*—thereby underlining the differences between himself and Merleau-Ponty I am seeking to articulate here.

25. Although she should not be held accountable for the content of these last paragraphs, I am indebted to Sandra Luft for asking the questions—listening sympathetically to my answers, and remaining unconvinced—that provoked the line of thought that led me to write them.

PART I
PROBLEMATICS

1

Merleau-Ponty and Derrida on the Phenomenon

Thomas W. Busch

Jacques Derrida's critique of Edmund Husserl's phenomenology revolves around the relationship of signs to consciousness. He once expressed the nature of his critique by saying that if phenomenology operates as a reduction *to* meaning, deconstruction effects a reduction *of* meaning. In other words, deconstruction aims to push the phenomenological reduction further by utilizing what turns out to be an even more radical, grammatological[1], reduction. Husserl's phenomenological reduction was to lay bare a realm of primordial givenness, while Derrida's critique aims to undercut this givenness. His critique of Husserl's phenomenology forms only an instantiation of the power of deconstruction to undermine all forms of primordial givenness constitutive of the Western metaphysical tradition.

Husserl was a philosopher of consciousness whose methodological tool was intuition, with its metaphor of vision, of direct seeing. Derrida's critique attacked this Husserlian method head-on by claiming that there was no sphere of "ownness," of interiority wherein consciousness had a direct access to its own interior life. Derrida's strategy was to show that Husserl's views on the relationship of meaning, language, and communication were mistaken. Husserl assumed that signs as indicators of expressions (meanings) were of use in communicating one's meanings to others, but were not needed in the inner life wherein consciousness communicates with itself. This happens, according to Husserl, because the objects and meanings of consciousness are clearly *present* to it. Derrida centers his criticism on a close examination of the temporality of conscious life. He argues that, on Husserl's own terms, the present, because it retains what is absent, slipping out of sight, compounds itself in a building up. Presence, then, is not simple, self-identical presence, but is constituted. According to Derrida, "indication takes

20

place whenever the sense-giving act, the animating intention, the living spirituality of the meaning-intention is not fully present."[2] This is admitted by Husserl in the case of one consciousness communicating with another. Now, Derrida claims, Husserl must admit the use of indication within the sphere of the ownness itself of one consciousness. This is to say that *alterity* enters consciousness as a condition of presence.

> As soon as we admit this continuity of the now and not-now, perception and nonperception, in the zone of primordiality common to primordial impression and primordial retention, we admit the other into the self-identity of the *Augenblick*; nonpresence and nonevidence are admitted into the *blink of the instant.* There is a duration to the blink, and it closes the eye. This alterity is in fact the condition for presence. . . ."[3]

Derrida's reduction of meaning reveals the life of signs, the fact that signs themselves produce presence, meaning. In his essay "Structure, Sign and Play in the Discourse of the Human Sciences," he points out that from the beginning philosophers had developed representational systems. However, these systems (of Western thought) always had "a point of reference, a fixed origin," a "center" in the form of an "arche" or "telos" which had the effect of stabilizing meaning, producing a "reassuring certitude" by which "anxiety can be mastered." The critical moment which challenges Western metaphysics was "the moment . . . in which language invaded the universal problematic."[4] The sciences of language disclose that there is no centrally signified, nothing brought to presence outside of a system of differences. What Derrida finds in the problematic of language, however, is not a new science but a "freeplay": "It is freeplay. . . . [which] is disruption of presence."[5] Derrida's reduction leads to a reduction of meaning, to an origin which is not an origin of meaning—*différance*, "literally neither a word nor a concept" but a "temporization" and "spacing." "*Différance* is the non-full, non-simple, structured and differentiating origin of differences. Thus, the name 'origin' no longer suits it."[6] This "structured and differentiating" origin which is not an origin is the arche-writing which makes speech and writing possible. Derrida stresses that on this level the spacing, the differential gap between signs, is a radical discontinuity, an emptiness, an abyss. This is the meaning of "dissemination," the proliferation of signs under no power, no law, no metaphysical constraint of gathering. Dissemination is the basis of deconstruction's liberating criticism. John Caputo catches this spirit when he depicts deconstruction as "a work of emancipation, a strategy or praxis of liberation. It is not a theoretical discourse about freedom but a textual operation performed in the name of liberation."[7] One must keep in mind that the practice of deconstruction unfolds from a *principled* argument about how signs work, what Caputo calls "a kind of a priori."[8] One does not wait to see if some further case of presence or teleology will submit to deconstruction. One knows from the start that presence and telos must yield under the disseminative character of signs. But this is, for Derrida, no reason to mourn. Dissemination and freeplay as liberation must be embraced not with a sense of loss and fit of nostalgia, but with a Nietzschean affirmation, "the joyous affirmation of the freeplay of the world without truth, without origin. . . ."[9]

Deconstruction's critical power emanates from this grammatological reduction, constituting a discourse of dissemination. Spacing conceived as dissemination gives deconstruction the critical tool it requires to undermine all totalities, all forms of unities of meaning. It marks the most radical extreme of Derrida's claims (and is the discourse most favored by many of his most vocal followers). On the other hand, there is also, intertwined in Derrida's works with this disseminative discourse, a discourse of facticity, marked by situatedness. There are always horizons. One always finds oneself already in a language, a set of discourses and practices, etc. One lives in a world or worlds. Philosophy, of course, forms one of those worlds or traditions of discourse, and Derrida accepts that one cannot get "outside" of such a discourse, to criticize it. He warns of the dangers in an attempt "to change terrain, in a discontinuous and irruptive fashion, by brutally placing oneself outside, and by affirming an absolute break and difference. . . . [for] the simple practice of language ceaselessly reinstates the new terrain on the oldest ground."[10] Similarly, Derrida is critical of Levinas, who would have us think that the metaphysical can be surmounted. While Derrida is immensely impressed with many aspects of Levinas's thought, one finds him offering a passionate defense of Husserl against Levinas's attack on him as representative of the worst in Western thought. Levinas sees in Husserl's phenomenology, particularly in intentionality, the reduction of Otherness to the Same. Levinas, in turn, claims that the Other is *absolute* other and is not reducible to the phenemonal condition.

> Levinas *in fact* speaks of the infinitely other, but by refusing to acknowledge an intentional modification of the ego—which would be a violent and totalitarian act for him—he deprives himself of the very foundation and possibility of his own language. What

authorizes him to say "infinitely other" if the infinitely other does not appear as such in the zone he calls the same, and which is the neutral level of transcendental description? ... If the transcendental "violence" to which we allude is tied to phenomenality itself, and to the possibility of language, it then would be embedded in the root of meaning and logos, before the latter had to be determined as rhetoric, psychology, demagoguery, etc.[11]

Here one finds Derrida coming to the defense of "phenomenality." The latter is indeed the very condition of facticity and situatedness. Derrida is, of course, critical of reduction of the other to the same, but his deconstruction finds the other always entangled in the same, repressed by the same. There is no "pure" same for him, nor "pure" otherness, no pure "inside" nor "outside." It is precisely this recognition that leads Derrida to criticize those who would assume a critical posture of "rupture."

Yet, because of his grammatological reduction, with its notion of "spacing" as radical discontinuity, one also knows that all horizons are unstable and ungrounded. There exists a critical tension between the discourse of dissemination as radical discontinuity and the discourse of situatedness with its inevitable horizons.

Rodolphe Gasché, one of Derrida's most well-known and ablest commentators, sees Merleau-Ponty as a precursor of Derrida's deconstructive project. He cites Merleau-Ponty's critique of reflective philosophies, culminating in the notion of "hyperreflection," as evidence of this. He notes that in Merleau-Ponty's view of reflection there is no possibility of a return to origins or centeredness, because "Merleau-Ponty discovers divergences so unsurmountable as to impede all internal adequation."[12] Reflection itself is a "blind spot," an invisible which in its operation cannot grasp itself. In the end, however, Gasché judges that Merleau-Ponty's work only "came close to anticipating ... deconstruction,"[13] because the deferral of coincidence in Merleau-Ponty's critique of reflection is judged to be merely temporal. For Gasché, this temporal falling away is responsible in Merleau-Ponty's work for a nostalgia for a lost origin, "a reverie about the language of philosophy,"[14] which, to Gasché, means a nostagia for presence.

Gasché is right to stress the impossibility of coincidence in Merleau-Ponty's views on reflection. However, he does not fully appreciate what Merleau-Ponty means by *écart*, for time is only one dimension of that invisible which precludes coincidence. It is true that in *Phenomenology of Perception* Merleau-Ponty defined transcendence in relation to an incomplete synthesis: "The thing and the world exist only in so far as they are experienced by me or by subjects like me, since they are both the concatenation of our perspectives, yet they transcend all perspectives because this chain is temporal and incomplete."[15] Gasché does not realize how far Merleau-Ponty, because he was dissatisfied with his earlier understanding of transcendence, moved away from transcendental phenomenology in his later work, in which he considered Being to be a diacritically structured field. "There is for example no absolute flux of singular *Erlebnisse*; there are fields and a field of fields, with a *style* and a typicality."[16] "It is the Cartesian idealization applied to the mind as to the things (Husserl) that has persuaded us that we were a flux of individual *Erlebnisse*, whereas we are a field of Being."[17] This field of Being is a "syntax," in which there are significations only by divergencies. The discourse of "conscious acts" and "objects" must be jettisoned, for in fact "the 'objects' of consciousness themselves are not something positive in front of us."[18] Transcendence (difference) in the field of Being as "syntax" has displaced his earlier subject/object position: "Transcendence is identity within difference."[19]

The characterization of Being as "syntax" marks Merleau-Ponty's appropriation of structural linguistics and its "spatial" difference. It also marks the elimination of any nostalgia for origins that may have haunted his earlier work. He is clear that philosophy's search "is not for the immediate, the coincidence, the effective fusion with the existent, the search for an original integrity, for a secret lost and to be rediscovered, which would nullify our questions and reapprehend our language."[20] He goes on to emphasize the difference with his early work: "If coincidence is lost, this is no accident; if Being is hidden, this is itself a characteristic of Being . . ."[21] (not of our inadaquacy). Merleau-Ponty would fully agree with Derrida when the latter said that "if totalization has no meaning, it is not because the infinity of a field cannot be covered by a finite glance or a finite discourse, but because the nature of the field—that is, language and a finite language—excludes totalization."[22] On the question of lack of coincidence and criticism of philosophies of presence, as well as criticism of any nostalgia about all of this, I find, against Gasché, agreement between Merleau-Ponty and Derrida. On the other hand, I find that the important difference between Merleau-Ponty and Derrida surfaces when Gasché insists on the relevance of the phenomenological reduction for Derrida. He writes: "Derrida's notion of writing and of the trace presupposes a phenomenological reduction of all the mundane regions of sensibility (but also of all the intelligible)."[23] This reference to grammatological reduction reminds us of Merleau-Ponty's refusal of Husserl's reduction in the *Phenomenology of Perception*: "The most important lesson which the reduction teaches us is the impossibility of a complete reduction."[24] This remains true for his later work as well. *Écart* is a divergence in the realm of the phenomenon and of lived experience. Perception itself is diacritical. Color, for example, functions as if it is "a certain differentiation, an ephemeral modulation of this world—less a color or a thing, therefore, than a difference between things and colors. . . ."[25] For Merleau-Ponty differences are always qualified contextually. Because of his commitment to the phenomenon he would surely resist the discourse of dissemination and free play, which, for him, would be an abstraction from the actual functioning of differences in perception, painting, discourse, action, etc.

I find in this regard that Merleau-Ponty would agree with Ricoeur and Habermas in their claim that Derrida does not sufficiently distinguish the semiological and the semantic. For Ricoeur we must distinguish what is meant by "spacing."

> The spacing found in discourse is not the same as what you find in the semiological order when a sign is distinct from another sign. . . . What's important is that discourse produces, by its own differences which are not semiological differences, effects of discourse which are not effects of signs. . . . What is absolutely important to me is the recognition of the discursive order as being settled by no discussion concerning the semiological order and as calling for its own analysis.[26]

In like vein, Habermas sees in Derrida "the transcendental primacy of the sign as against its meaning . . . the identity of meaning dependent upon the intersubjective practices of employing rules of meaning."[27] Derrida does not deny that there are different differences and even that this applies to semiological and semantic, but he does not draw the consequence from this that is drawn by Ricoeur, Habermas, and, I believe, Merleau-Ponty, that the semantic (the level of use and function) has an irreducible intelligibility and primacy. There is, in other words, for these thinkers, an irreducibility of meaning to a grammatological reduction. For Merleau-Ponty differences are always integral to a medium,[28] are always caught up in levels, dimensions, fields, contexts. Subjects are installed within these contexts and operate on their bases.

> With the first vision, the first contact, the first pleasure, there is initiation, that is, not the positing of a content, but the opening

of a dimension that can never again be closed, the establishment of a level in terms of which every other experience will be situated. The idea is this level, this dimension. It is therefore not a *de facto* invisible, which would have nothing to do with the visible. Rather it is the invisible of this world. . . .[29]

"Spacing" differentiates the various regions or dimensions of Being (sensible, linguistic, social, praxical), which overlap and develop contingently but dialectically (temporally). For Merleau-Ponty there is no "origin" beyond Being. While for Derrida *différance* is an "abyss," for Merleau-Ponty *écart* is a "hollow" or "fold" in Being. *Écart* belongs to a discourse of Being and dialectics of expression, whereas Derrida's empty space, as revealed through grammatological reduction, is prior to and productive of Being and dialectics. Being is dimensionality for Merleau-Ponty, and the body is its prototype, with its differentiations of sensible dimensions—vision, touch, hearing—and their overlapping in practice. The body's reversibility as seeing/seen, touching/touched, is the style of Being itself. There is *écart* as well as reversibility between language and silence, between one body and another, between one discursive tradition and another. Thus, *écart* is not a radical discontinuity but a "distance," which "is not the contrary of . . . proximity."[30] *Écart* is invisible, but the invisible and the visible belong to Being. In opposition to the view that differences cannot be understood outside of the media in which they function, the grammatological reduction has the effect of decontextualizing difference, of retiring signs from their specific functions in order to discover, as it were, their common decontextualized nature. While Merleau-Ponty shares with Derrida the critique of univocity and identity, his commitment to the phenomenon precludes him from accepting the discourse of dissemination because he finds that in its functioning all that is sensible and discursive circulates and overlaps, enjoys a certain "kinship." Perhaps it is Derrida himself, when responding to a question about his understanding of dissemination, who best articulates what I believe his principal disagreement might be with an ontological thinker such as Merleau-Ponty.

I distinguish in a number of places between polysemy and dissemination. Polysemy is a multiplicity of meaning, a kind of ambiguity, which nevertheless belongs to the field of sense, of meaning, of semantics, and which is determined within the horizon of a certain grouping, gathering together. . . . Dissemination is something which no longer belongs to the regime of meaning; it exceeds not only the multiplicity of meanings, but also meaning itself.[31]

Merleau-Ponty would certainly find much to approve of in Derrida's discourse of facticity, with its admission of inevitable situatedness. Indeed, Derrida realizes that "the simple practice of language" is enough to show that one cannot brutally place oneself outside, to affirm an absolute break. In this hermeneutic discourse one finds the closest relationship between the two thinkers. When Derrida presented his notion of *différance* in *Margins*, he noted that it is not a definable concept nor word. Yet, he pointed out, there is a certain unity in its usage, what he called "the general system of this economy." The non-univocal, nonconceptual unity of usage he called a *sheaf*: "The word *sheaf* seems to mark more appropriately that the assemblage to be proposed has the complex structure of a weaving, an interlacing which permits the different threads and different lines of meaning—or of force—to go off again in different directions, just as it is always ready to tie itself up with others."[32] I believe that the notion of "sheaf" is one that Merleau-Ponty would welcome as descriptive of the syle of Being itself, with its circulations and overlappings and encroachments without coincidences. The "readiness" to "tie up" for Merleau-Ponty is indication of kinship, not equivocation, of analogical echoes, of an ecology of Being, not a discursive anarchy of signs.

It is precisely the discourse of dissemination, the result of a radical reduction, of a difference which is a radical discontinuity, that Merleau-Ponty would find uncongenial. "The invisible is a hollow in the visible, a fold in passivity, not pure production."[33] Merleau-Ponty would contest the Derridean notion of "free play," just as he had contested Sartre's radical freedom, also achieved by a radical reduction, as an abstraction. While Sartre's radical freedom and Derrida's disseminative free play are powerful critical tools with which to contest constellations of meaning, for Merleau-Ponty freedom and critique must arise within lived experiences, in practices, in the possibilities, latencies, and pregnancies of the phenomenal situation and its expressive (wild) possibilities. Whether, then, it is a question of freedom or meaning, Merleau-Ponty places faith (*foi*) in the phenomenon, while Derrida views it with suspicion.

Notes

1. "Now if one considers that the critique of anthropologism in the last great metaphysical systems (Hegel and Husserl, notably) was executed in the name of truth and meaning, if one considers that these

'phenomenologies.'... had as their essential motif a *reduction to meaning*.... then one can conceive that the reduction *of* meaning—that is, of the signified—first takes the form of a critique of phenomenology." Jacques Derrida, "Structure, Sign, and Play in the Discourse of the Human Sciences," in Mackey and Donato, eds., *The Structuralist Controversy* (Baltimore: Johns Hopkins University Press, 1970), p. 134. On Derrida's "grammatological reduction" see John Caputo, *Radical Hermeneutics: Repitition, Deconstruction, and the Hermeneutic Project* (Indiana: Indiana University Press, 1987).

2. Jacques Derrida, *Speech and Phenomena*, trans. David Allison (Evanston: Northwestern University Press, 1973), p. 38.
3. Ibid., p. 65.
4. Derrida, "Structure, Sign, and Play," p. 249.
5. *Ibid.*, p. 263.
6. Jacques Derrida, "Différance," *Margins of Philosophy*, trans. Alan Bass (Chicago: University of Chicago Press, 1982), p. 11.
7. Caputo, *Radial Hermeneutics*, p. 193.
8. Ibid., p. 130.
9. Derrida, "Structure, Sign, and Play," p. 264.
10. Jacques Derrida, "The Ends of Man," *Margins of Philosophy*, p. 135.
11. Jacques Derrida, "Violence and Metaphysics," *Writing and Difference*, trans. Alan Bass (Chicago: University of Chicago Press, 1978), p. 125.
12. Rodolphe Gasché, "Deconstruction as Criticism," *Glyph*, Vol. VI (1979), pp. 186.
13. Ibid., p. 188.
14. Ibid.
15. Maurice Merleau-Ponty, *Phenomenology of Perception*, trans. Colin Smith (New York: Humanities Press, 1962), p. 333.
16. Maurice Merleau-Ponty, *The Visible and the Invisible*, trans. Alfonso Lingis (Evanston: Northwestern University Press, 1968), p. 121.
17. Ibid., p. 240.
18. Ibid., pp. 238–39.
19. Ibid., p. 225.
20. Ibid., p. 122.
21. Ibid.
22. Derrida, "Structure, Sign, and Play," p. 260.
23. Gasché, "Deconstruction," p. 180.
24. Merleau-Ponty, *Phenomenology of Perception*, p. xiv.
25. Merleau-Ponty, *The Visible and the Invisible*, p. 132.
26. "Philosophy and Communication: Round-table Discussion between Ricoeur and Derrida," included in Leonard Lawlor, *Imagination and Chance* (Albany: SUNY Press, 1992), p. 138–39.
27. Jurgen Habermas, *The Philosophical Discourse of Modernity: Twelve Lectures*, trans. Frederick Lawrence (Cambridge: MIT Press, 1987), p. 171.
28. This point is effectively made by Mark Yount in "Two Reversibilities: Merleau-Ponty and Derrida," in Busch and Gallagher, eds., *Merleau-Ponty, Hermeneutics and Postmodernism* (Albany: SUNY Press, 1992), pp. 213–26.
29. Merleau-Ponty, *The Visible and the Invisible*, p. 151.

30. Ibid., p. 135.
31. Cf. Raoul Morley, *French Philosophers in Conversation* (New York: Routledge, 1991), pp. 97–98.
32. Derrida, "Differance," p. 3.
33. Merleau-Ponty, *The Visible and the Invisible*, p. 235.

2

Chiasmatic Differences: The Separation of Sight in Merleau-Ponty and Derrida

David S. Ferris

If we wish to understand language in the origination of its operation, we must pretend to have never spoken, we must submit language to a reduction without which it would again escape from us while bringing us back to what it signifies to us, we must look at language as mutes look at those who speak, we must compare the art of language to other modes of expression, we must attempt to see it as one of these mute arts. It may be that the meaning of language has a decisive privilege, but it is in trying this parallel that we will perceive what will perhaps render that parallel impossible in the end.

—Merleau-Ponty, "Le Langage indirect
et les voix du silence."

To speak of *écart* or divergence in Merleau-Ponty and *différance* in Derrida risks the assumption of a relation that would promise neither divergence nor difference nor deferral. To speak of these terms in Merleau-Ponty and Derrida is thus to pose a question that cannot proceed by comparing Derrida and Merleau-Ponty and their remarks on seeing and writing, but rather by elaborating the question of how the relation of seeing and writing is thought within their work. While the elaboration of this question will involve those instances where Merleau-Ponty and Derrida explicitly treat the visual, what is at stake in their treatment of the visual can hardly be represented in visual terms. Rather, what is always at stake whenever writing and the visual are evoked is a concept of relation through which a theory of the visual (that is, the ability to see writing and seeing in terms of one another) could be elaborated. Through this focus, or, to be more precise, through a metaphor of the visual, this essay will take as its subject the operation of a reversibility that determines the possibility of any such concept of relation.[1] To be absolutely clear about what is meant by this reversibility, we need only turn to Merleau-Ponty, who points out in his essay "Eye and Mind" that what is at stake in this relation is nothing less than metaphysics itself.[2] In order to approach the operation of this reversibility in Merleau-Ponty and Derrida, my remarks will move toward their recourse to the figure of the chiasmus.[3] But, first, I will turn to what Merleau-Ponty refers to as the *écart* of language in order to trace the significance of this aspect of language for the reversibility of writing and visibility in Merleau-Ponty's work. Within this context, Derrida's evocation of the chiasmus in *La Verité en peinture* will be located.

At the beginning of his essay, "Indirect Language and the Voices of Silence," Merleau-Ponty uses *écart* to refer to Saussure's account of the relation between one sign and another:

> What we have learned from Saussure is that signs taken one by one do not signify anything, and that each one of them does not so much express a meaning as mark a divergence [*écart*] of meaning between itself and other signs.[4]

In these words, Merleau-Ponty appears to evoke what has now become a deconstructive commonplace in postmodern or poststructuralist philosophy and literary criticism: the arbitrariness of the sign. However, rather than rehearse the arbitrariness for which Saussure has now become a not so arbitrary sign, Merleau-Ponty picks up Saussure's account of signification by emphasizing the divergence which constitutes the possibility of reference and meaning for a sign. Such a divergence cannot therefore be construed as, or even confused with, an essentially empirical difference between language and things. This is why an external world is never at stake in any account of the linguistic structure of perception (at least to the extent that this perception involves a minimal presence of con-sciousness[5]). Indeed, in any reflection on language, the difference between language and things can never be an issue, and precisely because things have no determining role to play in either our un-derstanding of language or how it represents, which is to say, they have no determining role in *how we decide to understand percep-tion*. As a result, we are always led back to the *écart*, or as Merleau-Ponty remarks: "La perception m'a comme le langage" (*Le Visible et l'invisible*, hereafter *Visible*, 244). The question of perception—to the extent that it cannot be separated from consciousness—becomes a linguistic question in Merleau-Ponty, it is ultimately the question of a figure (see note 5). What this indicates is that any judicious account of Merleau-Ponty's understanding of perception must consider its indebtedness to an *écart* that belongs fundamentally to language. As Merleau-Ponty's account of Saussure emphasizes, this *écart* marks the divergence between a sign and its meaning as the effect of the relation of one sign to another; in other words, the *écart* occurs because of what constitutes language as language. Here, divergence defines meaning as the necessity of a detour through what makes a sign knowable as a sign, namely, divergence itself. So defined, the *écart* is not in any way the difference between a sign and what it refers to but rather the movement through which any reference to and any perception of a world can be said to take place.

By locating divergence as a movement proper to language, Merleau-Ponty's use of this term would appear to establish an easily graspable ground from which to derive a considerable congruence between his thought and that of Derrida. Moreover, Merleau-Ponty's use of terms such as *pli*,[6] and his description of meaning as that which "appears only at the intersection of and as it were in the interval between words" ("n'apparaît . . . qu'à l'intersection et comme dans l'intervalle des mots" ["Langage indirect" 53]) would suggest that there is at least a thematic correspondence between Derrida and Merleau-Ponty, since Derrida will also turn to notions of the "fold" and "spacing" in his reflection on mimesis in "The Double Session." Yet, as is well known, "fold" and "spacing" are only two among the many terms employed by Derrida in his writing. The recourse to such terms is strategic to the extent that it establishes a chain of terms that would follow the logic of *différance*—a term that cannot exclude itself from the chain it describes but can never originate. This strategy would already distinguish how Derrida and Merleau-Ponty develop the consequences of what they examine in terms of *écart* and *différance*. However, the question still needs to be asked: Does Merleau-Ponty's disinclination to develop the kind of discursive practice evident in Derrida's writings (if not a text that could be, perhaps, speculatively entitled *L'Écart postal*) involve a matter of philosophical style rather than an irreconcilable difference in the set of issues that their thought tends toward?

There are passages in Merleau-Ponty's essay "Indirect Language" that, if written today, might read like a parody of Derrida left over from the days when deconstruction survived as a mode of literary criticism. Take for example: "Nowhere does [language] stop and leave a place for pure meaning, it is always limited only by more language, and meaning appears in language only by being set in words" ("Nulle part il ne cesse pour laisser place à du sens pur, il n'est jamais limité que par du langage encore et le sens ne paraît en lui que serti dans les mots" ["Langage indirect" 53]). If Derrida and deconstruction are to be summarily dismissed as semiological reductionism, then, on the strength of statements such as these, Merleau-Ponty's thought and the direction it takes in his later writings must suffer the same dismissive fate. There are distinctions to be made here: what might be dismissed as a deconstructive gesture in the accultured 1990s should hardly be considered such *avant la lettre*, nor should the rallying cry of semiological reduction become an excuse to turn away from the development of French thought since Merleau-Ponty's death—as if one could reduce language to an Adamic world of perceptual presence without deconstruction. To decide the relation between Merleau-Ponty and Derrida according to such a reduction would be to ignore the specificity of the question that emerges from the late work of Merleau-Ponty, a question that Derrida has recently acknowledged in a text he prepared for an exhibition on visual self-portraiture.[7] Within the work of Merleau-Ponty, this is a question about the way in which the visual constitutes the issues that Derrida examines under the rubric of textuality.

In his essay "Indirect Language and the Voices of Silence," Merleau-Ponty introduces the visual only after an introductory section in which he expounds upon what he refers to variously as the obliqueness, the opacity, the autonomy of language. These characteristics are themselves indistinguishable from the indirectness and allusiveness that Merleau-Ponty summarizes under the name of the silence of language ("tout langage est indirect ou allusif, est, si l'on veut, silence" ["Langage indirect" 54]). It is to this silence that the comparison of writing and the visual will resort, as Merleau-Ponty not only makes this silence become the condition of both the writer and the painter but does so in a way that places both on the reverse side of their productions. The passage in which this occurs develops as follows:

> The true word, the word that signifies, the word that finally renders present *l'absente de tous les bouquets* ["what is absent from every bouquet"] and frees the meaning captive in the thing, is only silence with respect to its empirical usage since it does not go so far as to become a common name. Language is of itself oblique and autonomous, and, if it were ever able to signify a thought or thing directly, this would be no more than a secondary power derived from the inner life of language. Accordingly, the writer,

like the weaver, works on the reverse side: he works solely with language and it is because of this that he finds himself suddenly surrounded by meaning. If this is true, the writer's mode of operation is not very different from that of the painter. ("Langage indirect" 56)

Leaving aside for the moment why Merleau-Ponty should express caution with the phrase "if this is true," it cannot be overlooked that the comparison of the writer to the painter finds itself mediated by the position of the weaver who works on the reverse side of what is being woven. With respect to the writer, this reversed position arises from the silence that defines language as language. This is not, however, as Merleau-Ponty notes, a silence that denies language any signifying power—as if language could be reduced to an opposition between itself and silence. Rather, this silence allows language to signify even to the extent of permitting the absence of a sign to be understood as another sign. It is this movement from one sign to another that Merleau-Ponty describes as "an operation of language on language that suddenly decenters itself towards its meaning" ("une opération du langage sur le langage qui soudain se décentre vers son sens" ["Langage indirect" 55]). Accordingly, as the long passage just cited indicates, the occurrence of meaning is attributed to a second power (neither the object of thought nor thought itself), which Merleau-Ponty calls the "internal life of language." What Merleau-Ponty means by such a phrase is precisely the movement through which language is said to decenter itself. What is important to note here is that this movement is not, as we are so accustomed to assert, a decentering *away* from meaning (such an assumption is itself contradictory since language could only decenter itself away from a meaning that is autonomous to it and that precedes it). Instead, Merleau-Ponty describes this decentering as a sudden movement *toward* meaning. In other words, the divergence or *écart* that constitutes language defines the signifying movement of language as a silence, whose suddenness may only be known in terms of the language through which it occurred. To cite a metaphor used by Merleau-Ponty, divergence and thus meaning are related in the same way that "a footprint signifies the movement and effort of a body" ("Il porte son sens comme la trace d'un pas signifie le mouvement et l'effort d'un corps" ["Langage indirect" 56]). As this example points out, no signification takes place unless what is to be signified can be known as a sign that is inseparable from its reversed imprint.

Because the movement of signification is always a movement from one sign to another, Merleau-Ponty cannot avoid risking the truism that the writer can only work with language. This is only a truism, however, if what Merleau-Ponty means here is restricted to the empirical medium of the writer. Rather, what Merleau-Ponty articulates at this moment is the unavoidable condition of language: language cannot transgress the limit that makes it language, and this is especially so when it is a question of what language represents (to assume otherwise would be, in Merleau-Ponty's metaphor, to work always on the other side of language). It is because (*ainsi*) of this restriction that the writer also becomes, suddenly, surrounded by meaning, since meaning, in this case, is not what language represents but language's attempt to represent itself as meaning, in other words, its *vouloir-dire*. At this juncture, or rather at this point of divergence, language and meaning cannot be separated from one another in Merleau-Ponty. To repeat: the *écart* is not between language and things but within language, which is to say, it occurs between language and meaning (since meaning only arises from an *écart* within language, its meaning can only be traced to the divergence of one sign from another). For this reason, Merleau-Ponty emphasizes:

> As far as language is concerned, it is the lateral relation of one sign to another which makes each one of them significant, so that meaning appears only at the intersection of and *as it were* in the interval between words. ("Langage indirect" 53; emphasis mine)

Meaning may only be traced to where there is silence, to where one is unable to say whether or not something is absent. This inability to decide is the very condition under which absence itself may become a sign, whose capacity to speak of this intersection or interval turns it into a witness for the *écart* that prevents it from ever supplying a common name (to supply such a name would be to assert that a sign may become the very separation [*écart*] that allows it to become a sign, never mind to signify). As a result of this condition, language can never, as Merleau-Ponty states, signify directly a thought or a thing. This is why, if we are to speak or say anything, the relation of thought to language cannot be understood as an act of placing a word under each thought, since, as Merleau-Ponty also observes, "if we did this nothing would ever be said" ("Dire, ce n'est pas mettre un mot sous chaque pensée: si nous le faisions, rien ne serait jamais dit" ["Langage indirect" 55]). Nothing would be said because if every thought had a word, lan-

guage could not function as language. In other words, if we were
to place a word under every thought, the *écart* through which language becomes language could not exist. It is this constitutive condition of language that necessitates that the writer "like the weaver
always works on the reverse side [*à l'envers*]." What comes between the writer and what the written word represents is language,
and it is this eventuality that defines, through the example of the
weaver, the relation between writing and the visible as a relation
of reversibility.

Although Merleau-Ponty's choice of the weaver as a mediating
example may be traced to at least Plato's use of the same metaphor to define the relation of meaning to language in the *Sophist*,
what demands attention here is the reversibility introduced by this
example. Inasmuch as the weaver and the writer work on the reverse or wrong side (*à l'envers*) of their respective mediums, what
they produce may only be understood from a position that, in effect, repeats the position from which the writer and painter both
work. To be on the other side of the writer or weaver is to be in
the position of sight, the position of being able to see what is meant
to be seen, that is, to be able to see what the writer or weaver
cannot see. The analogy of the painter to the writer or weaver would
appear to undergo some strain at this juncture; for, what the painter
sees (the painting) would also be what everyone else sees. Here,
the reversibility that defines, on the one hand, the writer and the
weaver and, on the other, those who see their work does not appear to be operative: the same painting is seen by painter and spectator alike. But, is this difference what Merleau-Ponty means by
reversibility? Is being on the wrong side with the writer and weaver
the same as being on the side of the painter?

In one of the working notes appended to *The Visible and the
Invisible*, Merleau-Ponty speaks directly of the reversibility involved
in this example. In this reference, Merleau-Ponty not only locates
reversibility in the figure of the chiasmus, but goes on to speak of
an inability to decide between the two sides that make up any
reversible relation:

> The chiasmus, reversibility, is the idea that every perception is
> doubled by a counter-perception (Kant's real opposition), is an
> act with two faces, one no longer knows who speaks and who
> listens. Speaking-listening, seeing-being seen, perceiving-being
> perceived circularity (it is this that makes it appear to us that
> perception forms itself *in the things themselves*)—Activity = pas-
> sivity. (*Visible* 318)

This inability to decide between who sees and what is seen not only constitutes reversibility for Merleau-Ponty but, at the same time, is the double of the silence of language through which painting and writing will be compared by Merleau-Ponty.

After establishing the comparison of painter and writer by means of the metaphor of the weaver, Merleau-Ponty addresses that moment within painting that accords with the silence of language:

> It is usually said that the painter reaches us across the silent world of colors and lines, addresses in us a power of unformulated deciphering which we will only really control after having blindly exercised it, after having loved the work. The writer on the contrary, exists within already elaborated signs, in a world already speaking, and only requires of this a power of reordering our understanding according to the signs proposed to us. But if language expresses as much by what is between the words as it does with words? By what it does not "say" as by what it "says"? ("Langage indirect" 56)

From a difference between the mediums employed by the painter (which requires a power of unformulated deciphering) and the writer (which requires a lesser power of reordering), Merleau-Ponty moves to a question about the relation between what is said and what is not said by language. Such a question is no longer concerned with what language or writing would represent according to an established system of signs. Rather, it is a question about language's ability to express its silence, which is to say, a question about language's own origin. To such an origin Merleau-Ponty addresses the following remark:

> If we wish to understand language in the origination of its operation, we must pretend to have never spoken, we must submit language to a reduction without which it would again evade us while bringing us back to what it signifies to us, we must *look* at language as mutes look at those who speak, we must compare the art of language to other modes of expression, we must attempt to see it as one of these mute arts. It may be that the meaning of language has a decisive privilege, but it is in trying this parallel that we will perceive what will perhaps render that parallel impossible in the end. Let us begin by understanding that there is a silent language and that painting speaks in this manner.
>
> ("Langage indirect" 58–59)

The operation of language described in these sentences necessitates (*il nous faut*) a self-inflicted muteness as the condition of its understanding. Only by reducing language to this muteness can language's ability to escape from us be countered. Without this reduction, language would escape from us. The situation Merleau-Ponty describes here presents the origin of language as a deceptive reduction ("il nous faut feindre ... le soumettre à une réduction") whose function is to avoid the ability of language to escape from us even as it brings us back to what it means. Given this situation, the movement toward meaning is, for Merleau-Ponty, precisely how language escapes from us. Consequently, the very reduction Merleau-Ponty appeals to as a means of preventing the escape of language will also be how this escape happens. Because of this escape there will always be a silence that language can never give voice to but without which it could never speak. It is in this manner that painting, according to Merleau-Ponty, must be understood as speaking ("il y a un langage tacite et ... la peinture parle à sa façon"). At the same time, it should not be forgotten, as Merleau-Ponty points out, that this parallel may well prove its own impossibility. In other words, the reversibility of painting and writing, not to mention the relation of Derrida and Merleau-Ponty, may, of necessity, require a relation of divergence rather than resemblance, and especially so at that point where their thought seems so intertwined.

If reversibility depends upon a moment of resemblance in order for its exchange to take place, then the discourse through which this reversibility is defined must function not as a mirror but as if it could look into a mirror and also look at what it reflects at one and the same moment. Such an ability involves, as Merleau-Ponty clearly points out, a deception that not only reiterates the reductive feigning that allows the origin of language to be thought but also invokes the opacity that demands this reduction. In a passage from his last completed work, Merleau-Ponty makes the following remarks about resemblance, remarks that testify fully to its visual provenance as well as to the separation of sight in which resemblance takes place:

> If the reflection resembles the thing itself, it is because this reflection acts upon the eyes more or less as a thing would. It deceives the eye, it engenders a perception which has no object but which does not affect our idea of the world. In the world there is the thing itself, and outside this thing itself there is that other thing which is only reflected light rays and which happens to have an ordered correspondence with the real thing; there are two individuals, then, bound together externally by causality. As far as the thing and its mirror image are concerned, their

resemblance is only an external denomination; resemblance belongs to thought. The "cross-eyed" relation of resemblance is—in the things—a clear relation of projection. ("Langage indirect" 38)

What is here translated suggestively as "cross-eyed" requires a little more precision. Merleau-Ponty speaks of "Le louche rapport de ressemblance." *Louche* is used specifically to speak of something that lacks clarity, that is, in this sense, opaque. In a more precise medical sense, *louche* is also used to refer to the inability of a pair of eyes to focus on the same point at the same time. The relation of resemblance Merleau-Ponty refers to here is therefore not simply one of crossed eyes: in fact, no decision is possible as to whether the relation in question is cross-eyed or even wall-eyed. What is crucial is that Merleau-Ponty traces resemblance to the source of the visible, a source that is defined by eyes that fail to meet.[8] Hence, the necessary intervention of a projection or external denomination as the place of their meeting, as the place of resemblance.

If it is to the intervention of an external denomination that resemblance owes its meaning, then the relation of Derrida and Merleau-Ponty would have to face its failure to focus on both. Such is the outcome of this comparison, and precisely because this relation poses the question of whether what can be seen in one can also be seen in the other. Indeed, to elucidate one by the other is to have failed to have elucidated either the *écart* that predominates in so much of Merleau-Ponty or the *différance* that is so often pronounced in French, in order to tell the difference between difference and difference—as if such a difference could ever be told without the separation of sight. To tell this difference would be like one blind person describing the difference or *écart* of language as a visible phenomenon to another blind person.[9] We who are not blind will be unable to see the ludicrousness of this situation. Similarly, we who are not blind can always see, that is, we can always feign that we see what language or the discourse on painting is always about. Such feigning demands, however, that we become blind not in the sense of Oedipus but in the sense that we see the blindness we inflict upon ourselves (it is thus not the blindness of Tiresias either). To see such blindness is to see the origin of sight in the same way that Merleau-Ponty speaks of the attempt to see (or is it to hear?) the origin of language in the invisibility of its silence.

Given the logic that governs the relation between silence and language, invisible and visible, within which Merleau-Ponty locates the movement of divergence or separation, it is clear that Derrida's own attempt to think the limit of the discourse on painting must also turn toward the limit of a silence that is blind to the very language in which it is spoken (and *The Truth of Painting* is nothing more than the reiterated attempt to follow the movement of this limit in all its reversals and intertwinings in the discourse on art).[10] Yet, to think a limit here is not to come to a standstill, for the issue which is at stake is the possibility of thinking a limit that is not a decision between what is outside and what is inside, what is visible or invisible, silent or mute. In other words, it is a question of thinking what the deceptive reduction practiced by this decision responds to when the only answer repeats the evasion already signalled by the question. It is at this point that the chiasmus intervenes in both Derrida and Merleau-Ponty.

In the course of *The Truth in Painting*, Derrida invokes the figure of the chiasmus during his reading of drawings by Valerio Adami. This figure, referred to by its Greek name, χ (chi), appears as the anagrammatic inversion of the title (*Ich*) that Derrida gives to one of the drawings of Adami.[11] Derrida glosses his invocation of this figure in a text on the discourse of painting by citing two texts of his own. The first is to the preface ("Hors livre") of *Dissemination*, in which Derrida describes the figure of the chiasmus as a figure that "can always, hastily be thought of as the thematic of dissemination."[12] Derrida's thematic privileging of this figure does not occur in order to appeal to its history as a figure of reflexive totalization. As becomes clear from the second reference, the dissemination Derrida associates with this figure derives from an inequality that Derrida traces to the very form of its writing:

> Everything passes through this chiasmus, all writing is caught there—practices it. The form of the chiasmus, of the χ, interests me greatly, not as the symbol of the unknown but because there is there . . . a sort of fork . . . which is moreover inequal, one of its points extending its reach further than the other: figure of double gesture and crossing.[13]

If every writing is caught in what it practices, then it is unequal to the task of even explaining itself, never mind explaining the difference between itself and the referentiality from which this difference arises. Every writing is consequently incapable of seeing itself as it is seen, or, to put this in terms more familiar to Merleau-Ponty, no writing and no painting is capable of seeing either how it sees or how it is seen. In relation to itself each is unequal. Inasmuch as it would know what it sees, it must reverse itself. Yet to do so, it must be thought as a reflection upon itself as well as a reflection of itself. The consequences of this necessary step are outlined by Merleau-Ponty when he states: "There is the vision on which I reflect, I cannot think [vision] except as thought, the mind's inspection, judgment, a reading of signs" ("Il y a la vision sur laquelle je réflechis, je ne puis la penser autrement que comme pensée, inspection de l'esprit, jugement, lecture de signes" ["Langage indirect" 54]). From the separation in which perception is born there arises the necessity of a reading of signs. Reflection will therefore entail a folding back of the subject upon itself, but a folding back that affords no coincidence with itself because, like thought, it must face a reading of signs.[14] It is from the movement of reversal that takes place within this reflection that the inequal reach of the chiasmus may be traced. There is thus, in the movement of reversal, an incalculable divergence whose effect cannot be accounted for *avant la lettre*.

In tracing the movement of reversal that allows the figure of the chiasmus to function as a figure of divergence or *écart*, a discourse on the visual, a discourse on painting has arisen by necessity. This discourse demands the parallel of writing and painting, a parallel to be encompassed within one figure. This parallel turns, in the end, to what Merleau-Ponty refers to as a reading of signs, which is to say, a reading that produces the divergence to which it would now trace its origin. It is in such a tracing that every decision about the relation of writing to the visual, and vice versa, takes place. This trace is precisely the relation through which the visual, in the words of Derrida, does without *and* goes beyond this language—*(se) passe (de) ce langage*.[15] Yet, it is only through the discourse on painting, the discourse on the visual, that its silence may ever be said to take place. Is this the silence of language? How can two silences be compared when they can never have diverged from one another, when the visual is already the silence of language's attempt to see itself see? As one or the other could have written, "*par le jeu de cet* écart . . . *de ce silence qui (se) passe de (ce) langage.* . . ."

Notes

1. This essay originated as a paper presented in a special session on "Écart and Différance: Merleau-Ponty and Derrida on Seeing and Writing" organized by Martin Dillon at the 1993 IAPL Conference. I must thank

Martin Dillon for having organized this session as well as for a generosity that was combined with his forceful defense of a quite different
reading of Merleau-Ponty.

2. M. Merleau-Ponty "Toute théorie de la peinture est une métaphysique"
(*L'Oeil et l'esprit* [Paris: Gallimard, 1964], p. 42). Unless otherwise
noted, all translations from Merleau-Ponty's and Derrida's writings are
my own.

3. For other treatments of the relation between Merleau-Ponty and Derrida,
see the contributions of Gary B. Madison, Martin C. Dillon, Hugh J.
Silverman, and Joseph Margolis to the following two volumes,
Hermeneutics and Postmodernism, ed. Thomas W. Busch and Shaun
Gallagher (Albany: SUNY Press, 1992), and *Merleau-Ponty Vivant*, ed.
M. C. Dillon (Albany: SUNY Press, 1991); Hugh J. Silverman, "Merleau-
Ponty and Derrida: Writing on Writing," in *Ontology and Alterity in
Merleau-Ponty*, ed. Galen A. Johnson and Michael B. Smith (Evanston:
Northwestern University Press, 1990), pp. 130–41; and Bernard Flynn,
"Textuality and the Flesh," *Journal of the British Society for Phenom-
enology*, Vol. 15:2 (May 1984), pp. 164–27.

4. M. Merleau-Ponty "Le langage indirect et les voix du silence" (Paris:
Gallimard, 1960), p. 49. Subsequent references to this essay will be
given parenthetically in the text.

5. On this requirement, it is instructive to read a late remark about consciousness by Merleau-Ponty: "Avoir conscience = avoir une figure
sur un fond—on ne peut pas remonter plus loin" (Working Notes to
Le Visible et l'invisible [Paris: Gallimard, 1964], p. 245; referred to
subsequently as *Visible*). Since, as Merleau-Ponty writes here, being
conscious is equal to having a figure on a base, consciousness is to be
thought only through recourse to a rhetorical dimension, and only
then if it regards the figure as resting on a base. Beyond this recourse
one cannot go back any further.

6. Read, for example: "Si le signe ne veut dire quelque chose qu'en tant
qu'il se profile sur les autres signes, son sens est tout engagé dans le
langage, la parole joue toujours sur fond de parole, elle n'est jamais
qu'un pli dans l'immense tissu du parler. . . . Il y a donc une opacité
du langage: nulle part il ne cesse pour laisser place à du sens pur. [If
the sign means something only to the extent that it is profiled by
other signs, its meaning is completely involved in language, the world
always plays on the base of another word, it is nothing other than a
fold in the immense tissue of speaking. . . . There is therefore an opacity
of language: nowhere does it stop to allow place for a pure meaning]"
("Langage indirect," p. 53).

7. See, J. Derrida, *Mémoires d'aveugle. L'autoportrait et autres ruines* (Paris:
Éditions de la Réunion des musées nationaux, 1990), p. 56.

8. Note also the following passage from *Le Visible et l'invisible*: "Réfléchir
sur le deux, la paire, ce n'est pas deux actes, deux synthèses, c'est
fragmentation de l'être, c'est possibilité de l'écart (deux yeux, deux
oreilles: possibilité de discrimination, d'emploi du diacritique), c'est
avènement de la différence (sur fond de ressemblance donc, sur fond
de l'ὁμοῦ ἦν πάντα) [To reflect on the two, the pair, this is not two
acts, two syntheses, it is the fragmentation of being, it is the possibil-

ity of separation (two eyes, two ears: possibility of discrimination, of the use of diacritics), it is the advent of difference (on the basis of resemblance therefore, on the basis of the 'same was the many')]" (*Visible*, p. 270, [November 1959]).

9. Derrida noted a related effect in *Mémoires d'aveugle* (p. 11) when he described the sonorous aspect of language as precisely what remains invisible: "Il faut toujours rappeler que le mot, le vocable s'entend, le phénomène sonore reste invisible en tant que tel. Preoccupant en nous le temps plutôt que l'espace, il ne s'adresse pas seulement d'aveugle à aveugle, comme un code pur non-voyant, il nous parle en vérité, tout le temps, de l'aveuglement qui le constitue. Le langage se parle, cela veut dire *de l'aveuglement*. Il nous parle toujours de l'aveuglement qui le constitue."

10. "Les discours sur la peinture se destinent peut-être à reproduire la limite qui les constitue, et quoi qu'ils fassent et quoi qu'ils disent: il y a pour eux un dedans et un dehors de l'oeuvre dès lors qu'il y a de l'oeuvre" (*La Verité en peinture*, p. 16).

11. "χ, la lettre du chiasme, c'est *Chi* en sa transcription habituelle. J'appelle ainsi cette autre scène, selon si vous voulez l'inversion anagrammatique de *Ich*, ou de *Isch* (l'homme hébraïque)" (*La Verité en peinture*, p. 189).

12. Jacques Derrida, "Selon le χ (le chiasme) (qu'on pourra toujours considérer, hâtivement comme le dessein thématique de la dissémination)" ("Hors livre," *La dissémination* [Paris: Seuil, 1972], p. 52).

13. J. Derrida *Positions* (Paris: Minuit, 1972, 95).

14. This recognition may be read in the "Working Notes" to *Le Visible et l'invisible*: "All this leaves untouched the question about what it is 'to know,' 'to be conscious,' 'to perceive' in a Cartesian sense—a question that is never asked—Theses such as 'connection,' 'thought of seeing and thought of feeling' are discussed in the sense of presumption, 'meaning'—It is shown that a connector is necessary, that there must be a 'pure thinking (*pur denken*),' or a '*Selbsterscheinung*,' an auto-apparition, a pure appearance of appearance. . . . But all this supposes the idea of a for-itself and ultimately this cannot explain transcendence—To look in quite different direction: the for-itself as an incontestable but derived attribute [need one stress that the word translated here as attribute (*caractère*) carries as its first meaning the very foundation of written language, its characters?]: it is the culmination of separation in *differentiation* (*c'est la culmination de l'écart dans la différentiation*)—Presence to itself is presence to a differentiated world—Perceptual separation as making up the 'sight' (*vue*) such as is implied in the reflex for example,—and closing the being for itself through language as differentiation" (*Visible*, pp. 244–45). To look in the different direction proposed by Merleau-Ponty, is it not to look in the direction of language as the differentiation that establishes the *écart* of perception? It is in this question that one can see the necessity "pour toute une relecture du dernier Merleau-Ponty." If one can be even more explicit than the passage just cited, one need only cite the following: "There remains the problem of the passage from perceptual

meaning to language meaning (*sens langagier* [more precise than "language meaning" would be "meaning relative to language," or "language-like meaning"], from behavior to thematization. Thematization itself must however be understood as behavior in the highest degree: the relation of one to the other is a dialectical relation: by breaking the silence language realizes what silence wishes for but cannot obtain. Silence continues to envelop language; the silence of absolute language, of language thinking" (*Visible*, pp. 229–30). The problem of the passage between perception and meaning is the problem of a language that cannot obtain what is wished for. This problem is the problem of an *écart* that has no independent existence between perception and meaning but ex-ists as their effect.

15. "Quant à la peinture, sur elle, à côté d'elle ou par-dessus, le discours me paraît toujours niais, à la fois enseignant et incantatoire, programmé, agi par la compulsion magistrale, poétique ou philosophique, toujours, et plus encore quand il est pertinent, en situation de bavardage, inégal et improductif au regard de ce qui, d'un trait, (se) passe (de) ce langage, lui demeurant hétérogène ou lui interdisant tout surplomb [As for painting, any discourse on it, beside it or above, always strikes me as inane, both didactic and incantatory, programmed, driven by the compulsion to mastery, whether poetical or philosophical, always, and the more so when it is pertinent, in the setting of chitchat, unequal and unproductive in the sight of what, at a stroke, does without and goes beyond this language, remaining heterogeneous to it or denying it any overview]" (*La Verité en peinture*, pp. 175–78).

3

Expression and Inscription at the Origins of Language

Dorothea Olkowski

While much has been written about Merleau-Ponty's unquestionable indebtedness to Husserl's phenomenology,[1] it is not difficult to note the many steps Merleau-Ponty took to differentiate his own work from that phenomenology, steps that, at times, seem to have taken him to the point of creating an altogether new method of carrying out philosophy and interrogating the world. One area of Merleau-Ponty's thought in which this distancing and creation clearly takes place is his philosophy of language. The distancing orients itself around Merleau-Ponty's rejection of Husserl's "eidetic of language"; what Merleau-Ponty creates in the place of eidetic phenomenology is part of what this essay will address. Husserl's eidetic of language is a logic concerned with the formal properties of signification and their rules of transformation, resulting in a system of precise significations that translate all discourse into a clear language.[2] Merleau-Ponty objects to pure grammar because of its inability to either recognize or account for the confusions of everyday life. When language is construed as a pure sign representing a pure signification, speech is nothing more than coded thought, the pure "spectre" of language (*Prose of the World*, 7).

Given the alleged hostility of deconstructive theory to any form of phenomenology, it is somewhat surprising to find Derrida objecting to Husserl on much the same grounds. Keeping one eye on Husserl's metaphysical presuppositions, namely that the *form* of an object is given in a clear and present intuition, Derrida asks of Husserl how language can ever be used in reference to transient objects and circumstances, given that, on Husserl's account, language is constituted independently of them.[3] When the myth of the plentitude of presence is deconstructed, notes Derrida, it "remains for us to *speak*, to make our voices *resonate* throughout the

45

corridors in order to make up for [*suppléer*] the breakup of presence [insofar as] the thing itself always escapes" (*Speech and Phenomena* 104). As such, for Derrida, the inscription of the voice
guarantees the surplus of things over the ideal nature of signs.

Both Merleau-Ponty and Derrida initially embrace Saussure when
they turn away from Husserl, and it is this move in both that interests me more than their mutual suspicion of Husserl's eidetics.
That is, apart from the critical stance in relation to Husserl, what
values does each embrace? What is clear at the outset is that Merleau-
Ponty and Derrida operate in accordance with not merely different
logics, but also different purposes and methods. I am less interested in pitting one against the other in order to declare a victor,
than I am in delimiting the process by which each assesses language. What purposes are at work in each approach and what do
those purposes tell us about the respective method, agency, or effects of each philosophy?

In his search for a positive point of departure, Merleau-Ponty
orients his philosophy of language, not in terms of Husserlian intuition but strictly in terms of Saussure's diacritical theoretics.[4]
Thus, Merleau-Ponty begins with the declaration that, taken singly, signs are nothing.[5] Such a declaration, however, is dangerous.
It is dangerous if expressed without reservation or qualification,
because it opens the way to the conclusion that not only individual signs are nothing, but that *language* itself is in some sense
nothing insofar as language is radically contingent and radically
conventional. In this light language would be completely abstract.
It would be subject to a definitive lack of concern and, so, a dizzy-
ing drift. Ultimately, it might turn out that what Husserl hypoth-
esized as the foundation of language would turn out to be its telos.
If signs are nothing, form is all that is left, and all speech would
take its cue from the routinized formalizations of abstract signs
organized according to precise grammatical, syntactic, and semantic codes. Innovation, creation, change, and mystery would serve
no purpose, thus would cease to exist. Literary language, were it
to exist at all, would be limited to formal codes more restrictive
than any formal rhetorical rules, and would function only to provide the illusion of innovation without actually allowing it.

In order to escape the condemnation of language to its formal
organization, language demands some sort of non-external organizing concept that makes it possible for the grammatical, syntactic,
and semantic codes to not only operate formally, but to coexist as
a whole. Language is a whole that nonetheless moves and changes

in accordance with a kind of internal articulation of its various aspects. While signs may mean nothing singly, together they must, according to Merleau-Ponty, constitute a unity. Following Saussure, Merleau-Ponty claims that insofar as signs constitute a particular kind of unity, they exist below the level of words and below the level of meanings. At the "origin of words" linguistics discovers phonemes, "oppositive and relative principles" that function as "variations of a unique speech apparatus" ("Indirect Language" 40). The oppositive and relative character of phonemes determines that they are diacritical from the start, thus they are mutually differentiated. The mutual dependence of signs knits them into a whole, a unity, and by this means meaning is produced (p. 41).[6]

When Merleau-Ponty claims that meaning is produced, he is not investing in either a correspondence theory nor in a claim about essential meanings. Rather, he states, the mutual dependence of signs produces meaning, but only at the "edge." The edge of what? Where in this diacritically structured whole would one find an edge? Apparently, for Merleau-Ponty, everywhere. In the "interval" between words, but also insofar as each word is totally involved in language, in the language system that operates opaquely according to the logic of a woven fabric. Signs, though conditioned by formal linguistic rules, are nonetheless woven together, and it is this weaving that accounts for language. The nature of the conceptualization operating here remains somewhat obscure. Its clear that Merleau-Ponty is adopting some form of Saussurean diacritics; however, the terms of description and the resulting explanation are not those of Saussure's structural linguistics. Saussurean linguistics strictly separates signifier from signified, and constitutes the sign as an unmotivated cultural entity delimited by sound, reference, and the undeniably stable organization of grammar, syntax, and structure. This last, even though the sign is unmotivated, for the sign never ceases to be the combination of a concept and a sound-image. Merleau-Ponty, on the other hand, while accepting the diacritical nature of the sign, the eminence of the phoneme, and, in principle, the notion of structure, maintains a metaphoricity that undermines Saussurean structuralism.

In *The Prose of the World*, Merleau-Ponty acknowledges that Saussure has made it possible to make sense of how philosophy can leave behind Husserl's eidetics yet remain rational (*Prose of the World* 22). Thus Merleau-Ponty admires Saussure's insight into how semantic slippage takes place in language (diachronically). "Diachronic events," notes Saussure, "are always accidental and

particular" (*Course* 93). As Merleau-Ponty understands this, there
is no implication that, synchronically, "usage" is somehow reducible to the etymology of the word (*Prose of the World* 22). There
remains, according to Merleau-Ponty, an order, system, or totality
without which communication and any sort of linguistic community are impossible (the linguistics of speech) (p. 24). In language
as such, a totality, nothing is equivocal.

While Saussure declares that "speaking is necessary for the establishment of language, and historically, its actuality always comes
first" (p. 18), still, for Saussure the sign unites a *concept* and a
sound-image (p. 66); thus changes in meaning "always result in a
shift in the relationship between the signified and the signifier"
(p. 75). The "shift in relationship" occurs between concept and
signifier, both of which do change. So when, for example, "Latin
necare 'kill' became *noyer* 'drown' in French," and "[b]oth the sound-
image and the concept changed," what does not change is the nature
of the relation between some sound-image and some *concept*
(p. 75).

Is this what Merleau-Ponty means when he declares that speech
is a "fold" in the "immense" and "opaque" "fabric" that is language? The claim that language is opaque seems to refer to the
rejection of language as a "technique for ciphering/deciphering ready-
made significations" ("Indirect Language" 42). Language doesn't even
begin with words, but with phonemes, whose primary quality, in
Merleau-Ponty's assessment, is not that they are vocal (he never
even mentions this) but that they do not lend themselves to ready-
made signification. Saussure goes so far as to declare that a concept is "initially nothing," that is, any concept is only "a value
determined by its relations with other similar values" (*Course* 117).
Nevertheless, for Saussure, it is still the case that without such
concept-values signification would not exist.

On the other hand, it seems as though, for Merleau-Ponty, there
are never any concepts. If signs are equivocal, it is only insofar as
they are taken alone, outside of the totality of language; thus they
are so banal as to be without sense ("Indirect Language" 42). Were
there to be any concepts, they would simply be the product of
"common consent," a questionable status at best, for how long and
for how many speakers could such common consent endure? Instead, Merleau-Ponty maintains that language has the character of
an "immense fabric," "something like a universe," though one that
contains secrets that it can unveil or uncover and even teach to
every child (p. 43). What kind of organization could this be, since

unveiling is not, apparently, defined as correspondence between language's secrets and things? Rather, what is unveiled is a universe of meanings themselves. No correspondence, no translation, no cipher. Yet, just as in Saussure, there are two languages. One, empirical; the other true (p. 44). One the isolated thread; the other the fabric. One, where the signs themselves are equivocal and banal; the other, constituted out of the intercourse of signs, the between of words or even phonemes, existing in an immense universe of silence that is an allusive and indirect discourse and among whose "threads of silence" speech is mixed together (p. 46).

This is an odd formulation, quite unlike Saussure's: speech out of silence. In fact, Saussure is quite uninterested in determining what amounts to the origin of language, that is, the origination of utterances:

> No society, in fact, knows or has ever known language other than as a product inherited from preceding generations, and one to be accepted as such. That is why the question of the origin of speech is not so important as it is generally assumed to be. The question is not even worth asking: the only real object of linguistics is the normal, regular, life of an existing idiom. (*Course* 71–72).

This is no doubt related to the relative stability of the signifier. Both the individual and the community are powerless with respect to the signifier, which is always bound to the *existing* language system, not to language users, who remain by and large unaware of language laws and satisfied with the existing idiom: insofar as it is arbitrary, there is no motive to change the sign (*Course* 73, 74). Given also the seemingly unlimited number of signs involved and the fact that language as a system is ruled by *logic*, the very complexity of language makes it immutable (p. 73).

Thus, even though change does admittedly occur, "the principle of change is based on the principle of continuity" (*Course* 74). Language, for Saussure, is unlike other human institutions because it is not based at all on "the natural relation of things," and unlike, for example, the conventions of dress, language is not invariably "dictated by the human body" (pp. 75–76). No such limits exist in the relation of sound and concept—the only rule is that sound and concept must unite. So when language changes, it does so by means of social forces over time. No precise definition or explanation of this process is ever offered by Saussure. He lamely comments that time changes everything and language should be no exception. In fact, the situation here seems to be that the stability

of language, grounded in its logic and structure, overrides its ability to change: Saussure can point to real, historical changes, but
he cannot explain them. Saussure even admits that his description
of the forces of change gives us a language that is not really living
but only potentially so (p. 77). "Language is speech less speaking"
he says, hardly an enthusiastic endorsement of the role of speakers, whom he is quick to reenvelop within the community, whose
language is strictly tied to "social fact" (p. 77).

It is perhaps for this reason that the normal, regular life of an
existing idiom is precisely what Merleau-Ponty takes to be equivocal and banal—hardly worth considering. The ability of language
to signify, he states, is nothing more than a secondary, empirical
power, in and of itself uninteresting and without note. What interests Merleau-Ponty, on the other hand, is something he calls "the
act of expression," a term notably absent in Saussure's discourse.
As Derrida points out, for Saussure the expressive value of a signifier
is located in the sound-image, that is, in the psychological imprint
of a sound-image on the senses; thus its functioning is purely passive or receptive (*Speech* 46). Given Saussure's notion that language is diacritical, Merleau-Ponty concludes that what goes on
between words, or even between phonemes, is what matters, and
that the words themselves are banal. This, however, is a radical
reinterpretation of the Saussurean schema.

While it is true that, according to Saussure, "each linguistic term
derives its value from its opposition to all the other terms" (*Course*
88), the framework within which this statement occurs gives it a
much different import from that of Merleau-Ponty's context. Let
the full quotation speak for itself here:

> But of all comparisons that might be imagined, the most fruitful
> is the one that might be drawn between the functioning of lan-
> guage and a game of chess. In both instances we are confronted
> with a system of values and their observable modifications. A
> game of chess is like an artificial realization of what language
> offers in a natural form. (*Course* 88)

How does this differ from Merleau-Ponty's silent and indirect discourse?

Although it is true that the value of each chess piece depends
on its placement with respect to all the others, the overall conventions of the game are "unchangeable" and are therefore "constant
principles of semiology" (p. 88). Moves consist of passing from
one state of equilibrium to the next, moving only one chess piece

at a time (p. 88), and in chess (as in language) it is "perfectly useless to recall what had just happened ten seconds previously" because the change itself is not what matters, only the resulting state of affairs (p. 89). For Saussure, the analogy is weak only with regard to the player; the user of language has no intentions or consciousness with regard to what she does, but the chess player may be said to plot out her moves. On a certain level the realization of the distance between Saussure and Merleau-Ponty, on this point, is astounding. To elaborate, Deleuze and Guattari have pointed out that chess is a game of the state or of princely courts:

> Chess pieces are coded; they have an internal nature and intrinsic properties from which their movements, situations, and confrontations derive. They have qualities; a knight remains a knight, a pawn a pawn, a bishop a bishop.... Within their milieu of interiority, chess pieces entertain biunivocal relations with one another, and with the adversary's pieces: *their functioning is structural....* Chess is indeed a war, but an institutionalized, regulated, coded war, with a front, a rear, battles.... in chess it is a question of arranging a closed space for oneself, thus of going from one point to another, of occupying the maximum number of squares with the minimum number of pieces.[7]

In short, insofar as language operates like a game of chess, it is a hierarchized, courtly or warlike game whose elements are coded internally and rigidly structured. The relation between signifier and signified may shift, but there is always a word-image and always a concept. Even in the one case of genuine change in chess (when a pawn is transformed into a queen—a late addition to the game), one of the points of the game remains to keep this kind of transformation from occurring.

And Merleau-Ponty? Is this what he describes? It is striking that Merleau-Ponty does not foreground the structure of the social institution but, rather, emphasizes the speaker or the writer, what I would call the "*auteur*," in the process of expression. The *auteur* is less the author than the perpetrator, that name that lends itself to certain expressions. Thus Merleau-Ponty's is a peculiar kind of agency who ceases her banal utterances to interrogate the world of silence, out of which expressive language emerges, not passively but not under the control of the agent either. Clearly, in calling language an opaque fabric, allusive, indirect, or silent, Merleau-Ponty is not describing a hierarchized, coded language system. The differences between Merleau-Ponty's and Saussure's conceptions constitute an abyss. No expression takes place in Saussurean

linguistics, while it permeates Merleau-Ponty's. Expression (not signification), according to Merleau-Ponty, is what takes place between
words, or better yet, not even in between, which might indicate
some sort of vacuum, but expression takes place in the "intercourse
of signs" ("Indirect Language" 45). Expression is sexually generated out of a background of silence. Merleau-Ponty's analogy is far
from that of the chess game; it is the bodily gesture of the painter
who hesitates, then adds a brush stroke that makes the painting
"that which *it* was in the process of becoming" (p. 45, emphasis
added). But all acts of expression, whether speech or painting, must
be considered before they are spoken/painted against the silent
opaque fabric that "surrounds" them and in effect generates them
(p. 46). Such an origin cannot be merely a set of rules or a structure of laws, for, as what both surrounds and generates utterances,
it is like a womb or, at least, something living. Thus Merleau-Ponty
again counters the Saussurean claim that there is nothing "natural" about language, in the sense that it is nothing like clothing
that must be adapted to the demands of a body.

If Saussure's conception of linguistics leaves no room for acts of
expression, Merleau-Ponty's is often thought of as the opposite, as
nothing but expression, in particular the spoken expression of the
thinker. Yet, in the analogy to painting, Merleau-Ponty objects to a
reading that would either reduce the world to painter's formulas
(like structuralist semiology) or attribute painting to individual
sensation ("Indirect Language" 48). Further, it is paramount to
Merleau-Ponty's notion of expressive language that, insofar as linguistic expression is an "originating operation," it must be "mute"
like all other arts of expression (p. 46). That this is the case, for
Merleau-Ponty, seems to be related to what he says in *The Visible
and the Invisible* about the speaking subject:

> The Saussurean analysis of the relations between signifiers and
> the relations from signifier to signified and between the
> significations (as differences between significations) confirms and
> rediscovers the idea of perception as a *divergence* [*écart*] by re-
> lation to a level, that is, the idea of the primordial Being, of the
> Convention of conventions, of the Speech before speech.[8]

The speaking subject is no *cogito*, no consciousness of, but is the
kind of subject that can be called "nobody," and whose utterance
is only a divergence or separation (*écart*), at most an upheaval out
of opaque fabric and silence. This makes the utterance itself no
positive production, for, as in painting, the visible work is "but

the trace of a total movement of Speech," a trace produced through divergence (*Visible* 211). Again the description of painting operates forcefully, but Merleau-Ponty characterizes language in terms of neither speech nor writing; rather, he calls it a "phonematic system" which like painting (as I have noted above) is some kind of totality. What seems to be the case here is that neither language nor painting dominates, that language characterized in terms of the phonematic system is neither speech nor writing. So if philosophy is declared to be language (p. 213), this is not to elevate language but only to invest it with the task of rediscovering the silence necessary to any *écart*.

This is difficult to make sense of until Merleau-Ponty clarifies that perception itself is a "diacritical, relative, oppositional system" (*Visible* 213), a system in which sensibles ultimately prove to be *ungraspable* (p. 214). One could say in this regard that there is no perception. Or one could say, as Merleau-Ponty does: "Speech does indeed have to enter the child as silence . . . (*i.e. as a thing simply perceived*)" (p. 363, emphasis added). Here Merleau-Ponty's analysis of language breaks into ontology. There is no way to miss the intersection of language, painting, and perception, but perceptions should not be confused with pure intuitions. The silence of ungraspable sensibles is, we might imagine, a kind of inscription of the world upon our sensibility, no longer a pure phenomenology, but rather a divergence which, I suspect, would not be able to constitute a complete subject either.

Derrida has written that there is no such thing as perception (*Speech*) and this has often been taken as a denunciation of Merleau-Ponty's phenomenology. The question circulates throughout Derrida's essays on language: Does Derridean *différance* defeat a phenomenology that is no longer pure but has been transformed into phenomenological *écart*? In the essay titled *"Différance"* Derrida writes:

> Now Saussure is first of all the thinker who put the *arbitrary character of the sign* and the *differential character* of the sign at the very foundation of general semiology, particularly linguistics. And, as we know, these two motifs—arbitrary and differential—are inseparable in his view. There can be arbitrariness because the system of signs is constituted solely by the differences in terms, and not by their plenitude.[9]

Like Merleau-Ponty, Derrida recognizes and gives preeminence to the diacritical nature of language, so much so that he calls the concept of difference the "condition of signification" ("*Différance*" 10). Given this, however, Derrida goes on to what seems to be quite a different point. In making this point Derrida again follows Merleau-Ponty, because Derrida is also interested in the origins of language. And for Derrida, the language system disappears into the system of writing: "Language is first of all writing."[10] With this statement, Derrida's objection to Saussure's general linguistics emerges in a way that is, perhaps, critical to any understanding of Derrida's work insofar as he finds, in Saussure, the implication that writing is both the origin and the perversion of language.

In spite of the differential nature of the sign with regard to both its conceptual and phonic elements, Saussure defines language in terms of the exclusion of writing. We might say that this determination of general linguistics contradicts Saussure's own analysis of language as diacritical by excluding the very element that makes language both unmotivated and differential. Yet, Saussure insists that wherever we look and whenever we look, writing is effectively destroying language. On the one hand, Saussure writes:

> But the tyranny of writing goes even further. By imposing itself upon the masses, spelling influences and modifies language. This happens only in highly literate languages where written texts play an important role. Then visual images lead to wrong pronunciations; such mistakes are really pathological. (*Course* 31)

Derrida is immediately drawn to Saussure's characterization of writing as pathology, the tyranny that enslaves otherwise good men. But, equally interesting is the disparity between writing's influence on the "masses" and the "highly literate languages" of a society where presumably the masses read because "written texts play an important role" (p. 31).

Saussure seems to concede that writing *is* language, in that we must pass through the written "form" in order to reach language proper. But because the study of writing alone would deceive us, phonology (the physiology of sounds) provides us with "precautionary measures," descriptions of the sounds with which each language functions (p. 34). However, this may not be enough, for the pathology of writing is also a pathology of *reading* and of the masses; highly literate reading masses make wrong pronunciations when they encounter visual images. The pathology of writing is visual: we know this because if a rationalized, phonologically exact alphabet were given to the masses, it too would fail (*Grammatology* 38). All attempts to gain precision visually would "obviously" confuse the reader because they would "obscure what the writing was designed to express" (*Course* 34). And what writing is designed to express, according to Saussure, is clearly not what Merleau-Ponty thinks diacritical language expresses. Although he seems to say that writing exists to express or represent spoken language, on Saussure's account "language is a system of signs that express ideas" (*Course* 16). Thus writing is either a mode of expression of ideas in language, or it is completely useless because it would be a totally separate system, expressing nothing.

In Saussure's eyes, language is a matter for experts. Outside of science and the interests of scientists, phonological language is not very desirable—regardless of the fact that by means of it one should be able to speak any language more precisely. In keeping with his concern over how the masses contribute to the distortion of language, Saussure maintains that phonological language should be reserved for the use of linguists lest its plethora of diacritical marks "distress" the masses. If only the masses, even or especially the highly literate masses, could be kept from reading and writing, then there might be some hope of maintaining the purity of the language and protecting it from visual pathology. Writing and reading should be left to the linguists, whose phonological precautionary measures lend them a degree of protection that the masses do not share. The image of the hierarchized and ordered linguistic chess game certainly emerges out of such a prescription.

This is not the only sense in which the linguist must be wary of the tyranny of writing. Writing is dangerous insofar as it tends to substitute itself for its own origin. This tendency, though treated as a kind of usurpation by Saussure, is taken by Derrida as proof of "the essential possibility of nonintuition" (*Grammatology* 40). If writing can substitute itself for its origin, then it is unlikely that it only exists for the sake of representing spoken language. Moreover, it is odd that Saussure acknowledges that language without the written word is a "shapeless and unmanageable mass," and that apart from words sounds are vague notions (*Course* 32). Clearly something is blinding Saussure to his own insights. Here, careful attention to architectonics is everything. For Saussure,

> *a science that studies the life of signs within society* is conceivable; it would be part of social psychology and consequently of general psychology. . . . Linguistics is only a part of the general science of semiology. . . . To determine the exact place of semiology is the task of the psychologist. (*Course* 16)

The question Derrida raises explicitly concerning the architectonic that operates here has been raised implicitly by Merleau-Ponty. It is a question of the relation between Husserl and Saussure.

I have noted that for Saussure the sign is constituted out of the unity of a concept and a sound-image. This necessary unity of sense and *phoné* (sound) has the character of an "essential and 'natural' bond" that depends upon a Husserlian psychology of intuitive consciousness (*Grammatology* 40). The essential and natural unity of sense and *phoné* requires the "clear evidence of the sense" and the "full presence of the signified" given to an intuitive consciousness" (p. 40). Derrida relates this natural unity of sense and sound-image, arising in intuitive consciousness, to Saussure's moralizing over the pathology and danger of writing: a *"crisis"* threatens if the *"empty* symbolism of written notation" usurps the role of speaking. Avoidance or, at least, mitigation of writing's tyranny demands that if writing must exist at all, it should do so only phonetically, which at least is imitative with regard to sound. Nonphonetic writing usurps the clear evidence of sense and the full presence of the signified as they appear to intuitive conciousness in phenomenological reduction. Such a move would be dangerous to knowledge and destabilizing with regard to the subject.

However, the notion that the sign is arbitrary, in the sense of conventional, undermines Saussure's attempts to pathologize and exclude writing from language. Disregarding the exclusion of writing for a moment, what is arbitrary or unmotivated in language are the relations between any specific phonic signifier and any other specific signified, even though there is an "allegedly natural relationship between phonic signifiers and their signifieds *in general"* (*Grammatology* 44). But, given the thesis of arbitrariness, Derrida draws the following conclusion:

> Now from the moment that one considers the totality of determined signs, spoken, and a fortiori written, as unmotivated institutions, one must exclude any relationship of natural subordination, any natural hierarchy among signifiers or orders of signifers. (p. 44)

The implications of this conclusion are far-reaching. First of all, what is clear is that the attempt by Saussure to exclude writing from language fails miserably on his own terms; that is, if the sign is an unmotivated institution, it is so with regard to any and every signifier, since precisely what has been erased is the "natural" relationship between the concept and the sound, and with that any natural hierarchical relation between speaking and writing. Not even the analogy to the game of chess can save Saussure, for either he would have to claim that the hierarchy of the court that the pieces represent is natural or that the game represents a certain social organization of power. The former claim is absurd, the latter would defeat Saussure's purpose.

In and of itself, the discovery that the unmotivated nature of the sign eliminates all hierarchies within language would be of little importance to Derrida, a fluke, an oversight or inconsistency, but Derrida is not interested in this as an isolated phenomenon; nor does he care to carry out a critique of Saussurean linguistics so as to supplant it with his own. Derrida's "quarry," as he puts it, is the "uncritical tradition" which Saussure inherits (*Grammatology* 46). That tradition has been the focus of all of Derrida's work; the tradition is, of course, that of logocentric metaphysics and the privilege given to all that contributes to the metaphysics of presence. But my interest here is not the privileging of the metaphysics of presence nor even its critique. There is, rather, another element to Derrida's analysis that interests me and draws Derrida nearer to Merleau-Ponty at just the moment when they seem to be the farthest apart.

When Derrida reveals that the unmotivated nature of the relationship between "each determined signifier and its determined signified" unravels the natural privileging of the phonic over the written signifier, he has several things in mind. First, as I have noted above, the entire Husserlian phenomenological consciousness falls by the wayside. And this means that, like Husserl, Saussure assumes that an intuition is given to consciousness and that the content of this intuition is the fully present signified in its *truth*. Thus, as Derrida notes, both the natural unity of sense and sound and the privileging of the phonic signifier depend upon a Husserlian psychology of intuitive consciousness (*Grammatology* 40). For the psychologist, language takes place only in relation to the clear evidence of sense, and language is therefore a "social product deposited in the brain of each individual" (*Course* 23). If it is determined that writing is neither derivative nor outside the language system, the entire apparatus of intuition is suspect, for it appears not to be the case that sense is given to a consciousness, but that writing is somehow interior to langauge and expressions are not distinct from what is expressed.

Secondly, in Saussure there is the notion that while language evolves, writing remains stable and no longer represents the sound it is meant to record (*Course* 27). This is particularly maddening when it appears that the written word has a tendency to replace the spoken word in our minds (p. 26). Does this mean that the sense/sound structure of the sign is replaced by something else? This is what I have tried to suggest is taking place in Merleau-Ponty's reading of Saussure, and I would like to suggest that something very much like this takes place in Derrida's reading as well. He writes:

> If "writing" signifies inscription and the durable institution of a sign (and that is the only irreducible kernel of the concept of writing), writing in general covers the entire field of linguistic signs. (*Grammatology* 44)

In this sense any signifier that is instituted—conventional, hence without a "natural" (meaning intuited) relation to sense—is written. Now while this is in some sense Derrida's main point and not unrelated to what I am trying to show here, still, this alone is not the maint point of intersection between Derrida and Merleau-Ponty. As Hugh Silverman has written, the correlation between Merleau-Ponty's expressive linguistics and Derridean inscription is not obvious.[11]

While it is true that Merleau-Ponty maintains an ontology of expressive acts, while Derrida establishes the role of inscription as the very creation of actors, the articulation of *écart* and *différance* remain very close to one another. At the beginning of this essay I asked what purposes are at work in each approach and what those purposes tell us about the respective method, agency, or effects of each philosophy. The answer, I speculate, lies in this. What I have called Merleau-Ponty's *auteur* theory of expression is less an ontology of a subject than it is a world ontology, the discovery of a world in which creation or expression are at least virtual, and the name of the *auteur* is no more than a designation attached to such virtualities. Each name, each *auteur* is no more than a way of indicating the virtuality of a certain mode of expression, arising out of its inscription in the opaque fabric of existence. In this sense, Merleau-Ponty's phenomenology is a profound existentialism as well, but one that acknowledges the inscribed or written character of all existence. Derrida, on the other hand, is perhaps less confident about the recuperative and expressive powers of language and the world. He is deeply sensitive to the, at times, near deadly blows dealt to the sources and origins of expression. So he is attentive to the origins of language, the inscriptions that are to him no more than traces. If *différance* proclaims itself as writing (and *in* writing), it is to trace out the possibility of an ethics of thought that is, perhaps for the first time ever, sensitive to the always and ever originating functioning of thought as differentiation. Unlike Merleau-Ponty, whose *auteurs* may go unrecognized, even unnamed, but who never question their own emergence in acts of world expression, Derrida's *différance* seeks to secure a place, an acknowledgment, and perhaps a guarantee that no origination, regardless of how remote and incomplete, is ever overlooked.

Notes

1. See especially, M. C. Dillon, *Merleau-Ponty's Ontology* (Bloomington: Indiana University Press, 1988).
2. Maurice Merleau-Ponty, *The Prose of the World*, trans. John O'Neill (Evanston: Northwestern University Press, 1973), p. 16.
3. Jacques Derrida, *Speech and Phenomena and Other Essays on Husserl's Theory of Signs*, trans. David B. Allison (Evanston: Northwestern University Press, 1973), p. xv (Preface).
4. See Ferdinand de Saussure, *Course in General Linguistics*, ed. Charles Bally and Albert Sehehaye, trans. Wade Baskin (New York: McGraw-Hill, 1966).
5. Maurice Merleau-Ponty, "Indirect Language and the Voices of Silence," *Signs*, trans. Richard C. McCleary (Evanston: Northwestern University Press, 1964), p. 39.
6. My intent here is to make it clear that there is no unifying principle *outside* the level of discourse that gives language its order and sense. Merleau-Ponty's notion of expression will serve here as such an organizing concept. For whatever is expressed does not and cannot exist outside of its expressions, or rather, for Merleau-Ponty, the expressions are nothing outside of whatever is expressed.
7. Gilles Deleuze and Felix Guattari, *A Thousand Plateaus, Capitalism and Schizophrenia*, Vol. 2, trans. Brian Massumi (Minneapolis: University of Minnesota Press, 1987), pp. 352–53 (emphasis added). Deleuze and Guattari place these comments in the context of an analysis that delimits the difference between a state organization and a nomadic organization of power. The first is highly centralized and hierarchized; the second, dispersed with multiple power centers that are always shifting.
8. Maurice Merleau-Ponty, *The Visible and the Invisible*, trans. Alphonso Lingis (Evanston: Northwestern University Press, 1968), p. 201.
9. Jacques Derrida, *"Différance,"* in *Margins of Philosophy*, trans. Alan Bass (Chicago: University of Chicago Press, 1982), p. 10.
10. Jacques Derrida, *Of Grammatology*, trans. Gayatri Chakravorty Spivak (Baltimore: Johns Hopkins University Press, 1976), p. 30.
11. Hugh J. Silverman, "Merleau-Ponty and Derrida: Writing on Writing," in *Ontology and Alterity in Merleau-Ponty*, Galen A. Johnson and Michael B. Smith, eds. (Evanston: Northwestern University Press, 1990), p. 137.

4

The Flesh as *Urpräsentierbarkeit* in the Interrogative: The Absence of a Question in Derrida

Patrick Burke

At a strategic point in his groundbreaking essay, *"Différance,"* Jacques Derrida raises three questions: "What differs? Who differs? What is *différance?*"[1] He rightly challenges the sense and syntax of these questions in order to expose the questions that are begged by them, namely: does *différance* respond to such questioning, is there a "what" of *différance*, a "who" of *différance*? He intimates that the question of *différance* already presupposes the *différance* of the question, that is, the play of *différance* as the "constitutive source" of all questioning. But to ask the question of *différance* presumes that *différance* can double back upon itself, become present to itself, as a power, a force, or, what is worse, a subject, all of which is excluded by Derrida in principle because this doubling back pertains to reflection, to the self-givenness of something in consciousness. Derrida says that *différance* is removed from every possible mode of presence, like the unconscious of Freud, the force in Nietzsche, the Other in Levinas. So the question of *différance* must yield to the *différance* of the question and thus can never be asked, is forever absent. But here Derrida would reply: absence is itself a function of presence, a province of presence, and vice versa, so the question of *différance* is not absent, it simply cannot be asked, or else, perhaps, it is always deferred.

If the question of *différance* is always deferred or just downright unaskable, what consequences does this have for Derrida's thought about *différance*? If the play of *différance* is not auto-critical, is it not then auto-destructive? Does it not reduce itself to what Merleau-Ponty called in one place a "Zenonian reverie on movement,"[2] or

60

in another "the bad dialectic,"[3] such that there is no movement, no questioning at all? If the play of *différance* does not double back upon itself, does not submit itself to itself, does not differentiate itself from itself through the differentiating power of the question, is it not therefore static, or surreptitiously formulated into theses which, even though they are ostensibly under erasure, defy its essential instability, its internal discordance, the mutual confrontation of incompossibles within it? Does it not destroy the overtaking, the overlapping, the "metamorphosis (Rodin) of time" ("Eye and Mind," hereafter EM, 185) germane to all movement, to all play, to the dance? Since the ground of questioning is not itself in question, does not exemplify its own power by turning it upon itself, can it ground either differing or deferral, which are the primitive dimensions of every question and the language within which it is framed? In the end, the lens of *différance*, it would seem, is that of the photographer's mendacious camera and not the astonished eye of the painter.

What is at work in the argument strategy relative to *différance* is something akin to a transcendental argument Kantian style, and Derrida, it would seem, is the current keeper of the transcendental question. The analyses which surround the non-word, the non-concept *"différance"* function as stages in a transcendental deduction of *différance*. *Différance* is a kind of unconditioned ("without origin") (*Speech and Phenomena*, hereafter SP, 143) condition of language and all the human enterprises which rest within and upon it. It is the unconditioned condition of the experience of time, it is a temporalizing, "it is the origin or production of differences and the differences between differences, the play of differences" (SP 130). It is the unconditioned condition of meaning, which, as Saussure says, is a function of the differentiation, the spacing between signs, setting one off from the other, a setting-off which engenders meaning; "signification is the difference of temporalizing" (SP 138). It is the unconditioned condition at work as a pivot, a juncture in the ontic-ontological difference in Heidegger. Notice in all of this the language of transcendental reflection. Difference "is no longer simply a concept, but the *possibility* of conceptuality, of the conceptual system and process in general" (SP 140). It is also the *possibility* of words, "it is the structured and differing *origin* of differences" (SP 141), it is "the movement by which language becomes historically *constituted*" (SP 141), it "makes the movement of signification *possible*" (emphases added above).

In his chapter "Reflection and Interrogation" in *The Visible and the Invisible*, Merleau-Ponty submits the Kantian strategy at work

here to a rigorous critique. In a nutshell, Derrida, and Kant before
him, cannot think "the miracle of a totality that surpasses what
one thinks to be its conditions" (*The Visible and the Invisible*,
hereafter VI, 8), cannot think the power of differentiation in terms
of a metamorphosis relative to itself and what it differentiates, all
summed up in a statement Derrida could not have written, namely,
that "the conditioned conditions the conditions" (VI 22). Derrida,
like Kant, is engaged in a kind of regressive analysis (call it
deconstruction), the term of which is the play of *différance*, which
exposes the transcendental illusion of presence operative in ordinary experience and in philosophizing about that experience. Derrida
claims that this play of *différance* is never present, never given as
part of the fabric of the present, but this is his transcendental illusion. According to Merleau-Ponty, the play of *différance* is present
not in its pure state, which is at best only analytically deduced
(consequently violating this play which can never be pure), but in
its metamorphosed state as conditioned by that which it conditions, by the ever emerging totality of present experience. The key
to understanding this metamorphosis is the notion of "gestalt" to
which Merleau-Ponty reverts throughout his philosophical discourse,
namely, that a condition is taken up by and transformed by what
it conditions, such that the whole in which it functions as a condition is greater than and different from the sum of its parts, its
conditions, and these latter are thus different from themselves for
being part of this whole, greater than if they were isolated, caught
up as they are now in certain intertwined dimensions of variation
and participation which make up the flesh of the whole. The transcendental illusion operative in Derrida's analysis is that he believes in an unconditioned or irreducible condition, the play of
différance, which never factors in nor is transformed in the present.
For Merleau-Ponty, there is no unconditioned condition, no origin
of this kind:

> There is no longer the originating and the derived, there is a
> thought traveling a circle where the condition and the condi-
> tioned, the reflection and the unreflected, are in a reciprocal, if
> not symmetrical, relationship, and here the end is in the begin-
> ning as much as the beginning in the end. (VI 35)

Would not Merleau-Ponty, if he were reading Derrida today, be
tempted to show how Derrida himself is still conducting his thinking
within a metaphysics of presence? First of all, would he not attend carefully to the language which Derrida uses to describe

différance, the language of irreducibility and necessity (SP 134, 137, 139), and would he not suspect that the use of such language is justified by an apodictic insight into the indubitability of *différance* as an irreducible and necessary condition? Does such insight not assume its own self-transparency, or at least the self-transparency of the writer who expresses it and the language through which it is expressed? Does it not assume a perfect doubling-up, a perfect adequation of the subject and that which is expressed by him or her? If Derrida wishes to say that the subject is somehow the "effect" of *différance*, then is it not *différance* itself that grasps itself as irreducible and necessary? If Derrida denies this surrogate subject and this perfect coincidence, should he not then scuttle the language of necessity and irreducibility? Next, what is all this business about *différance* as deferral? Deferral to what? To some possible future which would be "full presence"? It would seem that the very language of deferral betrays the premise Derrida hopes to establish, that there is no coincidence of consciousness with itself in a full presence, that the talk of such is non-talk or pseudo-talk, that the sense of it is pseudo-sense or non-sense. The myth of presence is the myth of fulfillment and self-coincidence, and does not Derrida's use of the language of deferral simply prolong the myth? Why not just say with Lacan that the object of desire is lost forever because it was never really possessed in the first place?

Merleau-Ponty articulates a different notion of presence, which escapes the myth against which Derrida directs his project, and it is this notion which renders intelligible how the play of *différance* (call it dehiscence, *écart*, à la Merleau-Ponty) is present in a metamorphosed state, and how it is the questioning question at the root of all questioning. For Merleau-Ponty, there is an interrogative doubling back on the source of all differentiation, and the source is present in the subject, which, in its interrogative self-appropriation, gathers itself in the question that, nonetheless, further divides the subject from itself. Yes, there is agency, there is the subject as source of initiative, as, if you will, the conditioned which in its turn, in its self-appropriation, conditions the conditions, takes them up into itself, a taking up which is a metamorphosis of them and a self-metamorphosis through them, accomplishing thereby a differentiated self-presence. Derrida surreptitiously introduces a new binary opposition, *différance*/presence, and would repress presence rather than seeing, as does Merleau-Ponty, that *différance* and presence are accomplices of one another; Derrida's "*différance*" masks itself as what liberates philosophical thought from the metaphysics of presence. But Derrida condemns all modes of presence under the name of a presence which Merleau-Ponty himself deems to be impossible, namely, a pure, self-reflective presence, a pure co-inciding of self with self, an unmediated presence of self to self which would make possible a pristine and virginal *presence* of self to the world. For Merleau-Ponty, the metaphysics of presence that Derrida rejects is founded on this particularly idealized notion of *presence-to*. Merleau-Ponty, on the contrary, roots his new ontology in a notion of presence more fundamental than any version of "presence-to." Take, for example, this citation from *Phenomenology of Perception*:

> The analysis of time . . . discloses subject and object as two abstract "moments" of a unique structure which is presence.[4]

Already in this earlier work, Merleau-Ponty was denying that either subject or object is in the mode of the originating or founding, but both are distinct manifestations or articulations of the originating ground, which is primordial presence (*Urpräsenz*), that upon which their mutual relation of presence-to is also founded. Merleau-Ponty carries forward this notion of *Urpräsenz* into his later writings and ultimately identifies it with what he will call the "flesh." In "The Philosopher and his Shadow" (1959), Merleau-Ponty credits the Husserl of *Ideen II* with having articulated this new notion of presence.

Whereas Husserl had argued in *Zeitbewusstsein* that absolute consciousness was the purely noetic and constitutive source of the field of presence, in *Ideen II* Merleau-Ponty finds him arguing for a notion of consciousness rooted in sensible being, such that the field of presence is primarily neither a noematic correlate of consciousness nor the dynamic noetic domain of consciousness, but what is beneath such a distinction, what is fundamentally and originally meant by nature. Nature or sensible being is

> the being which reaches me in my most secret parts, but which I also reach in its brute or untamed state, in an absolute of pr2esence which holds the secret of the world, others, and what is true.[5]

By "absolute of presence" Merleau-Ponty does not mean merely that I reach sensible being in a condition of absolute presence, or that I live it in absolute presence. What must be noted here is the use of the genitive, through which Merleau-Ponty finds Husserl saying something more than "absolute presence" which can describe a strictly noetic domain. "Absolute of presence" signifies the "irrelative" of presence, its ground, its prototype, and its originary field: it signifies sensible being in its brute or savage state; it is found everywhere and is coterminous and coextensive with nature itself, with the flesh of the world. The body, through the reversibility which institutes it, is "incorporated" into things and they are incorporated into it, that is, they merge as one body or flesh. "Flesh of the world" is to be taken literally if by it is meant that "the world is made of the same stuff as the body" (EM 163), that is, the same intentional fabric, the crisscrossing of the touching and the tangible, of the seeing and the visible, so that flesh is not simply a property of the perceiving body relative to the world but is the "irrelative," the absolute of all relations of compresence and "presence-to," which encompasses the whole of nature or the world, persons as well as things. This original co-incorporation of the world and the body as one flesh, as the absolute of presence, is further clarified by an analysis of a footnote from *The Visible and the Invisible:* "The *Urpräsentierbarkeit* is the flesh" (VI 135).

Urpräsentierbarkeit means "original and fundamental presentability." What this means is that the flesh is primordial sensibility, visibility, tangibility, audibility, and so on, all modes of an original presentability. The emphasis in all of these words is on the last four syllables, a-bi-li-ty, which means potentiality in the two-fold sense of power and possibility. Merleau-Ponty tells us that he is offering here "a new notion of the possible, namely the possible conceived not as another eventual occurrence, but as an ingredient of the existing world itself, as general reality."[6] The possible is a dimension of power, the not-yet of power, is intertwined with it, and together they constitute the general activity of the doubling back of the sensible upon itself which is comprehended through the notion of flesh.

The source of all differentiation for Merleau-Ponty is this power to break forth, this original presentability, this pregnancy, this dehiscence, the perpetual splitting open of the tangible into the touching and the touched, or "this relation of the visible with itself that traverses me and constitutes me as a seer, this circle which I do not form, which forms me, this coiling over of the visible upon the visible" (VI 142). To claim that I am what is formed rather than what forms does not signal a reduction of the subject to the object, to the status of an "effect." For Merleau-Ponty, words like visible, audible, and tangible must be freed from the objectivist prejudices which govern their use in ordinary language. For

Merleau-Ponty, the visible is both pre-objective and pre-subjective. It is a term which is equally applicable to both subject and object. The flesh is the coiling over of the visible upon the visible, a coiling over which makes it possible that the visible be present to itself, which is what we mean when we say that there is a seer. The flesh is the "formative medium of the subject and the object" (VI 147). This means that we must not assume that this coiling over is that of an object upon itself, since, in fact, there is no object prior to this coiling over, prior to the advent of the subject, which is concomitantly the advent of the object. The object can be seen only if there is a seer, but the seer can see only because it can be seen, is itself visible. This coiling over is that by which they become mutually presentable as visibles. It is the secret of their visibility, of the fact that they can be seen. Therefore, visibility is not the gift of the seer to the world but is rather the original and differentiating presentability of the seer to itself, of the world to the seer, of the seer to the world, and of the world to itself through the seer.

The original visibility, as well as all the other modes of presentability, is thus characterized by a reversibility of the seer and the seen, of the touching and the touched, and is not a function of either term but of both, insofar as they are originally unified in the flesh. To say that they are unified implies that presence in its most original modality does not come about as the result of their ability to be present to each other, but is rather the most original form of that ability. In other words, they can be present to each other because they are already present in each other (*Ineinander*) in such a rudimentary way that it makes more sense to speak of a single but differentiated core of savage presence, the salient feature of which is reversibility, that by which both subject and object are within one another and yet differ from one another. Mindful of Derrida's critique of presence, it is important to note that reversibility does not mean identity, coincidence, or fusion of the seeing with the seen; between the touching and the touched there is a divergence, a spread, a deviation, a gap (*écart*) which keeps them from collapsing into one another, which prevents that perfect doubling back which would be achieved if I could touch myself touching, if the touching could be equally on the side of the touched. Merleau-Ponty agrees with Derrida that such a notion of self-presence or fusion is impossible. The originary presentability which is the flesh speaks to a rift, a chasm always gaping open, which is the secret of all appearing and all intimacy, since both are a function of distance. For Merleau-Ponty, this rift is the ur-trace of dehiscence, of a fission, a splitting open, which is eternal, and which is repeated in every process of embryogenesis and in every act of seeing and touching. It is a primordial opening, which is found and expressed in every act of questioning, an interrogation within Being by which Being becomes present to itself, the very mode of its self-presence. Consciousness is in the interrogative mode, the being of the world is in the interrogative mode, the *Urpräsentierbarkeit* which is the flesh is in the interrogative, in this originary mode of all presence.

It is in this coiling over of the sensible upon itself that the miracle of totality is born, that a configuration emerges which is greater than and different from the sum of its conditions, where "the subordinated each time slides into the void of a new dimension opened, the lower and the higher gravitate around one another, as the high and low (variants of the side-other side relation)" (VI 265). The higher stages of Being's self-differentiation and self-transcendence, the conditioned, are the obverse side of the lower stages, the revelation and articulation of this invisible "other side," the conditions which, although subordinate, are continually there, exercising their presence as metamorphosed by the totality which they condition. In this respect, for Merleau-Ponty (unlike Derrida), the play of *différance* does not exclude the presence which it articulates by differing and deferring, but is also articulated by it, taken up by it, and transformed (differed) by it.

Just a little word about language and predication! Like Derrida, Merleau-Ponty mounts a monumental effort to suspend or, if you will, place under erasure the descriptive and explanatory categories of traditional philosophical language and the ontological prejudices embedded within them. In order to presuppose nothing about the world, about Being, Merleau-Ponty proposes to speak "not according to the laws of the word-meanings inherent in the given language, but with a perhaps difficult effort that uses the significations of words to express beyond themselves our mute contact with the things, when they are not yet things said" (VI 38). The signification of words, independent of contexts of predication, is their lexical signification. If, as predicates, these words are always univocally related to their subject in predication, they are useless to an ontology which would grasp the meaning of Being prior to and motivating instituted language, which would find beneath the world as "a canton of language" (VI 97) (the world toward which, paradoxically, Derrida's analyses move) a world which is the silent interlocutor of all of our questions. As an indispensable condition of ontology, words must be able to be employed analogously and metaphorically, to call up or connote through acts of predication a sense of Being that grounds as well as transcends their lexically defined denotative use. Like Derrida, Merleau-Ponty questions the role of univocal predication in ordinary language. For example, he mentions experiences like seeing, speaking, and thinking, and notes that "they have a name in all languages, but a name which in all of them also conveys significations in tufts, thickets of proper meanings and figurative meanings, so that unlike those of science, not one of these names clarifies by attributing to what is named a circumscribed signification" (VI 13).

In ordinary discourse, predication ranges between the figurative and proper meanings of words, and reveals the "oneric world of analogy" (EM 171), within which is held the secret of all experience, language, and culture. Merleau-Ponty argues that analogy is the mainspring of vision and of language, including metaphor (which is so privileged by Derrida), that things can be seen and said because they have "an internal equivalent in me; they arouse in me a carnal formula of their presence" (EM 164). Merleau-Ponty compares this carnal formula to what in Scholasticism was called the "intentional species," that through which "the same thing is both out there in the world and here in the heart of vision, the same or if one prefers a similar thing, but according to an efficacious similarity which is the parent, the genesis, the metamorphosis of Being in vision" (EM 166). According to Merleau-Ponty ontological predication must be rooted in the efficacious similarity between the seeing and the seen. We must speak as we see, and we see analogically, that is, taking the term in its simplest etymological sense, "according to the logos," according to that "pre-objective Being, between the inert essence or *quidditas* and the individual localized at a point of space-time" (*Themes* 110). According to Merleau-Ponty, this pre-objective Being, or what he calls *logos endiathetos* (VI 170), is the principle by which there are words, concepts and things, the principle of their differentiation and relatedness that renders them analogous and which is, consequently, the matrix of all predication, including the metaphorical; it thus gives rise to *logos prophorikos*, that logos uttered whose internal structure sublimates our carnal relation with the world. It is the wild and playful force by which every word signifies according to its differentiated relation to other words, a relation which is never determinable once and for all since it is subjected to many and complex participations, variations, and reversals which define the domain of presence. This logos institutes a dialectic of operative speech and silence that is the primal stream of all significative thought and language. This wild and playful logos is the *Urpräsentierbarkeit*, the power to break forth, and it is present in the logos of the created language and the ideas which are expressed therein, its silent spirit, always prompting new and varied punctuations of silence within, and at times beyond, the limits of logic and grammar. It ceaselessly draws back into its silence all the powers which it released in the speaking language, so that in the end the speaking language is "the voice of no one, since it is the very voice of the things, the waves and the forests" (VI 155). It is the voice of primal presence, and it perpetually echoes the mystery that presence is only a voice, the elusive voice of Being in its incessant self-differentiation and self-disclosure.

Obviously, Merleau-Ponty reinstates here a kind of phonocentrism and logocentrism particularly repulsive to Derrida, who favors the metaphor of inscription over speaking when articulating the language which has the human. The voice intimates self-presence, inscription does not. If the voice is the privileged metaphor, then it makes sense to ask the questions with which this essay began, "What differs? "Who differs?" Questions which, for Derrida, are pseudo-questions. For Merleau-Ponty, on the contrary, because the interrogative doubling back which institutes consciousness is a function of Being itself, there are real and important questions. Across the successive and simultaneous community of speaking subjects, it is Being that wishes, speaks, and thinks itself by its own fission through which it institutes savage mind and wild-flowering world, its reversible modalities. This wild and playful logos, this Being of all beings, realizes itself in savage mind and finally in reflective consciousness, but it is not identical to either. It is the power that breaks forth into vision, speech, and thought, and institutes the cultural world: it is the "light which, illuminating the rest, remains at its source in obscurity" (VI 130). It is the interrogative power of originary presence, the *Urpräsentierbarkeit* of everything, and yet hidden in what it manifests, present within all presence as the invisible of the visible.

Despite all the similarities which can be drawn between this wild and playful logos and the play and dance of *différance* articulated by Derrida, it is, in the end, the "absence" of a question in Derrida that renders suspect his otherwise brilliant and incisive analyses, the question of *différance* which would appropriate and transform the *différance* of the question.

Notes

1. Jacques Derrida, *Speech and Phenomena, and Other Essays on Husserl's Theory of Signs*, trans. David B. Allison (Evanston: Northwestern University Press, 1973), p. 145. Henceforth cited as SP.
2. Maurice Merleau-Ponty, "Eye and Mind," trans. Carleton Dallery, in *The Primacy of Perception*, ed. James M. Edie (Evanston: Northwestern University Press, 1964), p. 185. Henceforth cited as EM.
3. Maurice Merleau-Ponty, *The Visible and the Invisible*, trans. Alphonso Lingis (Evanston: Northwestern University Press, 1968) p. 94. Henceforth cited as VI.
4. Maurice Merleau-Ponty, *Phenomenology of Perception*, trans. Colin Smith (London: Routledge & Kegan Paul, 1962), pp. 430–31.
5. Maurice Merleau-Ponty, *Signs*, trans. Richard C. McCleary (Evanston: Northwestern University Press, 1964), p. 171.
6. Maurice Merleau-Ponty, *Themes from the Lectures at the Collège de France, 1952–1960*, trans. John O'Neill (Evanston: Northwestern University Press, 1970) p. 78.

5

Eliminating Some Confusion: The Relation of Being and Writing in Merleau-Ponty and Derrida

Leonard Lawlor

[Our life] is constantly enshrouded by those mists we call the sensible world or history, the one [on] of corporeal life and the one [on] of human life, the present and the past, as a pell-mell ensemble of bodies and minds, promiscuity of faces, words, actions, with, between them all, that cohesion which cannot be denied them since they are all differences, extreme *écarts* of one same something.

—Merleau-Ponty, *The Visible and the Invisible*[1]

Does not this "dialectic"—in every sense of the term and before any speculative reconquest of this concept—open up living to différance, constituting in the pure immanence of lived experience the *écart* of indicative communication and even of signification in general?

—Derrida, *Speech and Phenomena*[2]

Perhaps more than anything else, this word, *écart*, has contributed to the belief that Merleau-Ponty's thought, especially that found in *The Visible and the Invisible*, anticipates, if not matches completely, Derrida's thought, especially that found in early texts such as *Speech and Phenomena*.[3] What is basic in each—différance in Derrida's case; the flesh in Merleau-Ponty's—is reversible. Both the flesh and différance are described in terms of contamination. There is ambiguity in Merleau-Ponty, undecidability in Derrida. Derrida and Merleau-Ponty share the same concern for difference and absence. It even seems possible to develop an ethics on the basis of their respective thoughts.[4] Yet, despite their undeniable proximity, one can establish distance between Merleau-Ponty and Derrida, first and foremost in the following way: Derrida is a grammatologist; Merleau-Ponty is an ontologist.[5]

The decisive point is, as Derrida says, that "différance, in a certain and very strange way, [is]' 'older' than the ontological difference or than the truth of Being."[6] This comment makes two claims. On the one hand, it claims that *différance* cannot be defined in terms of being. *Différance* refers to an absolute non-being.[7] Defined in this way, *différance* refers to a negation,[8] a nothing that can be defined neither as a dimension of one sole something nor as a variant of the real. We can come to understand this "nothing" only if we recognize that the element that Derrida interrogates is logic, or more generally, language, and most precisely, writing. In contrast, the element that Merleau-Ponty interrogates is the visible, or more generally, experience, and most precisely, being. On the other hand, the comment claims, due to the strange sort of priority that Derrida mentions, that *différance*'s structure is supplementary: what is second is first and nothing returns to it. In contrast, for Merleau-Ponty, the structure of the flesh is circular: what is first is first and everything else turns within it.

To demonstrate this, I am going to proceed in two steps. First, starting from the element of being, I am going to try to reconstruct the ontology that animates *The Visible and the Invisible*. Merleau-Ponty's thought amounts to a monism, hence the circular structure of the flesh. The test of any monism lies in the relation of language to being. For Merleau-Ponty, speech is homogeneous with being because spoken language is one of being's possibilities; in contrast, language as a formalized system is separated from experience and seems to befall the homogeneity of being like an accident. Writing makes the transition to Derrida. Starting from the element of language, I am going to reconstruct the grammatology that animates Derrida's writings. We shall see here that Derrida's thought amounts to a dualism, hence the supplementary structure of *différance*. Because of writing's formality, the homogeneity of being already contains separation; the accident is necessary. In Derrida, the impossible can happen. Only if we clarify these two differences with as much precision as possible—that of Derrida's grammatologism versus Merleau-Ponty's ontologism, and the structure of supplementarity versus the structure of circularity—will we be able to eliminate at least some of the confusion concerning their relation. And only then will we truly be able to move to what seems to be the most pressing question: the question of alterity.[9]

1

From his earliest writings, Merleau-Ponty's project has consisted in the overcoming of the mind-body duality.[10] In order to address this problem, Merleau-Ponty interrogates the visible, or more generally experience, and most precisely being. We can see that being is the interrogated element, for Merleau-Ponty, when, in *The Visible and the Invisible*'s fourth chapter, on the chiasm, he says that "the flesh is . . . an 'element' of Being" (*The Visible and the Invisible*, hereafter VI, 184/139).[11] That this element must be understood in terms of experience can be seen in the opening chapter, when Merleau-Ponty defines perceptual faith in terms of experience (VI 48–49/28). And finally, returning again to *The Visible and the Invisible*'s ultimate chapter, we see Merleau-Ponty speak of the element as the visible (VI 184/140); indeed, combining the terms, he says, "we would simply find again . . . scraps of this ontology of the visible mixed up with all our theories of knowledge . . ." (VI 185/ 140). Ontology, in *The Visible and the Invisible*, describes what Merleau-Ponty calls "ontological history" (VI 186), or "ontogenesis" (VI 30/14, 139/102, 266/213); it describes the genesis of meaning from experience (VI 146/109), from being (VI 148/110), or from being-in-the-world (VI 28/12).[12] As Merleau-Ponty says, "Thought cannot ignore its apparent history, if it is not to install itself beneath the whole of our experience, in a pre-empirical order where it would no longer merit its name; it must put to itself the problem of the genesis of its own meaning" (VI 28/12).

The comparative *plus vieux que*, the adjectives *préalable* and *postérieure*, the preposition *avant*, the verb *précéder*, and the prefix *pré-* occur repeatedly in *The Visible and the Invisible*. They refer to a specific sort of priority, the key to which lies in the prepositions *au-dessous* and *sur*. Priority, for Merleau-Ponty, is not equivalent to "a transcendental, intemporal order, as a system of *a priori* conditions" (VI 117/85). In fact, this sort of system, according to Merleau-Ponty, "is in principle posterior to an actual experience" (VI 69/45). It is not the case that conditions for the possibility precede experience; rather they "accompany" or "translate" or "express" experience (VI 69/45). Thus, the "originary," for Merleau-Ponty, while not excluding the "true past," cannot be reduced to what lies *derrière* us (VI 165/124). The originary is what is *below* and *over* us. Thus it is impossible to speak of logical or temporal priority (cf. VI 191/145); "before" means a lower level or tier (VI 153/114). Being is vertical.

Although Merleau-Ponty describes what is originary in terms of space,[13] he forbids us to think of the "over" in terms of "super-position" (VI 177/134). This interdiction goes along with Merleau-Ponty's constant criticism, in *The Visible and the Invisible*, of "high-altitude thinking" (*la pensée en survol*) and his sustained criticism of the notion of essence in the third chapter. Superposition, high-altitude thinking, and essence imply a real or ideal rupture with experience (cf. VI 161/120). Experience, however, is "homogeneous" (153/114). The "space of existence" (VI 150/111), the "milieu" (VI 154/114, 155/115, 156/117),[14] the "atmosphere" (VI 116/84) is "undivided" (VI 162/121; cf. 157/117). The originary is "one same something" (VI 117/84), "the same world" (VI 64/41, 27/11), "one sole Being" (VI 148/110), "the unique Being" (VI 157/117; cf. 64/41); and oppositions "belong to the same Being" (VI 114/82) and to "one same body" (VI 185/141). Although Merleau-Ponty speaks of ambiguity (VI 129/94), this is an ambiguity—it is "good ambiguity" and not ambivalence (VI 127/93)[15]—not lacking in univocity.[16] Although Merleau-Ponty speaks of a "hiatus" between touching and being touched, a hiatus which seems to imply a break or a cut, he adds immediately that this hiatus "is not an ontological void, a non-being" (VI 195/148). Perceptual faith "is not nothing" (VI 74/49; cf. 160/120); moreover, "one starts with an ontological relief where one can never say that the ground be nothing" (VI 121/88). Most importantly, "the negative . . . is borne by an infrastructure of being" (VI 160/120; cf. 134/98).[17] That the negative is carried by being can be seen in the following expression: experience "is of [Being] but is *not* it" (*qui 'en est,' mais n'est pas lui*, VI 164/123, my emphasis). The genitive *de* (or *en*) in such expressions (VI 92/63, 198/151, 200/153) is not an abyss.[18] Although, in the Introduction to *Signs*, Merleau-Ponty speaks of an "abyss" in what is fundamental, he adds immediately that we must not say that "this extremity is *nothing*"; in fact, in *The Visible and the Invisible*, Merleau-Ponty seems to think that the notion of an abyss represents a different way to conceive being than *écart* (VI 180/136–37). The genitive, we can even say, refers to an identity: the body "communicates this identity without superposition, this difference without contradiction, this divergence between the within and the without that constitutes its natal secret to the things upon which it closes" (VI 179/135–36); "my activity is identically [*identiquement*] passivity" (VI 183/139).

In the sense of an exterior relation between two individuals, there is no dualism in Merleau-Ponty nor is there a monism in the sense of one something containing individuals "as in a box" (VI 157/ 117, 182/138; cf. also 200/152, 53/32); the originary, he says, is "not of one sole type" (VI 165/124), of which other things would be mere instantiations or copies. Nevertheless, his ontology is a monism because of the notion of possibility. Everything in Merleau-Ponty, the Merleau-Ponty of *The Visible and the Invisible*, turns on the notion of possibility. Although Merleau-Ponty's ontology is not a materialism (cf. VI 184/139, 191/146), it is being's *content*, the real, which includes possibilities, and it is possibilities which generate differences, divergences, and negations.[19] Possibility determines the very structure of the flesh. The flesh, Merleau-Ponty says, is not synthetic, which would imply a gap to be bridged (VI 23/8, 186/141). Rather, the flesh is "one sole body," "one sole tangible" (VI 186/141) "pregnant with all visions one *can* have of it" (VI 166/124, my emphasis). The flesh is the real (VI 150/112); and rather than the real being a simple variant of the possible, "it is the possible worlds and the possible beings that are variants and are like doubles of the actual world and actual Being" (VI 150/ 112). This comment clarifies the notion of doubling in *The Visible and the Invisible*; the double—the touched of the touching, for example—is the actualization of a possibility. As the flesh's "extension" (VI 153/114), as "a variant of one common world" (VI 27/11), the flesh is "relatively continuous" (VI 28/12). Doubles—touching and being touched—are opposites only when they have been transformed into theses, propositions, or significations (VI 30/13, 27/11); as Merleau-Ponty says, "The 'natural' man holds on to both ends of the chain, thinks *at the same time* that his perception enters into things and that it is formed this side of his body. Yet coexist as the two convictions do without difficulty in the exercise of life, once reduced to theses and to propositions they destroy one another and leave us in confusion" (VI 23–24/8). When formulated, the compossibles appear as incompossibles (VI 49/29); since the compossibles appear as incompossible, Merleau-Ponty calls the world (or the flesh) the "impossible-possible" (VI 56/34).

Even though there is no contradiction in the flesh's reversibility, there is no coincidence (VI 162/122). The lack of coincidence is due to the fact that being is not the "immediate" (VI 162/122). Being is non-coincidence because it consists in a "double reference, the identity of returning into oneself with emergence from oneself, of lived experience with distance" (VI 165/124; cf. also 27/11, 130/95). This slogan—"to return into onself is to emerge from oneself" (VI 74/49)—implies that to actualize one possibility of being is to leave another possibility unactualized; as Merleau-Ponty says, I cannot "dominate all the implications of the spectacle" (VI 150/112). Opposed to *la pensée en survol*, for Merleau-Ponty, is *enlisé dans l'être*; thus, stressing the spatiality of the flesh, one must say that every possibility of being is situated. So, as Merleau-Ponty points out, if perception is a fusion with the thing, the perception is extinguished and I cease to exist; conversely, if perception maintains distance, which preserves me, then I am no longer with the thing (VI 163/122). Similarly, if memory amounts to the process of preserving the past in the present, if it really allows me to "become again what I was," then "it becomes impossible to see how it could open to me the dimension of the past" (VI 163/122). For Merleau-Ponty, in either process—perception or memory—it is always necessary to begin again. This double reference—this identity—is why the image of the circle is appropriate for the notion of the flesh in *The Visible and the Invisible*. Such a spatial image implies that what is first is "the total situation" (VI 57/35, 74/49, 121/88), being. None of the positions within the circuit have priority (cf. VI 56–57/35); always referring back to the whole, all the positions are second. Making sense only in terms of each other, none of the positions makes sense independently. The lack of independence keeps the circle restless. As Merleau-Ponty says, "If one wants metaphors, it would be better to say that the body sensed and the body sentient are as the obverse and the reverse, or again, as two segments of one sole circular course which goes above from left to right and below from right to left, but which is one sole movement in two phases" (VI 182/138; cf. also 125/91, 159/119, 185/140, 188/143).

Although one cannot, according to Merleau-Ponty, speak of "effective fusion" with being, which would bring the circular movement to rest, one can speak of "partial coincidence." This "good error" is made possible by language, but not by just any language (VI 166/124–25). The origin, Merleau-Ponty says repeatedly, is "silent" or "mute" (VI 17/3, 18/4, 57/35, 121/88, 138/102, 159/119, 167/125–26, 202/154). He says, for example, "language lives only from silence; everything we cast to the others has germinated in this great mute land" (VI 167/126). Moreover, he speaks of "the transition from the mute world to the speaking world" (VI 202/154); finally, he says that "It is as though visibility ... emigrated (*émigrait*) not outside of every body, but into another less heavy, more transparent body ... that of language" (VI200/153). Nevertheless, silence is not the "contrary of language" (VI 233/179). He says that "lived experience is spoken lived experience (*vécu-parlé*), that, born at this depth, language is not a mask over Being ... but the most valuable witness to Being" (VI 167/126). Being is not an "immediation that would be perfect without [language] ... vision itself, the thought itself are ... 'structured like a language'" (VI 168/126; cf. VI 169/127).[20] Thus, somewhat paradoxically, Merleau-Ponty can speak of "mute language" and "voices of silence" (VI 168/126–27).

That silence is not the contrary of language means that "the structure of [our] mute world is such that all the possibilities of language are already given in it" (VI 203/155). From these possibilities arise an "operative language or speech" (VI 202/154). It is only operative speech, creative language, that allows for the partial coincidence with being. In order to capture the mute character of "authentic language,"[21] Merleau-Ponty compares it to painting— Renoir's paintings "interrogated the visible and made something visible"[22]—and especially to music. Music such as the "little phrase" described by Proust in *Swann's Way* can sustain a meaning (*sens*) by means of its own arrangement (VI 201/153). Consequently, Merleau-Ponty describes operative language as one in which "sense and sound are in the same relationships as the 'little phrase'" (VI 201/153). This perfect unity of sense and sensible is the Merleau-Pontean *logos* (VI 168/126, 202/154). The Merleau-Pontean *logos* is

a language of which [the speaker] would not be the organizer, words he would not assemble, that would combine through him by virtue of a natural intertwining of their meaning, through the occult trading of the metaphor—where what counts is no longer the manifest meaning of each word and of each image, but the lateral relations, the kinships that are implicated in their transfers and their exchanges. (VI 167/125)

Insofar as the *logos* makes the things themselves speak, it is not only the language of poets but also, according to Merleau-Ponty, the language of the philosopher: "It is by considering language that we would best see how we are to and how we are not to return to the things themselves" (VI 166/125).

We are not to return to the things themselves by means of the language of linguists, "an ideal system, a fragment of the intelligible world" (VI 201/154).[23] While recognizing that such formal systems are the "occultation of the truth," "the reflective vice," "the first irretrievable lie," "forgetfulness of perceptual faith," for Merleau-Ponty ideal systems arise from creative language; in other words, this "object of science" (VI 202/154)—theses, significations, propositions—is generated by means of an idealization of the real (VI 70/46). Similarly, "pure idealities"—as in geometry—are generated from the real. As always with Merleau-Ponty in *The Visible and the Invisible*, the issue in "the passage to ideality" (VI 51/30) is to describe an absence that would not be the contrary of the sensible (cf. VI 188/142-143), a negativity that would not be nothing (VI 198/151), an invisible that would be the possibility of the visible.[24] Having, like and before Derrida, studied Husserl's *The Origin of Geometry*, Merleau-Ponty is well aware that the genesis of ideal objects—idealization—takes place through writing: books, museums, musical scores.[25] Nevertheless, Merleau-Ponty is also aware that writing becomes a "petrified meaning,"[26] that sense becomes "separated"[27] or "detached" (*coupée*) (VI 126/92). Based in writing, the philosophy of essences, according to Merleau-Ponty, "succeeds in detaching itself from all beings" (*à se déprendre de tous les être*) (VI 145/108); writing is "a generalized warping of my landscape" (*un gauchissement général de mon paysage*) (VI 159/119). Most importantly, "Lived experience can no longer recognize itself [*se retrouver*] in the idealizations we draw from it" (VI 120/87). He even admits that pure ideality, made possible by writing, "will pass definitely beyond the circle of the visible" (VI 189/144, 30/14).

If it is indeed the case—and here we make the transition to Derrida—that writing brings about such an alterity, can we say the following: "When the silent vision *falls* [*tombe*] into speech, and when speech in turn, opening up a field of the nameable and the sayable, *inscribes* itself in that field, in its place, according to its truth—in short, when it metamorphoses the structures of the visible world and makes itself a gaze of the mind, *intuitus mentis*—this is always in virtue of the same fundamental *phenomenon* of reversibility" (VI 203/154–55, my emphasis)? Can we account for "spirit" without reconceiving the fall into writing? Can we explain the "impossibility" of pure ideality by means of possibilities of the flesh? Mustn't we instead reconceive the interrogative element in terms of non-phenomenality, in terms of the nothing?

2

In "Violence and Metaphysics," Derrida appropriates Levinas's thought (cf. *Writing and Difference*, hereafter ED).[28] Derrida's questions, however, break with those of Levinas; he asks, at the close of "Violence and Metaphysics," "Can one speak of an *experience* of the other or of difference? Has not the concept of experience always been determined by the metaphysics of presence? Is not experience always an encounter of an irreducible presence, the perception of a phenomenality?" (ED 225/152, Derrida's emphasis). Because of the sedimentation associated with the word *experience*, for Derrida one must interrogate the element of logic, or more generally language; most precisely, it is only through an interrogation of writing that one can gain access to the "beyond" of being, to what exceeds ontology (as well as phenomenology). As Derrida says in *Of Grammatology*, "Even before being determined as human . . . or nonhuman, the *grammé*—the *grapheme*—would thus name the element. An element without simplicity. An element, whether it is understood as the medium or as the irreducible atom, of the archisynthesis in general, of what one must forbid oneself to define within the system of oppositions of metaphysics, of what consequently one should not even call *experience* in general, indeed, the origin of *meaning* in general" (DLG 9). We cannot, therefore, understand the element of writing either in terms of experience or even in terms of meaning. Nevertheless, Western metaphysics, the metaphysics of presence, as Derrida has infamously summarized Western philosophy, has so defined writing; the metaphysics of presence is a logocentrism.

For Derrida, what defines logocentrism is the attempt to conceive reason—the *logos*—as essentially independent from linguistic mediation. Logocentric philosophy conceives reason as the complete and perfect mastery over whatever it reasons about. In other words, what reason reasons about is conceived as completely present. This conception of reason refers to an "absolute *logos*" (DLG 25/13). Consequently, language is relative; it functions merely as a means of conveying already completed knowledge. In logocentrism—exemplified by Hegel, according to Derrida in "The Pit and the Pyramid"—language is a detour through which reason is able to return to itself (*Marges* 82/71). Logocentrism, for Derrida, is defined by circularity. We cannot miss the obvious comparison of logocentrism to what we saw in Merleau-Ponty.

In any case, in a logocentric philosophy not all types of language are "pro-visional." Logocentrism must privilege the voice over writing, the phonic substance (that is, the phonic carrier of meaning) over the graphic substance. Only speech seems to be a diaphanous membrane; voice seems best to preserve presence and to enable its recovery. Nevertheless, logocentric philosophy recognizes that if knowledge is to be universal, it must be capable of being written down. Writing is a necessary supplement. Again however, not every type of writing is well suited for this task; in order to assure the passage's safety, knowledge must be written in a phonetic alphabet, which seems to maintain the animation of breath. In contrast, nonphonetic writing such as Chinese remains opaque; this type of writing is breathless because it is formalistic. As formalistic (or structural), each character, of course, derives its meaning from its difference from other characters.[29] Such formalistic writing would include mathematics—indeed, mathematical language is the model for nonphonetic writing (DLG 20/9)—where mere rote learning of the forms can lead to the manipulation of the signs without thought or content. Nonphonetic writings, therefore, are the death of speech (*Marges* 123/105); in this case, writing functions as a mere supplement, something superfluous. Overall in logocentrism, writing, according to Derrida, is seen as derivative from speech; writing is even seen as an unfortunate accident afflicting speech from the outside.

For Derrida, grammatology, as the science of scienticity (DLG 43/27), is the science of logocentrism. Unlike Merleau-Ponty's ontology, grammatology is not primarily a genetic interrogation. Instead, it begins with the very "dry" (*seche*) question of essence (DLG 43/28),[30] which it then complicates through the question of genesis: "The grammatologist least of all can avoid questioning himself about the essence of his object in the form of a question of origin: 'What is writing?' means 'where and when does writing begin?'" (DLG 43/28).[31] For Derrida, however, the genetic questions always disclose that language is constitutive for the generation of any object—natural or cultural—or of any thought. The genetic question always leads back to the structural question. Grammatology therefore begins with the structural question (or the naive ontological question, as Derrida also calls it [VP 26/25]), complicates it by means of genesis, only to return to structure, to the structure which makes genesis possible, in a word, language.[32]

The grammatological movement can be seen already in Derrida's 1962 *Introduction to Husserl's The Origin of Geometry*. In order to understand the genesis of geometry and the method of reactivation of geometry's origin that Husserl describes here, it is necessary to investigate the structure of writing; writing, as Derrida shows (following Husserl), constitutes all ideal objects, indeed, all meaning, all truth, insofar as ideality must be intersubjective, omnispatial, and omnitemporal. As Derrida says, because the possibility of writing assures the absolute traditionalization of the object, its absolute ideal objectivity, "the possibility or necessity of being incarnated in something graphic is no longer simply extrinsic and factual in comparison with ideal objectivity: it is the *sine qua non* condition of objectivity's internal completion" (LOG 86/89). Writing's ability to make ideal objectivity possible—the *sine qua non*—implies that "writing creates a kind of autonomous transcendental field from which every actual subject can be absent" (LOG 84/88). In other words, according to Derrida, writing implies the death of actual subjects; how else to virtualize dialogue? Nevertheless, in order to be what it is, writing must depend on a writer or reader in general; a text must be haunted by a virtual intentionality; in principle it must be intelligible for a transcendental subject in general. Otherwise, a text is unreadable, "a defunct designation" (LOG 85/88). Yet, and this is the crucial point for Derrida, there are silent prehistoric arcana, buried civilizations, intentions lost and secrets guarded in tombs, illegible inscriptions. Such imperfect unities of sense and sensible disclose that, even though we can see that death has a meaning (that is, death serves the purpose of making ideal objectivity possible), the fact that writing must be able—that is, in principle be able—to separate itself from its origin implies the failure of that meaning (*sens*) or purpose (LOG 85/88). The separation makes nonsense intrinsic to sense.

In "Signature Event Context," Derrida describes the same structure of writing. In SEC (as Derrida calls this essay in *Limited Inc*[33]), in this very "dry" discourse, Derrida isolates certain characteristics of writing which seem to be implied by writing's "usually accepted sense" (*Marges* 369/311). He focuses especially on the characteristic of absence. According to Derrida, the absence of the actual sender or the intended receiver from writing is not an absence which happens sometimes, a factual absence; rather, in order for writing to be what it is, absence must be able to "be brought a certain absolute degree" (*Marges* 374/315). Writing must be able to be legible, or more precisely, must be able to function "in the absolute absence of the addressee or of the empirically determined set of addressees" (*Marges* 375/315). If absence is internal to the very constitution of what we call writing, then, as Derrida says, "this absence is not a continuous modification of presence; it is a break in presence, 'death,' or the possibility of the 'death' of the addressee, inscribed in the structure of the mark" (*Marges* 375/316). Parenthetically, Derrida reminds us immediately of what we saw in the *Introduction*, that "the value or effect of transcendentality is linked necessarily to the possibility of writing and of 'death' analyzed in this way" (*Marges* 375/316; cf. also VP 60–61/54).

The necessary link between the possibility of writing and transcendentality is precisely what Derrida calls *différance*. Or, to put this another way, for Derrida in *Speech and Phenomena* (and elsewhere), *différance* refers to the relation that holds between ideality and factuality. Facts exist as things in the world; in contrast, "authentic ideality" (*La Voix et le phénoméne*, hereafter VP, 4/6) "is *nothing* existing in the world" (VP 8/10, my emphasis). Yet, while existing in a non-worldly sense, authentic ideality does not exist as something outside of the world; this externality—inauthentic ideality—was Platonism's mistake. Thus the relation (or passage or transition) between fact and essence is neither, for Derrida, a monism in the sense of one homogeneous being nor a dualism in the sense of two separate things; yet, unlike the monistic relation in Merleau-Ponty, the relation in Derrida is a dualism. As Derrida says, one must conceive the relation between fact and essence as "a radical difference . . . one having nothing in common with any other difference, a difference in fact distinguishing *nothing*, a difference separating no state, no experience, no determined signification—but a difference which, without altering anything, changes all the signs" (VP 10/11, my emphasis).[34] As Derrida says, concerning the relation between the empirical (or psychological) ego and the transcendental ego, "my transcendental ego is radically different from my natural and human ego; and yet it is distinguished by nothing, nothing that can be determined in the natural sense of distinction" (VP 11/11–12).[35] This nothing is the nothing that distinguishes parallels. In other words, it is an empty space between, a void between, a division between, an *écart*, even an abyss which separates and joins (cf. VP 75/67). Maintaining an ontic identity, the relation is a duplication which is not a duplicity (VP 11/11). *Différance* is a re-flection, a folding back over, and such a superposition defines doubling in Derrida. The nothing makes the relation called *différance* undecidable and not ambiguous; while, as we saw, ambiguity supposes the relative continuity of the two poles, undecidability supposes the relative discontinuity of the two poles. Finally, we can say that, because of the nothing, being, for Derrida, is not homogeneous. The nothing is the absolute nonsense, the absolute nonbeing, that makes the different senses of being possible. *Différance*, therefore, refers to nothing and, unlike Merleau-Ponty's flesh, not to something.

We can see how the nothing functions in Derrida by examining his analysis of auto-affection in *Speech and Phenomena*'s Chapter

Six, "The Voice That Guards Silence." As Derrida says here, the
necessity of auto-affection to bring about ideal meaning can be seen
in Husserl's First Investigation move to interior monologue; in
addition to these, Derrida relies on the *Ideas I*, #124, descriptions
of the passage from experiential, and hence silent, sense to conceptual meaning, in short, the passage from experience to the *logos*.
On the basis of the #124 descriptions, Derrida realizes that interior
monologue, as a transition to ideality, must make use of a medium
or an element. As Derrida says, "Husserl is unable to bracket what
in glossamatics is called the 'substance of expression' without
menacing his whole enterprise" (VP 86/76–77). Since Husserl is
describing a monologue, this "substance" must be the voice. It seems
that hearing oneself speak, which relies on the phonic carrier, allows meaning to be constituted as both an ideality, and thus opposed to me, and also as something absolutely close to me and
thus still inside me (VP 83/75). Being diaphanous and alive, breath
allows the meaning to be present—thus appears as an ideality—
and not to pass outside into the world—it is still animated by my
intention (VP 87/77). In other words, auto-affection supposes "that
a pure difference comes to divide self-presence" (VP 92/82). This
difference is pure because, as constitutive of ideality, auto-affection "creates nothing"; ideality is neither a being nor a produced
object, neither a natural thing nor a cultural thing (VP 93/84).
Moreover, being constituted interiorly, ideality is engendered by
nothing (in the world) (VP 93/83). Pure difference must be a difference which is not a difference, that is, not a difference between
beings.

Yet, what makes it a difference is that ideality cannot be itself
unless it can be repeated indefinitely; the passage to ideality (or to
an ideal object) is a "passage to the limit" or to infinity (VP 84/75;
cf. LOG 146/134). The requirement of indefiniteness turns auto-
affection into synthesis and pure difference into impure difference,
in a word, into *différance*.[36] According to Derrida, Husserl (or Western
metaphysics in general) privileges the voice because it is temporal
(VP 93–96/83–86). As is well known from Derrida's own analyses
of Husserlian temporalization in *Speech and Phenomena*, Chapter
Five, retention is the possibility of indefinite repetition in what
appears now. As indefinite, retention always implies the absence,
the destruction, indeed, the death of each unique now; indefiniteness implies that a space must be open between the now and the
retention. The present in turn is a synthesis of the now and retention: a nothing that joins and divides. Moreover, as indefinite, this

retentional trace implies the possibility of externalization, of the world, and of space. As Derrida says, "Taking auto-affection as the operation of the voice, auto-affection supposes a pure difference comes to divide self-presence. In this pure difference is rooted the possibility of everything we think we exclude from auto-affection: space, the outside, the world, the body, etc" (VP 92/82). *Différance* therefore makes impurity intrinsic to purity.

On the basis of this analysis of auto-affection, we can sharpen the comparison with the flesh's structure in Merleau-Ponty. Most importantly, the inclusion of indefiniteness within auto-affection implies that auto-affection is a sort of writing. The internality of writing leads to the structure of supplementarity. The structure of supplementarity cannot be understood in terms of a circle. Everything, as we saw with Merleau-Ponty, is supposed to be understood in terms of the total situation; everything, even ideas made possible by writing, is supposed to return to or, better, turn within, being; being, for Merleau-Ponty, is first.

We see now, however, with Derrida, that the most basic characteristic of writing, absence or death, is internal to speech and therefore to thought (cf. VP 92/82). Writing's internality implies that what has traditionally been seen as second (or even third) is actually first, the *sine qua non* of thought. Writing even precedes being insofar as writing conditions history and all genesis. Thus writing is a supplement in two senses. On the one hand, it is a supplement in the sense of being superfluous, even in the sense of an accident; speech seems to be entirely and solely dependent on my animation. So, writing is second (or even third, nothing more than a simulacrum). On the other hand, writing is a supplement in the sense of being essential, even in the sense of being necessary; there could be no speech without "signifying forms" (or codes) whose indefinite iterability implies death, absence, the nothing (cf. VP 13/13, 55–56/50; *Marges* 378/318). So, writing is first; it is what Derrida calls arché-writing.

How are we to understand this structure of the supplement? Unlike Merleau-Ponty, for whom everything turns on the notion of possibility, for Derrida everything turns on the notion of impossibility. Everything, for Derrida, turns on the notion of impossibility because Derrida's thought, starting from writing, is a thought of formalization.[37] For Derrida, form is the only way to think the "beyond" of being; he says in "Form and Meaning: A Note on the Phenomenology of Language,"

One might think then that the *sense of Being* has been limited by the imposition of the *form* which, in its most overt value and since the origin of philosophy, seems to have assigned to Being, along with the authority of the *is*, the closure of presence, the form-of-presence, presence-in-form, form-presence. One might think, on the other hand, that formality—or formalization—is limited by the sense of Being which, in fact, has never been separated from its determination as presence, beneath the excellent surveillance of the *is*: and henceforth the thinking of form has the power to extend itself beyond the thinking of Being. (*Marges* 206–207/172; cf. also 206 n14/172 n16)

Writing is first of all defined by form, the letters. In order for writing to be itself, it must be separated from the one who draws it. The gap opened by formal repeatability, an iterability to infinity, implies that the same form can enter into different, even unforeseen contexts and utilizations. The same form can be used either seriously or non-seriously. Unlike Merleau-Ponty, for Derrida these superfluous accidents—sarcasm, parody, etc.—must be conceived as "necessary accidents" (cf. *Limited* 61–63). These "accidents" do not befall the forms; these impossibilities are of the forms (cf. *Limited* 48). Thus the accidents that come to be associated with letters cannot be separated from the formality of the forms. And, as Derrida says often, the forms of writing are at once the condition for the possibility and the condition for the impossibility of communication (*Limited* 61; cf. VP 113/101, LOG 84/87).[38] Being the condition for the possibility and impossibility, forms suffocate the intention and yet they remain. Like rote learning, a form is a remainder or remnant (*reste*) (cf. *Limited* 51–54), something dead and yet still moving; it survives, a spirit.[39] Or, as Derrida also calls writing, it is a machine, which through its functioning can produce the impossible and thereby exceed all circularity (cf. *Marges* 126/105).

We can summarize the differences between Merleau-Ponty and Derrida in the following way. Most basic is the difference between interrogative elements: being versus writing. Within this difference, we were able to see that while for Merleau-Ponty being is homogeneous, relatively continuous, and undivided, writing for Derrida is heterogeneous, relatively discontinuous, and divided. On the basis of this difference, the different structures of the flesh and *différance* arose: circularity versus supplementarity. What organizes the structure of the flesh in Merleau-Ponty is the notion of possibility; in contrast, for Derrida the notion of impossibility organizes the structure of supplementarity. For Merleau-Ponty, the circular structure of being—content—accounts only for differences as possibilities of being. In contrast, for Derrida, the structure of supplementarity—formalization—accounts for alterities which are impossible. In fact, this difference between possibility and impossibility allows us to define Merleau-Ponty's and Derrida's respective uses of the word *écart*. Nevertheless, as we know from the working notes for *The Visible and the Invisible*, Merleau-Ponty was trying to appropriate the Saussurean notion of diacritical difference for his descriptions of experience itself (VI 267/213). Perhaps, if he had succeeded in transforming his descriptions of experience in terms of diacritics, he would have had to push the notion of ambiguity into undecidability. We also saw that Merleau-Ponty recognizes that the idealizations made possible by writing lead to impossibilities. Speaking of the generation of ideas, he says, almost at the very end of *The Visible and the Invisible*'s completed part, that "We shall have to follow more closely this transition from the mute world to the speaking world" (VI 202/154). Who knows what would have happened if Merleau-Ponty had had the time to follow this transition more closely? Perhaps, if he had had the time, he would have felt compelled to change the title of this book one more time; perhaps he would have even felt compelled to change it from *The Visible and the Invisible* to something like *Ousia and Grammé*.[40]

Notes

1. Maurice Merleau-Ponty, *Le visible et l'invisible* (Paris: Gallimard. 1964), pp. 116–17; English translation by Alphonso Lingis as *The Visible and the Invisible* (Evanston: Northwestern University Press, 1968), p. 84. Hereafter cited as VI with reference first to the French, then to the English. At times, the English translation has been modified in order to be consistent with the commentary.
2. Jacques Derrida, *La voix et le phénomène* (Paris: Presses Universitaires de France, 1967), p. 77; English translation by David B. Allison as *Speech and Phenomena* (Evanston: Northwestern University Press, 1972), p. 69. Hereafter cited as VP, with reference first to the French, then to the English. At times, the English translation has been modified in order to be consistent with the commentary.
3. Cf. Bernard Flynn, "Textuality and Flesh: Derrida and Merleau-Ponty," in the *Journal of the British Society for Phenomenology*, Vol. 15:2 (May 1984), pp. 164–77; David Krell, "Engorged Philosophy II," in *Postmodernism and Continental Philosophy*, eds. Hugh J. Silverman and Donn Welton (Albany: SUNY Press, 1988), pp. 49–66; Françoise Dastur, "Perceptual Faith and the Invisible," in the *Journal of the British Society for Phenomenology*, Vol. 25:1 (January 1994), pp. 44–52, es-

pecially, notes 7 and 47; also by Dastur, "Merleau-Ponty and Thinking from Within," in *Merleau-Ponty in Contemporary Perspective*, ed. Patrick Burke and Jan Van Der Veken (Boston: Kluwer, 1993), pp. 25–36. Finally one should consult Rodolphe Gasché's classic article, "Deconstruction as Criticism" (*Glyph*, 6 [Baltimore: The Johns Hopkins University Press, 1979], pp. 177–15). Here, Gasché first compares Derrida's operation of deconstruction with what Merleau-Ponty, in *The Visible and the Invisible*, calls hyper-reflection; but then he concludes this comparison by saying: "Yet this *hyper-reflection* which is fundamentally self-critical, which does not model itself after any historically given form of dialectics, which resists the temptation of its being 'stated in these, univocal significations,' and thus its becoming 'what we call *a philosophy*,' still longs for the rediscovery of 'the being that lies before the cleavage operated by reflection.' The desire for such a pre-reflexive *being* keeps hyper-dialectics in the bonds of philosophy. It is not *a* philosophy, but, as Merleau-Ponty admitted, philosophy itself. Nonetheless, *hyper-reflection* came close to anticipating the *strictly speaking* no longer philosophical operation of deconstruction" (p. 188, Gasché's emphasis).
4. Over the last two decades, Derrida has developed an ethical discourse, for example, his discourse on law. And Merleau-Ponty promised an ethical discourse on the basis of his metaphysics, the metaphysics for which *The Visible and the Invisible* was to be the start; see Maurice Merleau-Ponty, "A Prospectus of his Work," in *The Primacy of Perception*, ed. James M. Edie (Evanston: Northwestern University Press, 1964), p. 11.
5. This way of dividing Merleau-Ponty and Derrida came about from a reading of Jean Hyppolite's *Genesis and Structure of Hegel's Phenomenology of Spirit* (*Genèse et structure de la Phénoménologie de l'esprit de Hegel* [two volumes] [Paris: Aubier, 1946]; English translation by Samuel Cherniak and John Heckman as *Genesis and Structure of Hegel's Phenomenology of Spirit* [Evanston: Northwestern University Press, 1974]) and *Logique et existence* ([Paris: Presses Universitaires de France, 1952]; English translation by Amit Sen and Leonard Lawlor forthcoming from the SUNY Press) and Derrida's and Merleau-Ponty's respective comments about Hyppolite and Hegel. For the personal relation between Hyppolite and Merleau-Ponty, see H. L. Van Breda's "Merleau-Ponty and Husserl Archives at Louvain," in *Texts and Dialogues: Maurice Merleau-Ponty*, ed. Hugh J. Silverman and James Barry Jr. (New Jersey: Humanities Press, 1993). For the personal relation between Hyppolite and Derrida, see Jacques Derrida, "The Time of the Thesis," in *Philosophy in France Today*, ed. Alan Montefiore (New York: Cambridge University Press, 1983). In their essays and books, both Derrida and Merleau-Ponty cite or mention both of Hyppolite's major works, *Genesis and Structure of Hegel's Phenomenology* and *Logique et existence*. Merleau-Ponty's "Hegel's Existentialism" (Maurice Merleau-Ponty, "Hegel's Existentialism," in *Sense and Non-sense*, trans. Hubert L. Dreyfus and Patricia Allen Dreyfus [Evanston: Northwestern University Press, 1964], p. 65) is based on a Hyppolite lecture, which is itself based on *Genesis and Structure*; Derrida's "The Pit and Pyramid:

Introduction to Hegel's Semiology" mentions Hyppolite's *Logique et existence* by name (Derrida, "The Pit and the Pyramid," in *Margins of Philosophy*, 81/71). Moreover, Derrida's "Genesis and Structure' and Phenomenology" was first a lecture presented at a Hyppolite-inspired conference and Hyppolite himself wrote articles about Merleau-Ponty. (See Jean Hyppolite, *Figures de la pensée philosophique* tome II [Paris: Presses Universitaires de France, 1971]). Derrida's *Introduction to Husserl's The Origin of Geometry* cites *Logique et existence* (LOG 58 n1/67 n62); Merleau-Ponty's "Philosophy and Non-Philosophy Since Hegel" (in *Philosophy and Non-Philosophy Since Merleau-Ponty*, ed. Hugh J. Silverman [New York: Routledge, 1990]) does the same (pp. 27, 48, 50, 53, 82–83, 309 n74, 310 n78).

6. Jacques Derrida, "Différance," in *Marges de la philosophie* (Paris: Minuit, 1972), p. 23; English translation by Alan Bass as *Margins of Philosophy* (Chicago: University of Chicago Press, 1982), 23/22. Hereafter abbreviated as *Marges* with reference first to the French, then to the English. Cf. also Jacques Derrida, *De la grammatologie* (Paris: Minuit, 1967), p. 38; English translation by Gayatri Spivak as *Of Grammatology* (Baltimore: The Johns Hopkins University Press, 1976), p. 23. Hereafter abbreviated as DLG with reference first to the French, then to the English.

7. One could also say that *différance* refers to an absolute invisibility, an invisiblility "which would have nothing to do with the visible." Cf. Jacques Derrida, *Mémoires d'aveugle* (Paris: Reunion, 1990), p. 56; English translation by Pascale-Anne Brault and Michael Nass as *Memoirs of the Blind* (Chicago: University of Chicago Press, 1993), 52. Here Derrida is commenting on the following passage from *The Visible and the Invisible*: "The idea is this level, this dimension. It is therefore not an invisible *in fact*, like one object hidden behind another, and not an absolute invisible, which would have nothing to do with the visible. Rather it is the invisible *of* this world, that which inhabits this world, sustains it, and renders it visible, its own and interior possibility, the Being of this being" (VI 198/151).

8. We can see the role of negation in Derrida's thought as early as *Le Problème de la genése dans la philosophie de Husserl* (Paris: Presses Universitaires de France, 1990), where Derrida says, "In all of these 'transitions,' which are so difficult to conceive if we keep to Husserl's analyses, negation assures the role of mediation. As such, negation appears to be the motor and movement of all genesis. Because it is mediation its status is ambiguous and participates simultaneously in the activity and passivity of all couples of contraries which can appear. Not elucidating the 'duplicity' of negation and giving it up to confusion, Husserl forbids the thematization of the true genetic movement" (197).

9. I would like to thank Ted Toadvine for the time he spent conversing with me about Merleau-Ponty and Derrida, and for his comments on earlier drafts of this paper.

10. Cf. Françoise Dastur, "Monde, Chair, Vision," in *Maurice Merleau-Ponty: Le psychique et le corporel*, ed. Anna-Teresa Tymieniecka (Paris: Aubier, 1988), p. 115.

11. We must not be misled by the phrasing of this sentence. It seems clear that the flesh is not *an* element of being, but *the* element of being, especially, insofar as Merleau-Ponty says: "But this domain [that of the flesh], one rapidly realizes, is unlimited. If we can show that the flesh is an ultimate notion . . ., [it] can traverse, animate other bodies as well as my own" (VI 185/140).

12. In *Hegel's Concept of Experience*, which Merleau-Ponty studied in "Philosophy and Non-Philosophy Since Hegel," Heidegger says, "What is it that Hegel names with the word 'experience'? He names the Being of beings. . . . Experience now is the word of Being, since Being is apprehended by way of beings *qua* beings. Experience designates the subject's subjectness. Experience expresses what '*being*' in the term 'being conscious' means—in such a way that only by this 'being' does it become clear and binding what the word 'conscious' leaves still to be thought" (113–14).

13. Although spatial metaphors abound in *The Visible and the Invisible*, it is not entirely clear that Merleau-Ponty is privileging space over time. He says, for example, that "Every ideation, because it is an ideation, is formed in a space of existence, under the guarantee of my duration [*durée*]. . . . Every ideation is borne by this tree of my duration and other durations, this unknown sap nourishes the transparency of the idea" (VI 150/111).

14. Merleau-Ponty, "Philosophy and Non-Philosophy Since Hegel," in *Philosophy and Non-Philosophy Since Merleau-Ponty*, p. 41.

15. Here in *The Visible and the Invisible*, Merleau-Ponty defines ambivalence in terms of "pure identity," that is, an identity which cannot contain multiple possibilities. Cf. also Maurice Merleau-Ponty, "The Child's Relations with Others," in *The Primacy of Perception*, ed. James M. Edie (Evanston: Northwestern University Press, 1964), pp. 103, 107.

16. Merleau-Ponty, "Philosophy and Non-Philosophy Since Hegel," in *Philosophy and Non-Philosophy Since Merleau-Ponty*, pp. 44, 49, 52.

17. Cf. Merleau-Ponty, "Philosophy and Non-Philosophy Since Hegel," in *Philosophy and Non-Philosophy Since Merleau-Ponty*, pp. 52–53.

18. Maurice Merleau-Ponty, *Signs*, trans. Richard C. McCleary (Evanston: Northwestern University Press, 1964), p. 21; see also Patrick Burke, "Listening at the Abyss," in *Ontology and Alterity in Merleau-Ponty* (Evanston: Northwestern University Press, 1990), pp. 81–97.

19. We could call Merleau-Pontean genesis dialectical. While everyone stresses Merleau-Ponty's notion of "hyper-dialectic" (VI 129/94) as a notion more radical than dialectic, it is important to recall the following comments from *The Visible and the Invisible*: "From the most superficial level to the most profound, dialectical thought is that which admits reciprocal actions or interactions . . ." (VI 123/89); "The dialectic is indeed all this, and it is, in this sense, what we are looking for" (VI 125–26/92); "what we exclude from the dialectic is the idea of a pure negative, what we seek is a dialectical definition of being that can be neither the being for itself nor the being in itself—rapid, fragile, labile definitions, which, as Hegel rightly said, lead us back from the one to the other—nor the In-Itself-For-Itself which is the height of ambivalence" (VI 130/95). Merleau-Pontean ontology defined

as dialectical genesis is "good dialectic," hyper-dialectic, while Hegel's ontologic explicated by Hyppolite and defined by its own sort of negativity and difference, its own element, is what Merleau-Ponty calls "bad dialectic" (VI 129/94). Concerning dialectic in Merleau-Ponty, one should also consult the following comment from "Indirect Language and the Voices of Silence," in *Signs* (trans. Richard C. McCleary [Evanston: Northwestern University Press, 1964]): "The Hegelian dialectic is what we call by another name the phenomenon of expression, which gathers itself up and launches itself again through the mystery of rationality" (73). Because of the connection between genesis and dialectic in Merleau-Ponty, the following comment from "Philosophy and Non-Philosophy Since Hegel" seems important; it is the primary reason why it seems that one can stress content in Merleau-Ponty (versus form in Derrida): "Dialectic is a *movement of content*, that is, of our ontological milieu, which is the 'experience' and which does not occur without a relation to someone who experiences" (41, Merleau-Ponty's emphasis).

20. Cf. Merleau-Ponty, "Indirect Language and the Voices of Silence," in *Signs*, p. 44.
21. Ibid., p. 44.
22. Ibid., p. 63.
23. Ibid., p. 44.
24. Cf. Maurice Merleau-Ponty, "Husserl at the Limits of Phenomenology," in *In Praise of Philosophy*, trans. John Wild and James Edie, John O'Neill (Evanston: Northwestern University Press, 1988), p. 188, where he says that "The true cannot be defined outside of the *possibility* of the false" (my emphasis).
25. Maurice Merleau-Ponty, "Phenomenology and the Sciences of Man," in *The Primacy of Perception*, ed. James M. Edie (Evanton: Northwestern University Press, 1964), p. 83; see also "On the Phenomenology of Language," in *Signs*, pp. 96–97; "Indirect Language and the Voices of Silence," in *Signs*, pp. 60–63.
26. Maurice Merleau-Ponty, "Husserl at the limits of Phenomenology," in *In Praise of Philosophy*, p. 187.
27. Merleau-Ponty, "Philosophy and Non-Philosophy Since Hegel," in *Philosophy and Non-Philosophy Since Merleau-Ponty*, 50.
28. Jacques Derrida, *L'écriture et la différence* (Paris: Editions du Seuil, 1967), p. 161; English translation by Alan Bass as *Writing and Difference* (Chicago: University of Chicago Press, 1978), p. 109. Hereafter ED with reference first to the French, then to the English.

Cf. Levinas's 1972 essay "Meaning and Sense," in *Collected Philosophical Papers*, trans. Alphonso Lingis (Boston: Kluwer, 1987), pp. 75–107. Here Levinas says that Merleau-Ponty's philosophy (especially as expressed in "On the Phenomenology of Language" [in *Signs*]) "guides the present analysis" (p. 80); but it guides the analysis insofar as Merleau-Ponty's philosophy circumscribes "the contemporary philosophy of meaning" that Levinas criticizes and from which he wants to distance himself. Thus, Levinas says, on the one hand, "It is then not surprising that Merleau-Ponty's thought seemed to evolve toward that of Heidegger. Cultural meaning is taken to occupy an exceptional place

between the objective and the subjective—the cultural activity dis-
closing being; the one that works this disclosure, the subject, invested
by being as its servant and guardian. Here we rejoin the schemas of
the last writings of Heidegger, but also the *idée fixe* of the whole of
contemporary thought—the overcoming of the subject-object structures.
But perhaps at the source of all these philosophies, we find the Hegelian
vision of a subjectivity that comprehends itself as an inevitable moment of the becoming by which being leaves its darkness, the vision
of a subject aroused by the logic of being" (p. 82). On the other, Levinas
says, "The 'term' of such a movement both critical and spontaneous
[ethics or desire] . . . is no longer called being. Here perhaps we can
catch sight of the necessity for a philosophical meditation to resort to
notions such as that of infinity or God" (p. 100). Cf. also Levinas's
comments on the notion of the lateral in Merleau-Ponty, pp. 88 and
100. Lastly, we should not forget this comment by Levinas: "'Where
does the resistance of the unreflected to reflection come from?', Merleau-
Ponty asked at Royaumont in April, 1957, in connection with problems that the Husserlian theory of phenomenological reduction poses.
Our analysis of *sense* perhaps responds to this fundamental question,
which Merleau-Ponty refused to resolve by simple recourse to the finitude
of the subject, incapable of total reflection" (pp. 98–99). Perhaps this
last comment by Levinas suggests that it is possible to interpret Merleau-
Ponty's later thought as an attempt to move toward absolute alterity.
If time had permitted, it would have been appropriate to examine
Merleau-Ponty's criticisms of Sartre in *The Visible and the Invisible*'s
second chapter. There Merleau-Ponty calls the experience of the other
"an impossible," but then interprets this impossibility as solipsism
which is overcome by means of language (VI 110–11/79). We shall
return to the possibility of interpreting Merleau-Ponty's later thought
as an attempt to move toward absolute alterity at the end of this paper.
     On the tension between Merleau-Ponty's thought and that of Levinas,
see Robert Bernasconi, "One-Way Traffic: The Ontology of Decolonization
and its Ethics," in *Ontology and Alterity in Merleau-Ponty*, pp. 67–
80. See also the Levinas essays on Merleau-Ponty in the same volume, pp. 53–66.

29. In spoken Chinese, according to Derrida, who is at this point quoting
    Hegel in "The Pit and the Pyramid," the meaning derives from "the
    connection, the accent, and the pronunciation" (*Marges* 122/104).
30. Derrida's starting point in structuralism, in the precomprehension of
    the meaning of a word, his privilege of the question "what is?", can
    be seen as early as the 1953–54 *Le problème de la genèse dans la
    philosophie de Husserl* (Paris: Presses Universitaires de France, 1990):
    "If we do not begin with a description of *a priori* essences, never will
    we be able to claim any rigor. In its most originary upsurge, existence
    itself will not be able to appear to philosophic contemplation. Also,
    every reproach addressed to this Husserlian essentialism in the name
    of an empirical or existential originality or in the name of some prior
    genetic moment, in order to make sense, will have to suppose an al-
    ready constituted eidetics. This postulate of all philosophy has opened,
    in all of its depth, the primary phenomenological procedure. The ab-

solute beginning of philosophy must be essentialist. This law, insofar as it is 'methodological,' insofar as it not founded on the actual movement of the genesis constituting and prior to the essences and where it rules all philosophic elucidation, makes of formalism or of idealism or, if you will, of eideticism, the inaugural moment of all real or possible philosophy. Every reflection must begin by assuming this idealism, without which it will always remain in confusion and in inauthenticity" (225–26, my translation). It can be seen as recently as *Given Time: 1. Counterfeit Money* (trans. Peggy Kamuf [Chicago: University of Chicago Press, 1992]): "For the gift to be possible, for there to be gift event, according to our common language and logic, it seems that this compound structure is indispensable. Notice that in order to say this, I must already suppose a certain precomprehension of what *gift* means. I suppose that I know and that you know what 'to give,' 'gift,' 'donor,' 'donee' mean in our common language. As well as 'to want,' 'to desire,' 'to intend.' This is an unsigned but effective contract between us, indispensable to what is going on here . . ." (11). Moreover: "it is a matter of . . . responding faithfully but also as rigorously as possible both to the injunction or the order of the *gift* ('give') as well as to the injunction or the order of meaning (presence, science, knowledge): *Know* still what giving *wants to say, know how to give* . . ." (30).

31. The combination of genetic and structural questions can be seen in "'Genesis and Structure' and Phenomenology," where Derrida interrogates the "structurality of the opening" (ED 230/155), and in "Structure, Sign, and Play," where he interrogates "the structurality of the structure" (ED 409/279).

32. Most important is the discussion which closes *Speech and Phenomena's* first chapter, "The Sign and Signs." Here, after setting up Husserl's essential distinction between indication and expression within the sign, Derrida says that there can be two readings of Husserl's move to solitary mental life, a move through which Husserl intends to separate out indication leaving behind pure expression. The first reading is structural; Derrida says, "Husserl seems to repress, with dogmatic haste, a question concerning the *structure of the sign in general*" (VP 23/23). In the First Investigation, Husserl has not asked the question of what is meant by a sign in general before moving to the separation of the sign's two functions. The second possible reading, according to Derrida, is genetic; this second reading itself can go in two directions. On the one hand, the absence of the structural question could be seen as critical vigilance (not as dogmatism), insofar as Husserl would be suspicious of our precomprehension of the notion of sign. Perhaps, two concepts are actually attached to the word *sign*; there is mere verbal unity but no conceptual unity. On the other hand, according to Derrida, we could see the repression of the essence question as an attempt to stop the subjection of the "sign to truth, language to being, speech to thought, and writing to speech" (VP 25/24). Husserl would be critically vigilant insofar as he does not suppose that the sign must satisfy truth but rather constitutes or produces it (VP 26/25). While, at this point, Derrida seems to privilege the genetic question, he immediately

adds that "this last move is not simple." He says, "This is our problem and we shall have to return to it" (VP 26/25). The reduction of structure, the return to an active constitution of meaning and validity, the return to the activity of a life which produces truth and validity in general through its signs, in short, the move to genesis, does not imply an escape from the metaphysics of presence. Another "necessity," Derrida says, confirms the metaphysics of presence; genetic philosophy needs to assure the pro-visonality of the passage. Because this need determines its interrogations, genetic philosophy fails to examine the structure of the sign—it does not start with the question of language in general—thereby failing to recognize the inseparability of voice and writing. All of *Speech and Phenomena* therefore amounts to a demonstration of this inseparability.

33. Jacques Derrida, *Limited Inc*, trans. Samuel Weber and Jeffrey Mehlman (Evanston: Northwestern University Press, 1988).
34. The first essential distinction that Husserl makes in the First Logical Investigation, indication and expression, is also a distinction of nothing. This distinction is not an ontic distinction or duplication; expression is not one sign and indication another. Rather the distinction is functional; any sign can be used indicatively or expressively. Thus nothing separates the two functions. As Derrida says, "The difference between indication and expression very quickly appears in the course of the description to be a difference more *functional* than *substantial*. Indication and expression are functions or signifying relations, not terms" (VP 20/20, Derrida's emphasis). In other words, as Derrida says in *Of Grammatology*, "the difference between signified and signifier is *nothing*" (DLG 36/23, Derrida's emphasis).
35. Cf. Jacques Derrida, "'Genesis and Structure' and Phenomenology," in *Writing and Difference*, 245–46/164.
36. In a note to "Violence and Metaphysics," Derrida says, "Pure difference is not absolutely different (from nondifference). Hegel's critique of the concept of pure difference is for us here, doubtless, the most uncircumventable theme. Hegel thought absolute difference and showed that can be pure only by being impure" (ED 227 n1/320 n91).
37. In fact, in *Speech and Phenomena*, Derrida links up the form (or *eidos* or idea)/matter distinction with that of act/potency (or reality/possibility) (VP 70/63).
38. Cf. also Derrida, *Given Time*, p. 103.
39. One can even say that the leftover has a ghostly existence (*geistige Leiblichkeit*). Cf. LOG 86/88; also Derrida, *Given Time*, p. 101 n18.
40. Or perhaps even into something like *Otherwise than Being or Beyond Essence*.

6

Merleau-Ponty and Derrida: *La différEnce*

G. B. Madison

"Le langage est une vie, est notre vie et la [vie des choses]....
C'est l'erreur des philosophies sémantiques de fermer le langage
comme s'il ne parlait que de soi: il ne vit que du silence; tout ce
que nous jetons aux autres a germé dans ce grand pays muet qui
ne nous quitte pas. Mais, parce qu'ayant éprouvé en lui-même le
besoin de parler, la naissance de la parole comme une bulle au
fond de son expérience muette, le philosophe sait mieux que
personne que le vécu est du vécu-parlé, que né à cette profondeur,
le langage ... n'interrompt pas une immédiation sans lui parfaite,
que la vision même, la pensée même, sont, a-t-on dit, "structurées
comme un langage," sont *articulation* avant la lettre....

Language is a life, is our life and the life of the things.... It is
the error of the semantic philosophies to close up language as if
it spoke only of itself: language lives only from silence; everything we cast to the others has germinated in this great mute
land which we never leave. But, because he has experienced within
himself the need to speak, the birth of speech as bubbling up at
the bottom of his mute experience, the philosopher knows better
than anyone that what is lived is lived-spoken, that, born at this
depth, language does not interrupt an immediation that would be
perfect without it, that the vision itself, the thought itself, are, as
has been said, "structured as a language," are *articulation* before
the letter....

—Maurice Merleau-Ponty,
The Visible and the Invisible

What is the relation between seeing and writing? Does one simply
write down what one sees ("telling it like it is"), or is it perhaps
not rather the case that what one thinks one sees is actually what
has already been written up by someone else, somewhere or other,
at some time or other?[1] The way traditional philosophy would respond to this question is well known. From classical metaphysics

to Husserlian phenomenology and beyond, the fundamental, sacro-sanct principle of referentialist-representationalism is that thoughts should directly mirror (refer to, represent) things, and that words should faithfully mirror thoughts. One should simply "put into words" ("write") what is there to be seen. "Truth" is a function of correctness in representation, in mirroring: *veritas est adequatio intellectus (verbum) ad rem*. This presupposes, of course, that there exists, "in itself," somehow, a "reality" that is just "there," laid out before a disinterested gaze, waiting to be seen and said, and that the supreme vocation of thought and language is merely that of copying this reality, with the least possible amount of linguistic gloss and embellishment.[2]

The answer to the question on the part of Derridian-style postmodern philosophy (if "philosophy" is still the appropriate word) is equally well known. Carrying on, as it were, with Nietzsche's *Destruktion* of all the great Idols of the Tradition ("Doing philosophy with a hammer"), Derrida informs us that there is no objective reality "out there," "present" to consciousness, simply waiting to be described with phenomenological impartiality. Whereas Husserl admonished his readers to shun empty words and "return to the things themselves" (*Zurück zu den Sachen selbst!*), for Derrida there are no *Sachen* to which, try as hard as we might, we could ever "return." Indeed, far from being the Origin, Source, or Criterion (*metron*), what metaphysics calls "reality" is nothing more than a "significant effect" of language (*un effet de signification*). Philosophers don't describe the world, they *write the world*. The world is nothing more than a semiological construct, a purely *intra*linguistic affair, a mirage produced by the limitless play of free-floating signifiers, in sum: a "bottomless chessboard." There is nothing outside of language—*Il n'y a pas de hors-texte; Il n'y a rien hors du text.*[3]

Derrida's work fully echoes the dominant leitmotif of contemporary thought, as much in evidence in analytic as in continental philosophy, viz., an overriding preoccupation with language (or linguisticality). Joining forces with Derrida, Richard Rorty likewise emphasizes the ubiquity of language. Language, he says, is not a mere medium between Subject and Object or a tool whose "adequacy" could be assessed in some "objective" manner.

> The latter suggestion presupposes that there is some way of breaking out of language in order to compare it with something else. But there is no way to think about either the world or our purposes except by using our language.... [O]ne cannot see

language-as-a-whole in relation to something else to which it applies, or for which it is a means to an end.[4]

Because Rorty maintains that language is something we cannot
"break out of," because, that is, he maintains that language is a
kind of prison (or a "padded cell," as Derrida might say),[5] his version of the linguisticality (or textuality)-thesis entails (protestations
on his part notwithstanding) a thoroughgoing cognitive *relativism*.
The motto of postmodernists such as Derrida and Rorty (or their
fellow travelers) could well be: There are no truths, only an endless proliferation of equally groundless or arbitrary interpretations.
Nietzsche's legacy with a vengeance!

In his attempt to advance "the anti-Platonic insistence on the
ubiquity of language," Rorty appeals to Gadamer, who had said:
"Human experience is essentially linguistic."[6] Gadamer's famous
dictum to the effect that "being that can be understood is language"
does indeed appear to be such as to warrant linguistic relativism
("textualism"). The fact of the matter, however, is that Gadamer
has strenuously refused to draw from the fact that human experience is essentially linguistic the conclusion that all understanding
is, for that reason, "language-bound" (i.e., language-relative).[7] Rorty
apparently realizes that it would be difficult to enlist Gadamer in
support of his version of the postmodern enterprise, for he goes
on to criticize Gadamer for being a "weak textualist" and expresses
his unqualified support for Derrida's "strong textualism."[8] This
amounts to an important admission on his part. As I have argued
elsewhere, although hermeneutics is an altogether *postmodern* form
of thought—in that it seeks to be genuinely postmetaphysical
("antifoundational")—it differs importantly from other forms of
postmodernism in that, while stressing the centrality and, indeed,
the inescapability of language and interpretation, it nonetheless
wishes to hold onto such traditional notions as "truth," "meaning," and "reality." In this it contrasts with the postmodernisms of
Rorty and Derrida, which are, I would argue, not genuinely
*post*metaphysical but only *anti*metaphysical.[9] Merely to substitute
language for reality, "writing" for "seeing," is not to move *beyond*
metaphysics; it is simply to engage in an inverse—indeed, per-
verse—form of metaphysics. If a genuine "overcoming" of metaphysics entails an overcoming of what amounts to the essence of
metaphysical thinking, viz., oppositional thinking, then hermeneutics
is indeed postmetaphysical in that it rejects the either/or that still
dominates the thinking of postmoderns of a Derridian or Rortyan
sort: *either* language *or* reality. For hermeneutics it is *neither* the

case that we merely "write" what we "see" *nor* that we merely "see" what we "write." It is rather a case of "both/and."

This brings us to Merleau-Ponty, whose reflections on both perception and language are such as to elucidate what it means to speak, hermeneutically, of a "both/and." Situating Merleau-Ponty in a hermeneutical context, as I am doing, involves not the least bit of textual violence (a "strong misreading," as some postmodernists would say, approvingly), since, viewed retrospectively, Merleau-Ponty was indeed both a proto-postmodern and a hermeneuticist.[10] In many ways, Merleau-Ponty was even more "progressive" or more "post" than Derrida, who would have us believe that Merleau-Ponty's phenomenology was nothing more than the last gasp of the moribund "metaphysics of presence." Merleau-Ponty's unfinished philosophical project was (or is) hermeneutical in that it sought to chart a course beyond both objectivistic metaphysics (what Merleau-Ponty referred to as *la pensée objective*) and relativistic semiologism. Herein lies the essential difference between Merleau-Ponty and Derrida, and it is this difference (*avec-un-e*) that I would like to explore in somewhat more detail.

There are a number of significant differences between Merleau-Ponty and Derrida, although they are not nearly as clear-cut as Derrida would have us believe, nor are they at all of the sort intimated by him (such as that Merleau-Ponty was still a "phenomenologist" and, therefore, unlike Derrida, a prisoner of the "philosophy of consciousness"). Between the two there is, in fact, not only difference or divergence (*écart*, so to speak) but also a very strange and interesting kind of proximity. Merleau-Ponty's project involved as much a rejection of the (metaphysical) "absolute" (*la pensée de l'absolu*) as Derrida's explicitly antimetaphysical one subsequently did, and, as a philosopher of ambiguity, Merleau-Ponty was in his own way as much a "deconstructionist" (of metaphysical comforts) as Derrida.[11] Indeed, he was no less as thoroughgoing a critic of the philosophy of consciousness (in the guise of Husserlian phenomenology) than was Derrida; in his *Speech and Phenomenon* Derrida was in fact building (without acknowledgment, to be sure) on Merleau-Ponty's own critique of Husserl. The key element in this pitiless critique was of course Merleau-Ponty's notion of the "flesh." One thing that has not received all the attention it deserves is the strange proximity between Merleau-Ponty's *flesh* and Derrida's *différance*, between which there exists a kind of functional isomorphism.[12] Although Derrida makes no reference to Merleau-Ponty in this respect (indeed, he rarely refers to Merleau-

Ponty in any respect), I cannot for my part easily imagine how such an uncanny *resemblance* could be completely fortuitous; Derrida, a voracious reader of anything and everything, must surely have given Merleau-Ponty a close reading as a young man. The lines of *dissemination* of the flesh have left their trace, not the least in Derrida's own *écriture.*

When once pushed to the wall (as it were), Derrida actually conceded that his own (mostly implicit) portrayal of Merleau-Ponty as a "logocentrist" was open to question. Nancy Holland has related how, as a visitor to a class of Bert Dreyfus on Merleau-Ponty, Derrida stated that Merleau-Ponty's work falls within the metaphysics of presence. Pressed to defend himself, Derrida (Holland relates) had to admit that "the case was not quite so clear-cut, given the breadth and complexity of Merleau-Ponty's work." And as she goes on to say: "He left us with an interesting thought—if one might argue that *The* [sic] *Phenomenology of Perception* falls within the metaphysics of presence, with *The Visible and the Invisible* 'it is even harder to say [these are Derrida's words].'" Holland herself remarks:

> What interests me more now than the question about the metaphysics of presence is the way in which much of what Merleau-Ponty says, even in *The* [sic] *Phenomenology of Perception*, denies any primacy to, or often even any possibility of presence. In this respect, Merleau-Ponty's work often seems to foreshadow some of the criticisms Derrida himself makes of traditional phenomenology. . . . Merleau-Ponty can be seen to exceed the tradition, often in words that echo Derrida's own texts before their time.[13]

These are suggestive remarks (Holland's last remark is, if anything, an understatement). Like Derrida later on, Merleau-Ponty was greatly taken with the Saussurean, or structuralist, conception of language; indeed, he was the first major French philosopher to attempt to incorporate Saussurean insights into his own philosophical undertaking—in particular Saussure's original thesis as to the *arbitrary and differential nature of the linguistic sign.*[14] If this "difficult idea," as he rightly called it, greatly fascinated Merleau-Ponty, it completely mesmerized Derrida, and was to serve as the basis for his entire philosophical "system." If Derrida is a "post"-structuralist (Saussure being for him attached still to the metaphysics of presence), it is only because he is in fact a *hyper*structuralist; his earlier work can be viewed as an attempt to generalize *without limit* (*sans limites*) Saussure's thesis that "in language there are only differences."[15] Going well beyond Saussure, Derrida in effect asserts that there is *nothing but* language and, *therefore*, nothing but *difference*, wherever you care to look. This is precisely what he calls *différance*. Given the diacritical nature of signifiers, meaning is something that is never decisively present; it is infinitely deferred, "undecidable." Like the structuralists, Derrida maintained that language has no "outside," only an "inside," and that it is therefore not "about" anything at all—experience, existence, the world, reality, whatever. Language "refers" only to itself, and the meaning of what it says to itself by way of *auto-affection* (*on sait bien ce que cela veut dire*) is forever deferred.[16]

We are thus approaching the point where the strange proximity uniting the two French thinkers "trembles" and gives way to a profound *divergence*. In the end we have to do not with a *chiasmic* intertwining (which, as Merleau-Ponty might say, at once *réunit et sépare*, but with an unbridgeable *chasm*, *qui sépare, et cela définitivement*. There were always, up to the very end, two poles to Merleau-Ponty's thinking: perception ("experience") and language. To be sure, for Merleau-Ponty these were not, as in traditional referentialist-representationalism, two separate and distinct "things" (just as for Merleau-Ponty, the "world" was not something metaphysically distinct from our consciousness of the world); the two are united in a relation of circularity.[17] Between "seeing" and "writing" there existed for Merleau-Ponty a dialectical intertwining; the two were "equiprimordial" (about which, more later). The case is quite otherwise with Derrida, as I have already intimated. For him there is only one "pole," and that is, of course, "writing" ("arche-writing," if one prefers). This is why Martin Dillon is in my estimation fully justified in labelling Derrida's thought a form of "semiological reductionism." As Dillon observes: "The semiological reductionism that defines postmodernism [and Derrida in particular] is an abject relativism because it reduces meaning to signification, and signification to a groundless play of signifiers."[18] I couldn't agree more. (It is perhaps worth recalling that reductionism is *the* classic move of metaphysics and its oppositional mode of thinking.)

In a quasi-Hegelian fashion (only quasi, because while Derrida "negates" he does not "preserve"), Derrida "sublates" (*relève*) perception, corporeality, and, in general, everything "existential" into the diaphanous realm of "writing," by way of a totally Immaculate Assumption (*relève*). (It is not Gadamer but Derrida who has to answer to Habermas's charge of "linguistic idealism.") The Derridian "writer" ("writer," not "author"),[19] impelled though he or she be by a *libido scribendi* of an extra-linguistic origin, is nonetheless the disembodied ghost of the real, flesh-and-blood (*chair et os, leibhaftig*) human subject. A pitiful, uprooted creature who knows well how to write (if not to write well, at least to write at interminable length on anything and everything) but who is at a lamentable loss when it comes to *acting*, since the ethical order of human *praxis* is nowhere to be found in the free-floating realm of Derrida's referentless signifiers.[20]

The "subject": that is indeed the word that names the essential difference between our two postmoderns. For Derrida, the notion of the subject is irredeemably metaphysical (the very epitome of the essence of "presence" itself). To the degree that, as a phenomenologist, Merleau-Ponty held onto the notion of the subject, he was to be counted as a lost cause, a hopelessly naive pre-postmodern or, as Gadamer says of Derrida's portrayal of him, "a lost sheep in the dried-up pastures of metaphysics." Merleau-Ponty's defense of the subject (like that of Paul Ricoeur after him)[21] was not, however, as simple (or simple-minded) as the poststructuralists/deconstructionists would make it out to be. Merleau-Ponty was no less an uncompromising opponent of modern subjectivism than was Heidegger, from whom Derrida learned his antihumanist (the "end of 'man'") lessons. Merleau-Ponty was, however, more sophisticated than Heidegger, and thus felt no need to denounce humanism as a metaphysical aberration (quite to the contrary, he realized full well that if humanism cannot be defended philosophically, neither can the idea of democracy [not that this would have disconcerted Heidegger in the least]). He realized that, as he said, "the thought of subjectivity" (*la pensée du subjectif*) is one of those thoughts which, once discovered, philosophy cannot simply annul (by returning, for instance, to some idyllic presocratic age of ontological innocence before philosophy began its long descent into the cosmic night brought on by the oblivion of Being); philosophy must, instead, correct them by divesting them of their metaphysical excesses.[22]

Contrary to what some postmodern deconstructionists would have us believe, writing does not simply write itself; it takes a real human subject to write whatever it is that, as a matter of fact, gets written; even deconstruction (which, as Rorty would say, is "a kind of writing") presupposes a subject who writes deconstructively, and thus who cannot be deconstructed without more ado. Derrida himself was once forced to concede as much.[23] And this subject is manifestly a corporeal, perceiving, personal subject (not just a bunch of disembodied words or "graphemes," a mere "scriptor" [as some poststructuralists would say]). Derrida's grudging recognition of the existential subject notwithstanding, he has never, in stark contrast to Merleau-Ponty, made any attempt to explore the corporeal and "perceptual" side of the seeing/writing couplet and to elucidate the complex and highly ambiguous relation that obtains between experience (perception) and expression (language).

The main thrust of Merleau-Ponty's work was precisely that of showing how subjectivity is indissociably, at one and the same time, *both* seeing (corporeality) *and* writing (language). The key concept in his earlier work was "experience," a phenomenological notion that Derrida would have us believe is irredeemably metaphysical.[24] But even in the *Phenomenology*, "experience" most emphatically did not mean "pure presence." What is "there" to be seen is never *fully* "there," and, moreover, there is no such thing as a "pure perception," "uncontaminated" by language. Seeing is itself thoroughly infused with words. Perception and language interpenetrate, they "flow into" (*einströmen*) one another, they are equiprimordial (*gleichursprunglich*). As Merleau-Ponty insisted: "There is no experience without speech, as the purely lived-through has no part in the discursive life of man."[25] This is admittedly a somewhat ambiguous remark, but then the stance taken by Merleau-Ponty, especially in the *Phenomenology*, was highly ambiguous, to the point almost of being, as he himself once said, a "bad ambiguity." On the one hand, he wanted, as a good phenomenologist, to insist that pre-verbal experience is already, in some important sense, "meaningful" (meaning is not, as logocentric analytic philosophy would have it, simply created by language and subsequently imposed upon an experience meaningless in itself) while, on the other hand, he felt the need to deny that the meanings embodied in lived experience are determinate meanings[26] (lived meaning [*sens*] becomes conscious or intelligible meaning [*signification*] only by being "spoken"); he even went so far as to assert at one point that "inner experience ... is meaningless (*ne veut rien dire*)."[27]

There are apparent inconsistencies here. (Can there be perception in the proper sense of the term without language or not?) But there is perhaps a way of getting around them, an issue to which I shall return. A remark later in the *Phenomenology* clarifies the matter somewhat: "It is true that the subject as an absolute presence to itself [lived experience] is something that we cannot circumvent. ... It is also true that it provides itself with symbols of itself in both succession and multiplicity, and that symbols *are* it, since without them it would, like an inarticulate cry, fail to achieve self-consciousness."[28] Merleau-Ponty's phraseology here (and elsewhere)[29] clearly underscores his attempt to get beyond oppositional thinking and to defend a "both/and" position.

Not only is the perceived world never fully present to the perceiving subject (such that it could be unambiguously "referred" to), the subject is never fully present even to itself. Self-consciousness ("subjectivity") means self-presence (the presence of the self to itself), but for Merleau-Ponty this presence was not of the "Husserlian" sort denounced by Derrida. The hold that the subject has on itself is always tenuous, at best. To the degree that the subject does achieve a passable degree of self-presence or self-knowledge, it is thanks to language. The subject *is* an interpretation ("thinking" is interpreting oneself to oneself; Merleau-Ponty referred to this as *la pensée interrogative*), and thus the self knows itself only by speaking or writing itself (cf. Montaigne).[30] The self is a "text," heavily imbued with "intertextuality" and amounting to a never-ending story. As Cornelius Castoriadis has very aptly remarked in speaking of Merleau-Ponty, the subject is "a being who can become what he will have been only in speaking of it."[31]

In regard to the matter at hand, this means that while, in one sense, lived experience ("seeing") precedes its expression ("writing"), in another sense it is itself a function of what is subsequently said about it. William James was getting at much the same point when he said:

> What we say about reality [i.e., our experience of reality] thus depends on the [interpretive] perspective into which we throw it. The *that* of it [its facticity] is its own; but the *what* depends on the *which*; and the which depends on *us* [on language]. Both the sensational and the relational parts of reality are dumb; they say absolutely nothing about themselves. We it is who have to speak for them.[32]

Between "seeing" and "writing," within the subject itself, there is therefore an *écart* or non-coincidence, which is not for all that pure *différance*. Let "/" stand for *écart*. To say that between the *sentant* and the *sensible*, for instance, there exists an *écart* then translates as: *sentant/sensible*. In the way Merleau-Ponty would use it, "/" is not a mere disjunctive (as in "either/or"); it means neither "≠" (or "−" [hyphen]) nor "&," for it both disjoins and conjoins (*sépare et réunit*), at one and the same time.

Because the human subject is a result of a *déhiscence* of the flesh (*la chair du sensible, du monde*), it is, and can never be, fully "present" to itself—but neither is it ever totally dispersed, a complete stranger to itself, "disseminated" in an endless series of self-effacing "traces." *Écart* means both proximity and distance, both presence and absence, both sameness and difference. Between seeing and writing, as between the subject and the world, there is (*il y a*) the "thickness of the flesh." In fact, the flesh is nothing other than this thickness itself.

I mentioned above that there may be a way of getting around the apparent inconsistencies in Merleau-Ponty's text. Perhaps the best way of clarifying the ambiguous relation between the two "equiprimordials" of seeing and writing—this "difficult idea"—would be to bring to bear on the issue an extremely interesting idea of Merleau-Ponty's that to my knowledge has not received a great deal of attention. The key to the problem, I hypothesize, lies in a notion Merleau-Ponty had come across in Bergson and to which he occasionally alludes under the heading *le mouvement rétrograde du vrai*. As Merleau-Ponty might say, *le vrai ne tient qu'en mouvement*.[33] Truth never holds still; it is in constant movement, and the direction in which it moves is *backward*, into the past; it is retrospective, retrograde. In other words, nothing is ever "true" at the split second it occurs (the absolute "now," Husserl's "living present," *lebendige Gegenwart*, which precedes all expression [*Ausdruck*]), and in this sense Derrida is quite right in denying the existence of what metaphysicians call "the truth." Like human existence itself (in Kierkegaard's reading of it), truth *is not*; rather it *becomes*. Anything that is true is true only *après coup*. That is to say, the truth of what-is always awaits its "veri-*fication*," its being-made-true, and thus its being-true, from the future.[34] Is it true that what I think I am now perceiving is "real" and not a mere hallucination? There's no possible way I can know (and thus be "in" the truth) until successive experiences either confirm or disconfirm the "present" one. Subsequent experiences—the interpretation process—always legislate retroactively for preceding ones. Thus, as James would say, "Truth is *made* . . . in the course of experience."[35] (One thing that this obviously entails is that, although we are indeed in the truth [this is just what *être-au-monde* means], we are never *fully* in the truth, since, like Peirce's series of interpretants, there is no end to this interpretive process, to the endless spiral of experience/expression/experience. . . .)

Recall Castoriadis: The subject is what, through an ongoing interpretive process of "becoming," he or she *will have been*. The crucial thing in this statement is the tense of the verbs. The intertwining of tenses, of past and future in the future past perfect, is the most faithful reflection of the structure of human understanding itself. As James once said, alluding to Kierkegaard ("a Danish thinker"): "We live forwards, ... but we understand backwards."[36] Or as Gadamer puts it: "All beginnings lie in the darkness, and what is more, they can be illuminated only in the light of what came later and from the perspective of what followed."[37] As truth-seeking beings we are, Merleau-Ponty said, quoting Bergson, like travelers on the back of a train who see only those places they have already left behind. When we truly "see" something, it is because it has already been "written." This is what Merleau-Ponty means when he says, speaking of an "exchange between the past and the present": "Expression antedates itself and postulates that being was going towards it."[38] Between experience and its own (*propre*) truth, there is always a certain *décalage* or temporal displacement ("distanciation," in hermeneutical terms), an *écart*, or "spacing," of a temporal nature, this distantiation being itself a necessary condition for the production of meaning.[39]

As Merleau-Ponty would readily admit, we seem here to confront a paradox. On the one hand, philosophy, the attempt to express experience, is manifestly a creative enterprise (Nature does not philosophize, only human subjects do). On the other hand, this creation presents itself as an "adequation." It is therefore "a creation that is at the same time an adequation." Creation is in fact the only way to obtain an adequation. The notion of a *creative adequation* may seem to be a contradiction in terms, but it is nevertheless the most apt way of characterizing the phenomenon of expression. The curious fact of the matter is that "art and philosophy *together* are precisely not arbitrary fabrications in the universe of the 'spiritual' (of 'culture'), but contact with Being *precisely as creations* [emphasis added]." The lesson that Merleau-Ponty draws from all this is that literature is nothing other than the "*inscription* of Being [itself]."[40]

The paradox of expression—"What I say of the sensible world is not in the sensible world, and yet it has no other meaning than to say what the sensible world means"[41]—ceases to be the insuperable aporia it is for traditional referentialist-representationalism; indeed, ceases to be a paradox altogether once we take into account the hermeneutical fact that human understanding, precisely because it is linguistic through and through, proceeds backward (forward into the past). This hermeneutical fact is also such as to enable us to escape the deadend of Derridian deconstruction and Rortyan relativism: the fact that human being is essentially "linguistic" (the fact that, as Wallace Stevens would say, "the world is a world of words to the end") does not mean that we are prisoners of language, cut off for all eternity from a truthful experience of reality, perpetually condemned to a kind of ontological Diaspora. It simply means that *language* is the way in which *reality* itself most properly exists (*existe en propre*) for us.

A prominent sub-theme in Merleau-Ponty's work, present already in *The Structure of Behavior*, is his notion that human understanding is of such a sort that it invariably tends to misunderstand itself. This phenomenon of self-misunderstanding is perhaps nowhere more in evidence than in what has to do with that most cherished ideal of human understanding: *truth*. With its referentialist-representational conception of truth as *adequatio intellectus et res*, traditional philosophy assumes that truth is a *static* affair: the coincidence, *in the present moment* (and totally *sans écart*), of ideas or words with things, a kind of undivided epistemological simultaneity or immediacy. A view of truth such as this—purely spatial, timeless view of truth, as it were—remains oblivious to the dynamic or processual nature of truth discussed above. Deconstruction is altogether within its rights when it sets out to deconstruct (*faire ébranler*) truth so conceived. What James referred to as the "rationalistic notion of 'the Truth' with a big T"[42] is indeed nothing more than a metaphysical will-o'-the-wisp, an illusion of the understanding created by understanding's ignoring of its own retrograde or interpretive nature.[43] Deconstruction does not itself escape the metaphysical trap, however, viz., the error of conceiving of truth, as James again would say, as "a stagnant [and fully present] property inherent in" a purely representational discourse about reality. Because truth as traditionally conceived is "stagnant," it tends to become putrid and give off noxious odors (as Nietzsche might say). This is why one of the main tasks Merleau-Ponty assigned himself was that of purifying consciousness of all the "psychological bric-a-brac" (sense impressions, hyletic data, etc.) traditional philosophy had cluttered it up with; as is especially apparent in *The Visible and the Invisible*, Merleau-Ponty's goal was that of airing out the stuffy attic of what philosophy had traditionally referred to as the "mind." Deconstruction, in fact, merely compounds the error. It errs when it takes the metaphysical conception of truth to be the true or proper one, and it errs again when, having exposed this conception for the illusion it is, it goes on from there to reject the notion of truth altogether.

As mentioned above, the "paradox of expression" (the notion of a "creative adequation") constitutes an *aporia*, a nasty Gordian knot for referentialist-representationalism. As an instance of semiological reductionism, deconstruction seeks not to unravel the knot but to cut it in one fell swoop, and thus (in merely "reducing" it) it does not really offer a "solution" to the paradox at all. If to be confronted with an *aporia* means "being stuck in a bind," deconstruction, in playing its game of double jeopardy, lands us in an insuperable double bind, a veritable *cul de sac*. The only viable way of overcoming the relativistic nihilism that follows upon the deconstruction of metaphysical illusions and of defending "truth" in a postmodern age is by moving beyond both metaphysical referentialism and semiotic reductionism. It is precisely such a move that Merleau-Ponty was attempting throughout his writings. Truth is never something that simply *is*; it is, if we're lucky enough and can conjoin *virtu* and *fortuna*, something that sometimes, *de temps à autre*, *happens* to us. Like "being" itself (as Merleau-Ponty conceived of it), truth is not an immobile *state-of-affairs* but a luminescent and, more often than not, a fleeting or evanescent *event*.

Merleau-Ponty's philosophy was not only a philosophy of ambiguity, it was also an ambiguous philosophy. This is not at all surprising, given the fact that the "greatest of French phenomenologists" (as Ricoeur once referred to him) was engaged in the supremely difficult task of exploring uncharted territory, beyond the boundaries of metaphysics, with few markers to serve as a guide along the way. Given the fragmentary nature of Merleau-Ponty's later, unfinished work, it is only with difficulty that the direction in which it points (its meaning, *sens*) can be discerned. And yet, I think it safe to say that it points us in a good direction, beyond *both* metaphysical referentialist-representationalism *and* semiological reductionism. *Contra* Derrida and other such postmoderns, there is indeed something like "reality," but its locus is not "out there," in the never-never-land of "transcendental signifieds"; reality is not some kind of stagnant in-itself to be "referred" to by transparent word-signs.[44] Strictly speaking, reality, like truth, *is not*; it becomes, it transpires, *elle s'écrit*, and the locus of its most eloquent (*parlante*) inscription is the human seeing/writing subject.

Notes

1. At the 1987 annual meeting of the Merleau-Ponty Circle in Kingston, Rhode Island, Claude Lefort chided Merleau-Ponty for having said that "nature is always for us as at the first day." Instead, Lefort remarked, "We should rather say that nature is always seen as having already

been seen by another" ("Flesh and Otherness" in Galen A. Johnson and Michael B. Smith, eds., *Ontology and Alterity in Merleau-Ponty* [Albany: State University of New York Press, 1990], p. 10). Lefort had a valid point. And one should add: not only as having been seen by others but, above all, as having been "spoken" by others. For the hermeneutical fact of the matter is humans inhabit the world they do only to the degree that they are, as Josiah Royce said, members of a Community of Interpretation. It is language, and language alone, that transforms a biological *Umwelt* into a genuine *Welt*.

2. As Aristotle admonished his student audience: "The arts of language cannot help having a small but real importance, whatever it is we have to expound to others: the way in which a thing is said does affect its intelligibility. Not, however, so much importance as people think [Derrida's sophist predecessors?]. All such arts are fanciful and meant to charm the hearer. Nobody uses fine language when teaching geometry" (*Rhetoric*, III, 1, 1404a5 [W.R. Roberts trans.]).

3. See Derrida, *De la grammatologie* (Paris: Editions de Minuit, 1967), pp. 227, 233.

4. Richard Rorty, *Consequences of Pragmatism* (Minneapolis: University of Minnesota Press, 1982), pp. xviii–xx.

5. See Derrida, *Positions*, trans. Alan Bass (Chicago: University of Chicago Press), p. 86.

6. Rorty, *Consequences*, p. xx. Actually, this is Rorty's own free transcription of what Gadamer says on p. 19 of his *Philosophical Hermeneutics* (Berkeley: University of California Press, 1976), where the text reads "the essential linguisticality of all human experience of the world."

7. See Gadamer, *Philosophical Hermeneutics*, p. 15, as well as my "Philosophy without Foundations," *Reason Papers* 16 (Fall 1991), pp. 26–27.

8. See *Consequences of Pragmatism*, p. 153.

9. In addition to my "Philosophy without Foundations," see also my "Coping with Nietzsche's Legacy: Rorty, Derrida, Gadamer," *Philosophy Today* (Winter 1991), pp. 3–19, as well as my "Beyond Seriousness and Frivolity: A Gadamerian Response to Deconstruction" in *The Hermeneutics of Postmodernity: Figures and Themes* (Bloomington: Indiana University Press, 1988), pp. 106–22 (reprinted in H. J. Silverman, ed., *Gadamer and Hermeneutics* [London: Routledge, 1991] pp. 119–35).

10. See my "Merleau-Ponty in Retrospect" in Patrick Burke and Jan Van Der Veken, eds., *Merleau-Ponty in Contemporary Perspective* (Dordrecht: Kluwer Academic, 1993), pp. 183–95. On the relation between Merleau-Ponty and Gadamer, see also, in this volume, James Risser, "Communication and the Prose of the World: The Question of Language in Merleau-Ponty and Gadamer," pp. 131–44.

11. See my "Merleau-Ponty's Deconstruction of Logocentrism" in M. C. Dillon, ed., *Merleau-Ponty Vivant* (Albany: State University of New York Press, 1991), pp. 117–52 as well as my "Between Phenomenology and (Post)Structuralism: Rereading Merleau-Ponty" in Thomas W. Busch and Shaun Gallagher, *Merleau-Ponty, Hermeneutics, and Postmodernism* (Albany: State University of New York Press, 1992), pp. 117–28 in which I attempt to situate my reading of Merleau-Ponty

(as a kind of proto-deconstructionist) in relation to those of Hugh Silverman and Martin Dillon.

12. See in regard to this my "Did Merleau-Ponty Have a Theory of Perception? in Busch and Gallagher, *Merleau-Ponty, Hermeneutics, and Postmodernism*, pp. 94–97.

13. Nancy J. Holland, "Merleau-Ponty on Presence: A Derridian Reading," *Research in Phenomenology* 16 (1986), pp. 111–12.

14. "What we have learned from Saussure is that, taken singly, signs do not signify anything, and that each one of them does not so much express a meaning as mark a divergence of meaning between itself and other signs. Since the same can be said for all other signs, we may conclude that language is made of differences without terms; or more exactly, that the terms of language are engendered only by the differences which appear among them" (Merleau-Ponty, *Signs*, trans. Richard C. McCleary [Evanston: Northwestern University Press, 1964], p. 39).

15. See Ferdinand de Saussure, *Cours de linguistique générale* (Paris: Payot, 1964), p. 166.

16. I am drawing here on my "Being and Speaking" forthcoming in John Stewart, *Beyond the Symbol Model* (Albany: State University of New York Press).

17. For an extended discussion of the notion of "circularity" in Merleau-Ponty, see my *The Phenomenology of Merleau-Ponty* (Athens: Ohio University Press, 1981), Chapter One.

18. See Dillon, *Semiological Reductionism: A Critique of the Deconstructionist Movement in Postmodern Thought* (Albany: State University of New York Press, 1995).

19. See *Of Grammatology*, p. 68.

20. A point stressed by Calvin O. Schrag; see his *Communicative Praxis and the Space of Subjectivity* (Bloomington: Indiana University Press, 1986).

21. In regard to Ricoeur, see my "Ricoeur and the Hermeneutics of the Subject" in *The Hermeneutics of Postmodernity*, reprinted in E. Hahn, ed., *The Philosophy of Paul Ricoeur*, The Library of Living Philosophers (Chicago: Open Court, 1995), pp. 90–105.

22. See Merleau-Ponty, *Signs*, pp. 153–54, and, for a discussion of the matter, my "Merleau-Ponty and Postmodernity" in *The Hermeneutics of Postmodernity* and "Merleau-Ponty Alive," *Man and World* 26 (1993), pp. 19–44 (previously published under the title "Merleau-Ponty je ziv," *Filozofska Istrazivanja* 11; 3 [Zagreb, 1991]).

23. In response to a question put to him following a public presentation of his "Structure, Sign, and Play," Derrida stated: "The subject is absolutely indispensable. I don't destroy the subject; I situate it. That is to say, I believe that at a certain level both of experience and of philosophical and scientific discourse one cannot get along without the notion of the subject. It is a question of knowing where it comes from and how it functions" (*The Languages of Criticism and the Sciences of Man: The Structuralist Controversy*, ed. Richard Macksey and Eugenio Donato [Baltimore: The Johns Hopkins University Press, 1970], p. 271).

24. Cf. Jacques Derrida, *Of Grammatology*, trans. G. Spivak (Baltimore: Johns Hopkins University Press, 1976), p. 60: "As for the concept of experience, it is most unwieldy here. Like all the notions I am using here, it belongs to the history of metaphysics and we can only use it under erasure [*sous rature*]. 'Experience' has always designated the relationship with a presence, whether that relationship had the form of consciousness or not."

25. Merleau-Ponty, *Phenomenology of Perception*, trans. C. Smith (London: Routledge, 1962), p. 337. See also Merleau-Ponty's remark on p. 392: "[S]peech itself *brings about* that concordance between me and myself, and between myself and others, on which an attempt is being made to base that thought."

26. Compare with *The Visible and the Invisible*, trans. Alphonso Lingis (Evanston: Northwestern University Press, 1968), p. 171: "Yet there is a world of silence, the perceived world, at least, is an order where there are non-language significations—yes, non-language significations, but they are not for all that *positive*."

27. *Phenomenology of Perception*, p. 276.

28. Ibid., p. 76. It is tempting to compare what Merleau-Ponty says about "symbols . . . in both succession and multiplicity" with Peirce's notion of *interpretants*. Like Merleau-Ponty, Peirce stressed the linguistic constitution of the self, the self being for him *a process of semiosis*: "At any instant then man is a thought, and as a thought is a species of symbol, the general answer to the question what is man? is that he is a symbol" (*Collected Papers*; vols. 1–6, ed. C. Hartshorne and P. Weiss, vols. 7–8, ed. A. W. Burks [Cambridge: Harvard University Press, 1931–58]; 7.583); "my language is the sum total of my self" (CP; 5.314).

    It would also be interesting to *contrast* Peirce with Derrida. Derrida states that according to Peirce we think only in signs. That is correct ("all thought whatsoever is a sign, and is mostly of the nature of language" [CP; 5.421]). However, Peirce most definitely does not maintain, as Derrida nevertheless says he does, that "there are nothing but signs" (see *Of Grammatology*, p. 50). In his semiological (mis)reading of Peirce, Derrida chooses to ignore what Peirce has to say about the relatedness of signs to the domain of *action* and *praxis* (see in this regard *The Hermeneutics of Postmodernity*, p. 113).

29. Cf., for instance, *Signs*, trans. Richard C. McCleary (Evanston: Northwestern University Press, 1964), p. 153: "Subjectivity is neither thing nor substance but the extremity of both particular and universal."

30. Cf. *Signes* (Paris: Gallimard, 1960): "La connaissance de soi chez Montaigne est dialogue avec soi. C'est une interrogation adressée à cet être opaque qu'il est et de qui il attend réponse, c'est comme un 'essai' ou une 'expérience' de lui-même" (p. 252).

31. C. Castoriadis, "The Sayable and the Unsayable" in *Crossroads in the Labyrinth*, trans. K. Soper and M. H. Ryle (Cambridge, New York: MIT Press, 1984), p. 143.

32. William James, "Pragmatism and Humanism" in *Pragmatism: A New Name for Some Old Ways of Thinking* (*William James: Writings 1902–1910* [New York: Library of America, 1987]), p. 594. The affinities between James and Merleau-Ponty are numerous and profound, and

this is no accident, since the central project of both of these thinkers
was that of overcoming metaphysics (rationalism).

33. Merleau-Ponty's phrase is "L'être ne tient qu'en mouvement." Being
and truth are, of course, one and the same.

34. I am, of course, invoking James here: "The truth of an idea is not a
stagnant property inherent in it. Truth *happens* to an idea. It *becomes*
true, is *made* true by events. Its verity *is* in fact an event, a process:
the process namely of its verifying itself, its veri-*fication*. Its validity
is the process of its valid-*ation*" ("Pragmatism's Conception of Truth,"
William James: Writings 1902–1910, p. 574).

35. Ibid., p. 581.

36. Ibid., p. 584.

37. Gadamer, *Reason in the Age of Science*, trans. F.G. Lawrence (Cambridge: MIT Press, 1981), p. 140.

38. Merleau-Ponty, *In Praise of Philosophy*, trans. John Wild and James
M. Edie (Evanston: Northwestern University Press, 1963), p. 29; translation modified ("L'expression s'antidate elle-même et postule que l'être
allait vers elle").

39. As Gadamer has said: "Contrary to what we often imagine, time is not
a chasm which we could bridge over in order to recover the past: in
reality, it is the ground which supports the arrival of the past and
where the present takes its roots. 'Temporal distance' is not a distance in the sense of a distance to be overcome.... Actually, it is
rather a matter of considering 'temporal distance' as a fundament of
positive and productive possibilities for understanding" ("The Problem of Historical Consciousness" in P. Rabinow and W.M. Sullivan,
eds., *Interpretive Social Science: A Reader* [Berkeley: University of
California Press, 1979], pp. 155–56).

40. *The Visible and the Invisible*, p. 197.

41. *In Praise of Philosophy*, p. 29.

42. James, "Pragmatism and Humanism," p. 592.

43. Bergson describes the error in this way: "Toute la difficulté du problème
qui nous occupe vient de ce qu'on se représente la perception comme
une vue photographique des choses, qui se prendrait d'un point
déterminé avec un appareil spécial, tel que l'organe de perception, et
qui se se développerait ensuite dans la substance cérébrale par je ne
sais quel processus d'élaboration chimique et psychique (*Matière et
mémoire: Essai sur la relation du corps à l'esprit* [Paris: Presses
Universitaires de France, 1959], pp. 35–36. He later states: "*Les questions relatives au sujet et à l'objet, à leur distinction et à leur union
[écart?], doivent se poser en fonction du temps plutôt que de l'espace*
(p. 74; emphasis in original). In a later work (*L'Evolution créatrice*
[Paris: PUF, 1966]) he stated: "Notre manière habituelle de parler, laquelle
se règle sur notre manière habituelle de penser, nous conduit à de
véritables impasses logiques" (p. 312).

What makes Bergson's views on (veridical) perception particularly
relevant to those of Merleau-Ponty is that, like Merleau-Ponty after
him, Bergson was breaking with a long-standing philosophical tradition in attempting to conceptualize perception in terms not of *images*
but of *action*.

44. As in the case of Gadamer, the basic thesis of Merleau-Ponty's philosophy of language (which takes not *la langue* but *la parole* as paradigmatic) is that *words are not signs*. This is why his approach to language is neither metaphysical (referentialist) nor semiological (reductionist). For a more thorough discussion of this issue see my "Being and Speaking."

7

Philosophical Extravagance in Merleau-Ponty and Derrida

Joseph Margolis

Reflecting on Merleau-Ponty and Derrida, I find myself drawn to two remarkable observations that may seem eccentric, possibly of no relevance at all. I draw them in to confirm a deep convergence between Anglo-American and continental European philosophy that is regularly neglected and that helps to place Merleau-Ponty and Derrida in the right light and tempers their characteristic philosophical extravagance. Both observations are well known; neither is quite canonical, even within the analytic literature. The first is Wittgenstein's, though Wittgenstein was hardly a standard specimen of an English philosopher. The second is Wilfrid Sellars's.

Here is Wittgenstein's remark:

> If language is to be a means of communication there must be agreement not only in definition but also (queer as this may sound) in judgments. This seems to abolish logic, but does not do so. It is one thing to describe methods of measurement, and another to obtain and state results of measurement. But what we call "measuring" is partly determined by a certain constancy in results of measurement.[1]

I take this to signify that the validity of philosophical theorizing is inseparable from the contingent uniformities of a society's way of life (*Lebensform*) in which it arises: in particular, it signifies that seeming discoveries about what is self-evident or necessarily true or prior in the way of understanding are a function and artifact of the consensual reliability of what the active members of a society count as the ordinary constancies of their experience. Alternatively put: Wittgenstein is drawing attention to the inseparability of would-be logical and factual truths, to what (therefore) can only be the conditional priority of conceptual necessities, to the impossibility of defending any form of cognitive privilege from within the routine effectiveness of societal practices, to the sense in which discerning all *that* is the contingent result of a reflexive conjecture, hardly a necessary truth itself.

Here is Sellars's remark—well, several remarks pieced together:

> The direct perception of physical objects is mediated by the occurrence of sense impressions which latter are, in themselves, thoroughly non-cognitive. Furthermore, this mediation is causal rather than epistemic. Sense impressions do not mediate by virtue of being known.[2]

> Strictly speaking, sensa do not *seem*. They belong to a highly sophisticated account of the world, and simply do not belong to the framework of perceptual consciousness.[3]

> I have ... been claiming that [for instance] *being red* is logically prior, is a logically simpler notion, than *looking red*; the function "x is red" to "x looks red to y." In short, that it won't do to say that *x is red* is analyzable in terms of *x looks red to y*.[4]

I take these remarks to signify that the supposed immediacy, the subjectivity or interiority, and the pretheoretic standing of sensory experience ("impressions") is entirely compatible with such experience's being a theoretical posit of some explanatory sort, lacking any cognitive priority at all. Alternatively put: Sellars is dismantling what he calls the "Myth of the Given," which he finds (metonymically) in Descartes and Locke, and is affirming (again, as a reasonable conjecture or bet) that there are no privileged cognitive sources that escape the formative contingencies of our theories and the conceptual resources embedded in our language.

In somewhat different ways, both Wittgenstein and Sellars draw attention to the deep contingency of philosophical claims to penetrate to the original sources of cognitive certainty. They confirm by their insistence the protean vitality of the "Cartesian" intuition and the need to combat it even now. That may serve to fix the family connection between Wittgenstein and Sellars, on the one hand, and Merleau-Ponty and Derrida, on the other. Cartesianism is their common target, though that alone is hardly worth mentioning.

Merleau-Ponty and Derrida might have been sympathetic with Wittgenstein's and Sellars's claims. More quarrelsomely: even Husserl might have supported both up to a point—insofar, that is, as they might have been judged to be critical of the "naturalistic" stance.[5] But Husserl, of course, believed *he* could recover a source of cognitive assurance deeper than whatever might limit the "naturalistic," a subjective source that would escape the constraints just drawn from Wittgenstein and Sellars.

They would not have thought that possible. That is implicitly why Wittgenstein joins conceptual and factual truths within the same *Lebensform*—which is holistic and incompletely fathomable in any case. Sellars offers a related lesson, namely, that the presumption of a cognitively favored pre-linguistic sensory or experiential immediacy is utterly fatuous: not because "empirical knowledge has *no* foundation," not because "I [Sellars] should deny that observings are *inner* episodes, [or] that *strictly speaking* they are *nonverbal* episodes"; but rather because no such concessions could possibly bring "aid or comfort to epistemological givenness."[6]

For his part, Husserl only appears to make a comparable concession, acknowledging that the work of phenomenology obtains within the horizonal constraints of our *Lebenswelt*.[7] Especially after his attempt to accommodate Frege's criticism of the early "psychologism," Husserl tried to disjoin the cognitive sources of the "naturalistic" and the "phenomenological"; then to admit the separable sources of both within the same *lebensweltlich* experience; and then to admit that the effectiveness of the search for conceptual invariances must work through and only through the horizonal limitations of our *Lebenswelt*. Husserl never believed, however, that such concessions ever disqualified the pretensions of "pure" reason to penetrate to the universal invariances of conceptual imagination. Here, Derrida's rather less than convinced reading of Husserl and Merleau-Ponty's troubled loyalty converge and, thus converging, converge as well with the spirit of Wittgenstein's and Sellars's remarks. Derrida's theme, *différance*, and Merleau-Ponty's, *écart*, are, finally, no more than two quintessentially—late twentieth-century—French versions of the never-ending effort to dismantle the Cartesian confidence that lies at the base of modern Western philosophy. Nevertheless, I say they are great extravagances. The modesty of the Wittgensteinian and Sellarsian options begins to show a more promising way of avoiding the Cartesian presumption—which is hardly to favor their views over Derrida's or Merleau-Ponty's. (I shall venture nothing about their respective profundity.)

The single theme that unites Wittgenstein and Sellars and Merleau-Ponty and Derrida is this: thinking and perceptual experience cannot be detached, in the epistemic sense, from the tacit contingencies of acquiring conceptual powers through mastering the cognizing practices of a particular historical society—hence, cannot exceed its horizonal limitations. Differences in philosophical style prevent me from pursuing the comparison more closely. It would not be fruitful. In any case, whatever may be thought to be "phenomenological" in Wittgenstein and Sellars (the term is not altogether inapt), the local problems that occupy Merleau-Ponty and Derrida are very different from those that occupied the others. More than that, I am bound to say that Merleau-Ponty's and Derrida's problems are very different from one another's. Nevertheless, those differences do not altogether disallow our discerning a remarkable convergence between what Merleau-Ponty has in mind (speaking of *écart*) and what Derrida has in mind (speaking of *différance*). I concede that it is too easy to pretend that the two notions play the same role in their respective philosophies: they do not; but it is also too easy to miss what is common ground, which, by an economy (but surely more than that), is focused in a perceptive critique of Husserl. Certainly, neither Merleau-Ponty nor Derrida is merely a destructive critic. But understanding their challenge of Husserl fixes (I should say) a theme essential for our own end-of-century. There are other ways of approaching this discovery: that was in fact what led me to begin with Wittgenstein and Sellars.

I

I should like to proceed carefully and in an uncomplicated way. We are addressing two notoriously "stylish" writers. Let me offer a few preliminaries.

Derrida's "deconstruction" is not a philosophy. *Différance*, as Derrida says, "is literally neither a word nor a concept."[8] I take him at his word. Deconstruction is a parasitic strategy—not unlike skepticism but *not* a form of skepticism—which adopts a "host" idiom (and *its* doctrinal claims) in order to subvert them in the deconstructive way; doing that, it returns us to the problematic of *différance* (or to one or another of its analogues: "radical alterity," the *arche-trace*, *supplémentation*, the "infinite deferral" of the "transcendental signified," *arche-écriture*, the presumption of *présence*, and the rest of Derrida's florid tactical menagerie.

If deconstruction had been a form of skepticism, it would have been a philosophical theory about the limits of our cognitive powers; as a consequence, it would have had to address directly the familiar paradox that directly confronts skepticism. (It would have victimized itself.) It escapes the paradox in a canny way because it is not (it refuses to be) a form of skepticism; and it escapes what would otherwise have been the counterpart paradox of deconstruction (viewed as philosophy) because it is not (it refuses to be) a philosophy at all. I must disagree, therefore, with what may be the best attempt to construe deconstruction as a philosophy—Rodolphe Gasché's *The Tain of the Mirror*. It is not true, I think, that Derrida, functioning as a deconstructionist, "is primarily engaged in a debate with the main philosophical question regarding the ultimate foundation of what is."[9] For that to be true, *différance* would have had to be "a word [or] a concept." For similar reasons, I must disagree with Christopher Norris's spirited defense of "deconstructive criticism" as disputing "the kind of privileged status [philosophy] has always claimed as the sovereign dispenser of reason"; or "contest[ing] the idea that philosophy could work its way back to a logic of meaning and experience derived from the immediate data of consciousness itself."[10]

I hope I am not misunderstood: I *do* hold that Derrida has a philosophical thesis, I *do* believe deconstruction serves that philosophy in the parasitic way I've suggested. It's only that deconstruction *cannot* be a philosophy, or a philosophical "activity," leading (however informally) to a "method" (Kristeva's, not Derrida's, term) or a doctrine.[11] That is, *when* Derrida is pursuing philosophical work he is *not* functioning deconstructively, and when he is doing deconstruction he is not pursuing philosophical arguments. Deconstruction *is* an ingenious adjunctive strategy that serves Derrida's *philosophical* purpose; but deconstruction and philosophy are necessarily disjoint.

If you ask what Derrida's philosophical doctrine is, I think there can be little doubt that it is adumbrated in the following: "Il n'y a pas de hors-texte"—there is no "outside-text"; *not* that there is nothing "outside the text," or that there are only texts, or that there is a supreme text within which everything there is obtains.[12] I don't deny that Derrida is interested in the philosophical projects Gasché and Norris assign him. I don't deny these projects belong to the *philosophical* work of Derrida's analysis of Husserl's essay, "The Origin of Geometry," the early essays of *La Voix et le phenomène*, the mixed text of *Of Grammatology* (which moves between philosophy and deconstruction), and other later texts. I insist only that deconstruction is not philosophy and cannot be. The comparison between *écart* and *différance* depends on it.

The picture is suddenly very complicated, baffled by the surface extravagances of Derrida's double undertaking, yet remarkably simple in the clarification it promises—and, I think, delivers. There can be little question that Derrida's analysis of Husserl's "Origin of

Geometry" is his earliest and most sustained philosophical labor. The "Origin" is also one of Husserl's last efforts to come to grips with the puzzle of construing science as a historical tradition that intrinsically preserves (in its evolving work) the a priori structures of the conceptual imagination of the whole of mankind. The question haunts Husserl's earlier work, marks his explicit preoccupation with the historicity of the *Lebenswelt* and the meaning of the deep contingency—the "relativism"—of the cultural life of different societies (especially so-called primitive societies, not yet caught up with the supposedly universal themes of European science).[13] That question is also, as it happens, the site of some of Merleau-Ponty's most ardent efforts to reconcile Husserl's phenomenology with his own refusal to claim a privilege where none can be vouchsafed. It is here that the comparison between *écart* and *différance* is most instructive.

What I claim is that, in the discussion of the "Origin" essay, also in *La Voix et le phenomène*, Derrida brings his philosophical strategy up to its characteristic form—even up to an exceptional clarity; doing that, he provides a backdrop against which the parasitic game of deconstruction functions as the freewheeling play it is. The early essay confirms the fact that Derrida does indeed have a philosophical "doctrine" and a "method." But Derrida tires of the labor of isolating the unsecured premises of Husserl's phenomenology. He finds an essential clue already in Merleau-Ponty, who cannot bring himself to expose Husserl's papering-over of the essential worry Husserl had isolated. Husserl must have grasped, in some twilight sense, the fatal weakness of his venture: how to draw the universal conceptual structures of European science out of the sheer contingencies of the *different* modes of life of all the societies of the world. In this sense, Merleau-Ponty and Derrida are merely the late articulators of what is no longer subterranean in Husserl. But Husserl never exposes his own irresolution and never solves its deeper puzzle: he falls back forever to the unexplained presumption of Cartesian privilege. *He treats the uncognizable cognitively.* Merleau-Ponty repudiates such maneuvers in his own work, but he cannot accuse Husserl of having failed to do so in his. That is the theme of the *écart*, or a large part of it. Derrida is hardly filial in the same sense. But he tires of philosophical wrangle—rather too quickly, I should say—and favors instead the exhilirating *jeu* of deconstruction. That is the theme of *différance*.

In the first instance, therefore, the strategies of deconstruction are meant to remind us of the unanswered—the unanswerable—

question that lies behind Husserl's project (as well as those of others that, like Saussure's, Derrida believes are infected in the very way Gasché and Norris isolate but wrongly assign as deconstruction's *philosophical* targets).

In short, Derrida's and Merleau-Ponty's distinctive strategies are ultimately intended to subvert Cartesianism and to facilitate the birth of a "philosophical" idiom that might resist falling back to its tentacular influence. Derrida is pretty clear about his purpose almost from the start: *différance* is introduced in a deliberately provocative way. But Merleau-Ponty came to realize only dawningly that to escape the infelicities of Husserl's evolving vision—which remained tethered to its Cartesian convictions the more it changed— it would be necessary to escape Husserl's entire idiom of method, categories, subjectivity, and lifeworld and replace it with an idiom that would expose any backsliding into Husserlian phenomenology (at the "originary" point). That is what Merleau-Ponty's *écart* envisions. But it takes form too late, too problematically—for instance, in the Working Notes for *The Visible and the Invisible*—to provide a sufficient clue about its final form. What we have is the evidence for a strategy of escape, not the full outline of the new philosophy.

II

You must turn back to Derrida's analysis of the "Origin" essay to get your bearings. But let me remind you, first, of certain commonplaces that collect the mystery at stake. For one thing, when I use a general predicate ("blue," say, or "tragic"), validly extending its use beyond the paradigms through which it was first introduced ("agreement . . . in judgments," to remember Wittgenstein's phrasing), do I, *must* I, know or understand, or "preunderstand" (that is, be capable of isolating by some explicit intellectual exercise—Husserl's "eidetic variations," say), certain ulterior conceptual invariances in virtue of which a seemingly changeable predicate is rendered universally intelligible? This is, of course, the classic puzzle about universals. But what is interesting about it is this: there is no way to show that such universals *ever* obtain, and there is no way to show that understanding a general predicate *must* implicate such a universal even if we cannot identify it explicitly. Furthermore, if that is so, then there is no sense in which we can be sure we are *ever* approaching the invariant limits of the conceptual imagination of mankind by eidetic exercises. For, of course, *if* those exercises are a function *of* the contingent predicates, paradigms, historical experience that the argument presupposes, then our sense of universality and invariance is an artifact of the same experience. In that case, the bare intelligibility of discourse *cannot* be made to depend on universal and invariant concepts.

There are two possible "species" of "historical a priori" here: one is Foucault's, which is, in effect, only the historical "impression" of conceptual necessity under one or another limited or horizonal *episteme*[14]; the other is Husserl's, which claims that the very intelligibility of the divergence or "relativism" of contingent modes of life—of history and historicity—presupposes the ultimate invariances of our conceptual powers invoked (in some phenomenologically effective way) within our quotidian understanding. But as soon as we grasp the subtlety of the example of any random general predicate, we see that the mystery extends to self-understanding over time, to the dawning understanding of children learning their first language, to understanding one another within the same *Lebenswelt*, and to the understanding that holds between the denizens of very different human "worlds."

The stakes are clear. *If* the contingencies of any society's language, thought, and practice are in some sense known (or foreknown) to be congruent with the invariant universal possibilities open to mankind, then: (a) the subjective competence that considers the ideal possibilities and limits of conceptual imagination cannot be constrained by the anthropological facts; and *if* that competence *is* constrained by such facts, then (b) it must be impossible to go beyond anything more than a horizonal sense of conceptual limits. Certainly, in Husserl's early work, in the *Cartesian Meditations* for instance, the autonomy of the inquiring Ego in favor of the option (a) is clearly intended:

> Our meditations . . . have in the main fulfilled their purpose, namely, to show the concrete possibility of the Cartesian idea of a philosophy as an all-embracing science grounded on an absolute foundation. To exhibit this concrete possibility . . . means exhibiting a necessary and indubitable beginning and an equally necessary and always employable method—whereby, at the same time, a systemic order of *all senseful problems is predelineated.*
>
> But there is only one *radical* self-investigation, and it is phenomenological. . . . universal and eidetic self-explication signifies mastery of *all the conceivable constitutive possibilities "innate" in the ego* and in a transcendental intersubjectivity.[15]

Derrida traces the theme in Husserl's "Origin of Geometry" and "Philosophy as Rigorous Science."[16] But he mentions Merleau-Ponty's citation of Husserl's letter to the anthropologist Lévy-Bruhl (March 11, 1935), written a year earlier than the "Origin," regarding which Merleau-Ponty remarks:

> Husserl was struck by the contact which Levy-Bruhl had established, through his book, with the actual experience of primitive man. Having made this contact with the author's aid, he now says that it is perhaps not possible for us, who live in certain historical traditions, to conceive of the historical possibility of these primitive men by a mere variation of our imagination. For these primitives are non-historical [geschichtlos]. There are certain "stagnant" societies, as they are sometimes called, in which our conception of history is simply absent.[17]

Merleau-Ponty ponders the possibility that the Freudian view of sexual phenomena may be limited in a similar way; and other have raised the possibility that Husserl's notion of "time-consciousness" may be similarly horizonal and "relativist" in nature.[18] Merleau-Ponty pursues the issue raised by the Lévy-Bruhl letter—in the following way:

> Suppose the philosopher no longer lays claim to the unconditioned powers to think his own thought through and through. He agrees that his "ideas" and his "certainties" are always to some extent naive, and that caught up as they are in the fabric of the culture he belongs to, they cannot be truly known by just being scrutinized and varied in thought, but must be confronted with other cultural formations and viewed against the background of other preconceptions.... Since we are all hemmed in by history, it is up to us to understand that whatever truth we may have is to be gotten not in spite of but through our historical inheritance.[19]

This certainly shows that Merleau-Ponty repudiated the notion of the "autonomy" of phenomenology, the notion of its independence from "naturalistic" sources. He must have supposed that phenomenology and naturalism were ultimately similar—in terms of the failure of cognitive privilege. Which is the way (I take it) Merleau-Ponty reads Husserl's well-known remark from *The Crisis*: "Transcendental subjectivity is intersubjectivity."[20] (There is surely an equivocation on "intersubjectivity" here. Husserl seems to believe that the solipsistic practice of phenomenological analysis can still be "intersubjective"; Merleau-Ponty surely abandons all that.)

Derrida challenges both Husserl and Merleau-Ponty at this point. For Husserl, struck by the implication of Lévy-Bruhl's work, admits, on Merleau-Ponty's interpretation: "Historical relativism is now no longer dominated at one stroke by a mode of thought which would have all the keys of history and would be in a position to classify all possible histories before any factual inquiry."[21] Merleau-Ponty understands this to mean, and apparently favors the sense, that "In order to grasp the essential structure of a human community, one must himself take into account, and relive, the whole milieu [*Umwelt*] of this society. Historical knowledge is a coexistence with the meanings of a people and not merely the solitary reflection of a historian. The eidetic of history cannot dispense with factual investigations."[22] About this, Derrida says: "Is such an interpretation justified?"[23] (Derrida treats it as another Cartesian formula.)

Now, it is here, I think, that the difference between Derrida's *différance* and Merleau-Ponty's *écart* makes itself felt. Both reject what Husserl *seems* (but only seems) willing to repudiate, the cognitive autonomy of phenomenology from its historical and factual "foundations." Derrida thinks the phenomenological project is thereby defeated (together with Saussurean and other analogues); Merleau-Ponty transforms phenomenology itself. Husserl, I am bound to say, becomes increasingly arbitrary, since, while grasping the import of his understanding of Levy-Bruhl's work, he never actually relents—he never stops to explain just how phenomenological universality (apodictic, exceptionless, necessary) *can* be discerned within the horizonal limits of any *Lebenswelt*.

III

It may well be that we cannot finally *state* the difference between Derrida's *différance* and Merleau-Ponty's *écart*: simply because both Derrida and Merleau-Ponty are pursuing what is unsayable in the inclusive milieu of what can be said. Yet there *is* a difference in their respective "pursuits"; and *that* can be stated. One way of casting the difference is this. Derrida proceeds deconstructively to expose the fatuousness of every attempt (notably, Husserl's—also, Saussure's, on a rather strained reading of the latter that is meant to ensure the lesson drawn from Husserl) to fix the originary *différance*; whereas Merleau-Ponty invents an *ur*-phenomenology by which to limn the "genesis" of the phenomenological competence of the originating subjectivity that "first" constitutes the intelligibility of the experienced world. Derrida proceeds by mimicking discourse at a (would-be) postulated point, at which it cannot possibly function in the way it mimes: that is what deconstruction both "does" and exposes. Merleau-Ponty reconstructs, by way of a mythical (*not* a fictional) conjecture, our sense of the condition of infancy from which (and continuously through which) we must have emerged as the perceiving and thinking beings we are. Derrida pretends to be a phenomenologist and a structuralist in order to expose the impossible task of each; whereas Merleau-Ponty carries out certain thought-experiments—for instance, by reading the Freudian psychogenesis of the ego in terms of Heidegger's analysis of the "ontological" structure of *Dasein*—by which to convey the insuperable contingency, the artifactual, constructivist, protean, but (also) familiar and regularized mode of functioning of the creatures we discern to be sentiently apt subjects and (even) selves— namely, ourselves, who are always and already the exemplary site of the question posed about the aptitudes of infants.

Derrida's philosophical motivation is to expose all forms of logocentric privilege; Merleau-Ponty's is to ponder how our perceptual and thinking competence is possible—beyond the conceptual fixities offered by Kant and Husserl. Both undertakings are discursively impossible (that is, in the way of discovering the truth, of glimpsing the conditions of intelligibility *beyond* cognition itself): Derrida realizes that to discard deconstruction in favor of first philosophy would be to claim to know what he takes to be "radically" unknowable; Merleau-Ponty explores instead a kind of imaginative cosmology (not a cosmogony) of the intelligible world— an interior analogue, so to say, of something provisionally like the "Big Bang" theory. Derrida exposes the "alterity" at the base of every Cartesian conception of cognizing subject and cognized object; Merleau-Ponty conjectures about the original "singularity" from which the complexities of the subject/object relation (deformed by the Cartesian presumption) must (or might conceivably) have evolved. I think this must be the meaning, for instance—from Merleau-Ponty's own side—of the following Working Note, written fairly close to the end of Merleau-Ponty's life:

> The essential is to describe the vertical or wild Being as that pre-spiritual milieu without which nothing is thinkable, not even the spirit, and by which we pass into one another, and ourselves into ourselves in order to have *our own* time. It is philosophy alone that gives it——
>
> Philosophy is the study of the *Vorhabe* of Being, a *Vorhabe* that is not *cognition*, to be sure, that is wanting with regard to cognition, to operation, but that envelops them as Being envelops the beings.[24]

It is simply philosophically hopeless to suppose there is a valid reading of any such remark. (The Working Notes appended to *The*

Visible and the Invisible are almost entirely of this kind: what I called "mythic" a moment ago.) I don't deny that we can fathom Merleau-Ponty's meaning; but I deny that there is any sense in which the utterance itself is a discursible "thesis"—any more than is Heidegger's "ontology" of *Sein* and *Dasein*. Both are (mythic) "singularities" in a sense (remotely) akin to that in which contemporary physical cosmologies speculate about the origin of our universe. (Merleau-Ponty's conjecture is plainly informed by Heidegger's.) About *cosmologies* proper, we must remember, the (singularity of the) Big Bang is entirely exhausted discursively by its being fitted to *all* the evidence we claim to have about our perceived world: *it draws on no independent evidence whatsoever*. Merleau-Ponty's singularity (Heidegger's as well) differs from the cosmological precisely in pursuing the "origin" of *our cognitive aptitude. To complete* Merleau-Ponty's work, therefore, would be to fall back (with a vengeance) to the Cartesian thinking that was so impressively perfected by Kant and Husserl. Of course Merleau-Ponty ultimately opposes any such venture as untenable. He falls back to "mythic" conjectures, namely, to what, as the cognitively apt creatures we are, we "suppose" lies at the point at which cognizing competence "first" emerges—in the natural course of the world—*from noncognizing processes already apt for the other!* What is at stake is a dilemma: *if* he supposed (if Heidegger had supposed) that the myth of the "flesh" (or the myth of *Sein/Dasein* was discursive— was no myth at all—then Merleau-Ponty would have been a philosophical fool; but if he grasped that this trap was indeed what was at stake, then he surely grasped the sense in which his own final speculations were utterly unlike the "Cartesian" efforts of Kant and Husserl that he exposes, and perhaps exposes in Heidegger as well.

This may explain something of the puzzlement produced by the recent dispute between Claude Lefort and Martin Dillon and what Merleau-Ponty must have meant by *écart*. Textually, there is evidence supporting each view, at least in different places; philosophically, there cannot be a defense of either, for each would then attribute a fully "Cartesian" reading to Merleau-Ponty's final reflections. Such a reading (either Lefort's or Dillon's) would be drawn out of the *ur*-structure of the subject/object relationship—which Merleau-Ponty now rejects.

I have no intention of taking sides in this dispute.[25] But I find its deep ambiguity already at work in Merleau-Ponty's instructive paper, "The Child's Relation with Others," which belongs to a course offered at the Sorbonne (1960): I find it as reliable a source of

Merleau-Ponty's latest thinking as *The Visible and Invisible* (and the Working Notes appended to the French edition and the translation). As editor of *The Visible and the Invisible*, Claude Lefort perceptively remarks:

> The intention [of *The Visible and the Invisible*] is to direct the reader toward a domain which his habits of thought do not make immediately accessible to him. It is a question, in particular, of persuading him that the fundamental concepts of modern philosophy—for example, the distinctions between subject and object, essence and fact, being and nothingness, the notion of consciousness, image, thing, which are in constant use—already implicate a singular interpretation of the world and cannot lay claim to special dignity when our intention is precisely to go back to face our experience, in order to seek in it the birth of meaning.[26]

Lefort's comment is meant to accord at least with Merleau-Ponty's own, in "The Child's Relations with Others":

> What classical academic psychology calls "functions of cognition"—intelligence, perception, imagination, etc.—when more closely examined, lead us back to an activity that is prior to cognition properly so called, a function of organizing experience that imposes on certain totalities the configuration and the kind of equilibrium that are possible under the corporeal and social conditions of the child himself.... [Similarly] the employment of language, which is an effect and also one of the most active stimuli of intellectual development, does not appear to be founded on the exercise of pure intelligence but instead on a more obscure operation—namely, the child's assimilation of the linguistic system of his environment in a way that is comparable to the acquisition of any habit whatsoever: the learning of a structure of conduct.[27]

Here, I may say, I find an affinity with the views of Wittgenstein and Sellars already cited, although Merleau-Ponty's conjectures are far deeper than theirs. Still, two difficulties arise. For one, Merleau-Ponty's remark is occupied with a perfectly standard question shared by naturalism and phenomenology, namely, that of the conjectured route by which the human infant first internalizes the discursive intelligence of the adult world. For another, Lefort's advice is noticeably inexplicit as to whether *he* means no more than what Merleau-Ponty is palpably talking about in the passage just cited, *or* whether he (also) means to signal that Merleau-Ponty has, in *The Visible and the Invisible*, hit on a deeper conjecture that (as I say) *cannot* be straightforwardly compared or reconciled with the conjecture just admitted. Here I suggest that when he reports Merleau-Ponty as exploring "the truth of our situation," "the mystery of our relation with being," the philosopher's "myth of the 'root'," Lefort is going beyond the conjecture of "The Child's Relations with Others" *and* beyond the point of his differences with Dillon.[28] (Merleau-Ponty's own phrasing—"an activity that is prior to cognition properly so called"—is already equivocal: it may signify what is involved in learning a first language, or it may signify a mode of functioning underlying the cognitive that is not "cognitive" itself but enables the cognitive to emerge.) It is certainly here that *différance* and *écart* invite comparison.

Merleau-Ponty finally escapes the clutches of Husserlian phenomenology of course. In a very late Working Note (April 1960), Merleau-Ponty could not be more explicit:

> The whole Husserlian analysis is blocked [he says] by the framework of *acts* which imposes upon it the philosophy of *consciousness.* It is necessary to take up again and develop the *fungierende* or *latent* intentionality which is the intentionality within being. This is not compatible with "phenomenology," that is, with an ontology that obliges whatever is not nothing to *present* itself to the *consciousness* across *Abschattungen* and as deriving from an originating donation which is an *act,* i.e. one *Erlebnis* among others. . . . It is necessary to take as primary, not the consciousness and its *Ablaufsphänomen* with its distinct intentional threads, but the vortex which this *Ablaufsphänomen* schematizes, the spatializing-temporalizing vortex (which is flesh and not consciousness facing a noema).[29]

There can be no doubt that Merleau-Ponty separates intentionality from consciousness, therefore abandons the Husserlian model, therefore assigns a "prior" intentionality to "flesh" (*la chair*)—which, of course, is the "site" of *écart* (by way of a "Cartesian" recovery). But the passage does not tell us explicitly (in the spirit of Lefort's and Dillon's disagreement) the nature of the conjecture in which that supposition is advanced—though it mentions the "vortex."

I take "vortex" to be an image like "flesh," like "chiasm," like "reversibility," like *écart*, when applied to this new puzzle. Remember: there is a prior "intentionality" assigned to "it"; but the "it" that is "prior" (to the intentional acts of "consciousness") is not discernible in the world in which the "other" form of intentionality is. Here, Merleau-Ponty is at his most cryptic. In addressing reversibility, he offers the image of "the finger of the glove

126 PROBLEMATICS

that is turned inside out": "There is no need," he says, "of a spectator who would be *on each side*"; the "fecund negative . . . is instituted by the flesh, by its dehiscence——the negative, nothingness, is the doubled-up, the two leaves of my body, the inside and the outside articulated over one another——Nothingness is rather the difference between the identical——."[30]

Here, Merleau-Ponty mentions the difference between his view and Sartre's: Sartre treats nothingness entitatively, he says; he himself regards "Being and the imaginary" as "'elements' (in Bachelard's sense), that is, not objects, but fields, subdued being, non-thetic being, being before being—and moreover involving their auto-inscription[;] their 'subjective correlate' is a part of them."[31] His intention is to baffle every effort to bring *this* speculation *within* the competence of phenomenology. The trick is to reassign (mythically) whatever is phenomenologically discerned—that is, when and as suitably transfigured *for the purpose*. Thus, all the normal rules of identity/nonidentity, affirmation/negation, subject/object are *suspended*: philosophical language becomes a figurative instrument for conveying *what cannot be said*—*in* the context of what can be said and is said (there). "What we are calling flesh," Merleau-Ponty warns, "this interiorly worked-over mass, has no name in any philosophy . . . . We must not think the flesh starting from substances, from body and spirit—for then it would be the union of contradictories—but we must think it, as we said, as an element, as the concrete emblem of a general manner of being."[32]

The *écart* is the decisive figure in terms of which the indissoluble "sameness" and "difference" and "unity" of *all* the oppositional notions that function in naturalistic and phenomenological discourse (regarding perception and cognition) are reclaimed: nonoppositionally, "chiasmically," "reversibly," in the originary "field" of the "flesh." But, in reclaiming these notions, Merleau-Ponty transmutes them figuratively, collects them in a mythic rather than a discursive mode, conjectures *beyond* any form of cognition but for the sake of overcoming the *aporiai* of the (standard) Cartesian and Husserlian accounts of cognition (those accounts that concern the connectedness—indeed, the "reversibility"—of the cognizing and the cognized). This does not mean that the language appropriate to cognizing and cognized (at the naturalistic or phenomenological levels) can simply be reversed or interchanged intelligibly. No. Nothing of the sort. What it shows rather is that *every* use of "cognizing" or "cognized" distinctions implicates, in an indissoluble way, the distinctions of the other matching category, *which the classical accounts utterly fail to accommodate.* Sympathetically read, this is the point of Merleau-Ponty's notoriously acrobatic prose. It is also the analogue (for another purpose) of Derrida's equally acrobatic use of *différance.*

Certainly, therefore, Merleau-Ponty gives up the doctrine of the "tacit *cogito*" developed in the *Phenomenology*: for we now see that it generates the same puzzle as the "spoken" *cogito* of Descartes. This is important, for, of course, the entire Chapter 1, Part III of the *Phenomenology*—Merleau-Ponty's summing up of the first phase of his philosophical career—is devoted to the "tacit *cogito*'s" contribution. In the Working Notes, Merleau-Ponty says very plainly: "What I call the tacit cogito is impossible." What he means is that he failed to account for the connection between thought and language, between perception and the expressions of what is perceived: that is, he failed to account for the fact that the "tacit *cogito*" is itself linguistically constituted. To follow the logic of his argument, was, Merleau-Ponty discovered, to go beyond phenomenology, to discern in Husserl the ineradicable vestiges of Cartesianism. Nevertheless, he says, "there is a world of silence [the pre-linguistic,] the perceived world, at least . . . an order where there are non-language significations—yes, non-language significations, but they are not accordingly *positive.* There is for example no absolute flux of singular *Erlehnisse*; there are fields and a field of fields, with a *style* and a typicality[.]"[33] Plainly, to renege here, to return to discursivity, would be to abandon the thrust of his entire labor. To continue is to escape the Cartesian—utterly.

Merleau-Ponty is entirely explicit:

> The taking possession of the world of silence, such as the description of the human body effects it, is no longer this world of silence, it is the world articulated, evaluated to the *Wesen,* spoken—the description of the perceptual *logos* is a usage of *logos prophorikos.* . . . What will this silence be? [It] will not be the *contrary* of language.[34]

In fact: "*One cannot make a direct ontology,*" Merleau-Ponty insists. "My 'indirect' method (being in the beings) is alone conformed with being—'negative philosophy' like 'negative theology.'"[35] Once again, the comparison with Derrida looms.

IV

Finally, it needs to be said that there is an altogether unnecessary extravagance in both Derrida's deconstructive work and Merleau-

Ponty's "negative philosophy" of "flesh" (*la chair*). I don't fault either for his extravagance, as his critics do. I see nothing incoherent or inappropriate in either program. But I do think both programs are vastly overblown and, if not actually unnecessary, much less important than the philosophical undertakings each displaces. The fact is that both Derrida and Merleau-Ponty had shown first-rate analytic abilities before their preference for *différance* and *écart*. In some curious way, both have evidently been pursuaded that certain philosophical excesses (the Cartesian) were so important to offset, or so dangerously attractive, that they found themselves obliged to give up more moderate philosophical undertakings for the sake of the extreme game each has favored. I think they have misjudged matters—and wasted a good part of their remarkable talents. For one thing, *deconstruction does not preclude philosophy: it serves it by non-philosophical means.* For another, *the "negative philosophy" of "flesh" is not philosophy at all (cannot be philosophy): it is only a mythic projection grounded in certain philosophical concessions.* Both are ways of opposing the Cartesian menace, it's true; and each is rather different from the other.

The extravagance of each lies in the plain fact that Merleau-Ponty and Derrida have little more to do than fall back to inquiries that refuse (Cartesian) privilege—which each has already secured! In the examination of Husserl's "Origin of Geometry," for instance, Derrida certainly shows the arbitrariness of Husserl's philosophical treatment of the contexted grounding of mathematical thinking[36]; and we have just seen how, in the Working Notes to *The Visible and the Invisible*, Merleau-Ponty traces the untenable presumption of the privileged *cogito* from Descartes to Husserl to himself. What Merleau-Ponty grasps here is that he has exhausted the resources of all our would-be cognitive powers: there is no way to recover, *cognitively*, the *noncognitive* ground of the cognitive, the forestructuring preparation *of* cognition itself. The unity of difference that is "flesh," before and through the initiation of its "dehiscence," by means of which our cognitional powers *are* "first" "constituted" as what they are, cannot be an object of discernible inquiry. Thus construed, it would violate conditions "anterior" to its own dehiscence. That is what I mean by the "mythic" conjecture that *The Visible and the Invisible* so bafflingly pursues.

More than that: I say that Derrida *could* not rightly apply his deconstructive techniques to Merleau-Ponty's "negative philosophy"— although *it* tolerates philosophy proper, and although neither it nor the philosophy it draws from shows the least tendency toward the "logocentric" disorders Derrida is so fond of exposing. Contrariwise, Merleau-Ponty plainly misperceives the focus of the Cartesian threat: for, if he had not done so, he would have seen the unnecessary labor of the "philosophy of flesh." For what, after all, is it that Merleau-Ponty accomplishes? The *philosophical* point—or at least its essential clue—is already fully in sight, once the chiasmic image of one hand touching the other is put before us.[37]

In the *Phenomenology*, Merleau-Ponty moves on (as he says) "to approach the analysis of the thing as an inter-sensory entity."[38] What he needed to do—what he does at long last—is to draw *from* the chiasmic exemplar itself the deeper thesis that "active" and "passive" in perception and entities perceived and perceiving are both prone (but only *prone*) to the Cartesian *cogito*. Nevertheless, he should have seen (perhaps he did: it is difficult to be sure) that the grammatical distinction between subject and object—hence, the perceptual distinction, hence the ontological distinction—may be kept from falling in with the purposes of the Cartesian *cogito*. Instead, Merleau-Ponty talks about "a world of science. . . . an order where there are non-language significations" that are not (that cannot be) "positive."

Yes of course. *But that's all there is to it! Any* articulation of "such" significations (it is already too much to speak of "*such*" significations) raises once again the matter of escaping from the *cogito*. If it can be made good (that is, escape), it can be made good through the exemplar of the touching hands; and if it cannot, then it surely cannot be by "negative philosophy"—which, in any case, is parasitic, is no more than the mythic projection of an idiom that figuratively mirrors what is to be denied as the fixed discursive structure of subject and object. That explains the enormous attraction of the positive images of *The Visible and the Invisible*—as distinct from their negative function. But it also baffles its unguarded readers, who find themselves wondering what the discursive rules are by which the "reversible" linkage between perceived and perceiving, visible and invisible, self and other, may be characterized. There are no rules: unless you suppose that one rule holds that you may say whatever you may say discursively, and that another rule holds that the idiom of negative philosophy should not obscure that fact, and that a third holds that we may experiment with predicative talk in order to see how language might be altered if the saliences of our experience were not what they are, or how they might be altered compatibly with the saliences that are in place, and so on.

In short, the extravagance is due to the impression that Merleau-Ponty is trying to get negative philosophy *right*. But there is no way to do that, except in the sense that all its maneuvers are meant to help preserve the minimal structures of cognitive discourse (subject/object, perceived/perceiving, self/other, and the like) that we appear unable to displace but by means of which, in spite of "failing" thus, we manage to escape the ubiquitous *cogito*. Beyond that, the work that is required is philosophically modest. It is also philosophically viable. It might have taken the form of a phenomenology without privilege. Or, it might have taken the form of explicating what (for Derrida) is implicated in the thesis *il n'y a pas de hors-texte*. Or, it might have taken the form of the line of reasoning that leads to Wittgenstein's and Sellars's simplifying conjectures. The point is, there is nothing else to salvage—and there is no need for more. But that says nothing yet about the conceptual power of competing philosophies.

Notes

1. Ludwig Wittgenstein, *Philosophical Investigations*, trans. G. E. M. Anscombe (New York: Macmillan, 1953), I, §242.
2. Wilfrid Sellars, "Phenomenalism," *Science, Perception and Reality* (London: Routledge and Kegan Paul, 1963), pp. 90–91.
3. Sellars, "Phenomenalism," p. 103.
4. Wilfred Sellars, "Empiricism and the Philosophy of Mind," *Science, Perception and Reality*, p. 142.
5. See Edmund Husserl, "Philosophy as Rigorous Science" (1911), in *Phenomenology and the Crisis of Philosophy*, trans. Quentin Lauer (New York: Harper and Row, 1965).
6. Sellars, "Empiricism and the Philosophy of Mind," p. 170.
7. See, for instance, the extraordinary claim in Edmund Husserl, *The Crisis of European Sciences and Transcendental Phenomenology: An Introduction to Phenomenological Philosophy*, trans. David Carr (Evanston: Northwestern University Press, 1970), p. 139 (§36).
8. Jacques Derrida, "Différance," *Margins of Philosophy*, trans. Alan Bass (Chicago: University of Chicago Press, 1982), p. 3.
9. Rodolphe Gasché, *The Tain of the Mirror: Derrida and the Philosophy of Reflection* (Cambridge: Harvard University Press, 1986), p. 7.
10. Christopher Norris, *Deconstruction, Theory and Practice* (London: Methuen, 1982), pp. 18, 42.
11. See Norris, *Deconstruction*, p. 48.
12. See Joseph Margolis, *Interpretation Radical But Not Unruly* (Berkeley: University of California Press, 1994), Chapter 5. I discuss the alternative readings briefly.
13. See Gail Soffer, *Husserl and the Question of Relativism* (Dordrecht: Kluwer, 1991), Chapter 5.

14. Michel Foucault, *The Order of Things*, trans. (New York: Vintage, 1970), Chapter 10.
15. Edmund Husserl, *Cartesian Meditations; An Introduction to Phenomenology*, trans. Dorion Cairns (The Hague: Martinus Nijhoff, 1960), Conclusion, pp. 153, 154; italics added, except for "radical" in the second citation.
16. See Husserl, *The Crisis of European Sciences and Transcendental Phenomenology*, Appendix VI; and "Philosophy as Rigorous Science." See, also, Jacques Derrida, *Edmund Husserl's Origin of Geometry: An Introduction*, ed. David B. Allison, trans. John P. Leavey, Jr. (Stony Brook: Nicholas Hays, 1978), pp. 108–10.
17. Maurice Merleau-Ponty, "Phenomenology and the Sciences of Man," trans. John Wild, in *The Primacy of Perception and Other Essays on Phenomenological Psychology, the Philosophy of Art, History and Politics*, ed. James M. Edie (Evanston: Northwestern University Press, 1964), pp. 90–91.
18. I have benefited from an unpublished paper by Shaun Gallagher, "Disrupting Seriality: Merleau-Ponty, Lyotard, and Post-Husserlian Temporality," presented at the Merleau-Ponty Circle, Muhlenberg College, September 1993.
19. Maurice Merleau-Ponty, "The Philosopher and Sociology," *Signs*, trans. Richard C. McCleary (Evanston: Northwestern University Press, 1964), pp. 108–109.
20. Merleau-Ponty, "The Philosopher and Sociology," pp. 92–97. See, Husserl, *The Crisis of European Sciences*, §§53–54.
21. Merleau-Ponty, "Phenomenology and the Sciences of Man," pp. 91–92.
22. Merleau-Ponty, "Phenomenology and the Sciences of Man," p. 92.
23. Derrida, *Edmund Husserl's Origin of Geometry*, p. 112.
24. Maurice Merleau-Ponty, *The Visible and the Invisible*, ed. Claude Lefort, trans. Alphonso Lingis (Evanston: Northwestern University Press, 1968): Working Notes, p. 204 (September 1959).
25. See Claude Lefort, "Flesh and Otherness," and M. C. Dillon, "*Écart*: Reply to Claude Lefort's 'Flesh and Otherness,'" in Galen A. Johnson and Michael B. Smith (eds.), *Ontology and Alterity in Merleau-Ponty* (Evanston: Northwestern University Press, 1990).
26. Claude Lefort, "Editor's Foreword," *The Visible and the Invisible*, pp. xxii–xxiii.
27. Maurice Merleau-Ponty, "The Child's Relations with Others," trans. William Cobb, in *The Primacy of Perception*, ed. James M. Edie (Evanston: Northwestern University Press, 1964), p. 99.
28. Lefort, "Editor's Foreword," p. xxvi. I should say the conjecture was "Heideggerean" both in Lefort and Merleau-Ponty.
29. Merleau-Ponty, Working Notes, p. 244.
30. Merleau-Ponty, Working Notes, p. 263 (November 16, 1960).
31. Merleau-Ponty, Working Notes, pp. 266–67 (November 1960). See *The Visible and the Invisible*, p. 147.
32. Merleau-Ponty, *The Visible and the Invisible*, p. 147.
33. Merleau-Ponty, Working Notes, p. 171.
34. Ibid., p. 179.
35. Ibid., p. 179.

36. See Joseph Margolis, "Deferring to Derrida's Difference," in Graham White (ed.), *European Philosophy and the American Academy* (La Salle: Open Court, 1994).
37. See Merleau-Ponty, *Phenomenology of Perception*, trans. Colin Smith (London: Routledge and Kegan Paul, 1962), for instance at pp. 315–19.
38. Merleau-Ponty, *Phenomenology of Perception*, p. 317.

PART II
EXPANSIONS

8

On the Pre-Noetic Reality of Time

Shaun Gallagher

In the early years of the twentieth century, two influential philosophers, John Ellis McTaggart and Edmund Husserl, investigated in different ways the relationship between consciousness and time. McTaggart, who was explicitly concerned about the metaphysical status of time, argued that precisely because time is something produced by human consciousness it lacks objective reality.[1] Husserl, intent on avoiding the very question of time's metaphysical status, provided a phenomenological description of time-consciousness. McTaggart would have been unhappy with Husserl's lack of metaphysical commitment. Perhaps he would have encouraged Husserl to agree that, since time is constituted by consciousness and therefore has a transcendental (although McTaggart would have said "merely psychological") status, then time is not real.

More recently, Jacques Derrida, taking a quite different approach, has shown that Husserl's analysis is unavoidably a metaphysical one. Indeed, Derrida claims that all analyses of time are metaphysical since the concept of time itself is metaphysical.[2] Rather than providing a metaphysical theory of time, Derrida's program involves the deconstruction of various theoretical discourses about time. Thus, even more so than Husserl, he attempts to avoid the metaphysical question of the reality of time. Yet, Derrida is the first to admit that in the practice of deconstruction one does not simply escape or avoid metaphysics. More to the point, despite his refusal to commit himself on the issue of the metaphysical status of time, his reading of Husserl's analysis of time-consciousness, and his discussion of the temporality of *différance*, leave open the possibility of at least two different conclusions in this regard.

For purposes of this essay let us set aside the question of whether it is possible to develop a postmetaphysical conception of time. Rather, let us assume that Derrida's proposition, that time is a metaphysical concept, is correct. Within the framework set by that assumption I want to face up to the traditional question that had been renewed by McTaggart concerning the reality or unreality of time. Specifically, I want to raise the question in a post-Husserlian context by examining two possible responses. The first response is one that I will force Derrida to make on the basis of his own critical assessment of Husserl. The second response is suggested by Merleau-Ponty in his critique of Husserl's analysis of time.

1. DIFFÉRANCE AND THE TEXTUALITY OF TIME

For Husserl, time-consciousness is the condition of possibility for all experience, the fundamental level of constitution, the very flux of human subjectivity. Experience is shaped by the temporal structure found in the retentional-impressional-protentional flow of consciousness. In this flow there is continuity rather than discontinuity. Husserl accounts for the continuity and unity of the flow in the double intentionality of the retentional structure of consciousness.

Each momentary phase of an enduring act of consciousness is structured by three functions: primal impression, retention, and protention. In its retentional function consciousness has an intentional awareness of a just-past phase of consciousness that contains its own (now elapsed) primal impression, and its own retention of the "just-just-past" phase. According to Husserl, this retentional continuum has a double intentionality. Longitudinal intentionality (*Längsintentionalität*) refers to the fact that each phase of consciousness intentionally retains the previous phases of consciousness as they elapse into the short-term past. But because consciousness retains the whole of each of the previous phases of consciousness, it also retains the previous primal impressions that have intended (or sensed) the object. So, indirectly, each phase of consciousness retains, in a "transverse" intentional manner (*Querintentionalität*), the previously intuited objects, for example, the notes of a melody.[3]

Husserl, by casting his analysis in terms of intentional functioning, solves a number of problems found in theorists such as Hume, Lotze, and James concerning the simultaneity of sense-data.[4] Transverse intentionality provides the intentional unity of the appearing object and thereby allows consciousness to perceive the object in its continuity. Transverse intentionality, however, is possible only on the basis of longitudinal intentionality, which unifies consciousness itself. The succession of phases of consciousness is tied together, not externally, as if it were a Humean bundle of disconnected and momentary perceptions or sense data, but internally in a unified, intentional structure of consciousness.

The auto-affective unification of longitudinal intentionality thus accounts for the continuity and identity of consciousness. The unity of consciousness in self-presence is not broken up by differences or by disrupting forces that would be alien to the pure, self-constituting, intentional immediacy of self-consciousness, which Husserl refers to as "absolute subjectivity." From the ground up, the phenomenological analysis of absolute subjectivity depends upon the structure of the now-phase of consciousness, with its intentional inclusion of the just-past and just-future in the immediacy of the "living present."

In his deconstructive reading Derrida shows how Husserl's own analysis undermines the immediacy and non-difference of the living present. According to Derrida, the immediacy of self-presence is always already disrupted by the mediation of the retentional function that is built into the very structure of the now-phase of consciousness. "One then sees quickly that the presence of the perceived present can appear as such only inasmuch as it is *continuously compounded* with a nonpresence and nonperception, with primary memory and expectation (retention and protention)."[5] Retention introduces something not present, something disruptive into presence, that is, something absent, the past, a trace of the past, a sign of the past. "This alterity is in fact the condition for presence, presentation, and thus for *Vorstellung* in general . . ." (*Speech and Phenomena*, hereafter SP, 65). This difference, which is a *différance*, a deferral of presence, is not introduced into the present phase of consciousness from the outside but, as Husserl insisted, is essentially built into the structure of presence, and thereby it "destroys any possibility of a simple self-identity" (SP 66).

The living present, which for Husserl guarantees the possibility of the self-identity of consciousness, is at bottom a system of differences. The *différance* of temporality disrupts the identity of presence with a trace. "The living present springs forth out of its nonidentity with itself and from the possibility of a retentional trace. It is always already a trace" (SP 85).

We can add, in the spirit of Derrida's reading, that against all of Husserl's good intentions, his analysis of the self-identity of consciousness demonstrates the impossibility of self-presence for the most basic now-phase of consciousness. The structure of the living present, as Husserl describes it, is entirely ek-static. Each of the three structural functions of the now-phase is intentionally directed away from itself, and none of them is directed toward either of the others. Retention is directed toward a past phase; protention toward a future phase; and primal impression not toward a phase of consciousness at all, but toward the present object. Husserl neither finds nor provides for a self-reflective function built into the now-phase itself. So even if the retentional structure of the now-phase explains how consciousness can be reflectively aware of itself, the self-awareness happens only after the fact, and thus at the cost of a lack of self-presence. The now-phase is an absence to itself, at the very heart of the process. There is nothing to capture the "living present" *in the act*. The living present turns out to be a living absence that can only be made self-*present* when it is just-past, and therefore *self*-present, not to itself but to a new and different phase of consciousness.

Derrida's reading of Husserl is not intended as an argument against Husserl, nor as an alternative phenomenology that sets out to correct his analysis. Rather, Derrida attempts to show that Husserl's phenomenology holds within itself conclusions that Husserl himself failed to draw—conclusions that undermine the claim for the primordial nature of pure self-presence and identity. In this reading, which motivates Derrida to think about time in terms of *différance*, he does not break out of the analysis of time-consciousness but enters more deeply into it. "In the ordinary temporalization and the movement of relationships with the outside, as Husserl actually describes them, nonpresentation or depresentation is as 'originary' as presentation. *That is why a thought of the trace can no more break with a transcendental phenomenology than be reduced to it.*"[6] But does this also mean that to think of time in terms of *différance* is to think of time as a transcendental that belongs to the realm of consciousness? And following along McTaggart's way of questioning, would this mean that time is not real?

Derrida struggles against this kind of interpretation. He maintains that the "movement of *différance* is not something that happens to a transcendental subject; it produces a subject" (SP 82). In Husserlian terms, the subject is not a self-constituting absolute origin; rather, "the concept of *subjectivity* belongs *a priori and in general* to the order of the *constituted*. . . . There is no constituting subjectivity. The very concept of constitution itself must be deconstructed" (SP 84–85 n9). *Différance* transcends the flow of consciousness. It involves an opening to otherness rather than a self-enclosed sphere.

Constituting and dislocating it at the same time, writing [trace, *différance*] is other than the subject, in whatever sense the latter is understood. Writing can never be thought under the category of the subject . . . the substantiality of a presence unperturbed by accidents or . . . the identity of the selfsame [*le propre*] in the presence of self-relationship.[7]

In itself différance is nothing (see SP 83) and requires as "compensation" a supplement "to *make up for* a deficiency . . . to compensate for a primordial nonself-presence" (SP 87).

In Derrida's terms, and in contrast to Husserl's view in which pure immediacy would exclude signs (see SP 58), *différance* has the structure of the sign (SP 88–89). The retentional trace *indicates* and thereby *signifies* something other than living presence. As such it is an interweaving, a "text," an arche-writing, a language in the most basic sense. This textuality of temporality is not produced by the subject; the subject is produced in it.

Subjectivity—like objectivity—is an effect of *différance*, an effect inscribed in a system of *différance*. . . . [T]he subject is not present nor above all present to itself before *différance*, [rather] the subject is constituted only in being divided from itself. . . ."[8]

Could we argue, then, that to the extent that the temporal flux of consciousness is dependent upon, or shaped by, or produced by a sub-personal, infrastructural textualizing, temporality has a trans-subjective reality? To the extent that temporality is written by writing, language, arche-trace; to the extent that the "subject of writing is a system of relations between strata (the [Freudian] Mystic Pad, the psyche, society, the world);"[9] to the extent that *différance*, which gives us time, transcends subjective consciousness, can we say that time is therefore objectively real? But objectivity, like subjectivity, "is an effect of *différance*." So Derrida would deny to temporality the status of objective reality, since objectivity itself is part of that same system of already constituted presence. *Différance* can never be thought under the category of object, objective identity, self-same substance. If this is so, must we give up the reality of time?

Of course, it is difficult to force Derrida to answer this question. Not unlike Husserl, yet following a very different style of inquiry, he would do his best to avoid it. But in a post-Husserlian inquiry into the status of time, unavoidably a metaphysical inquiry as Derrida tells us, we require an answer that would not lead us back to the old metaphysical dualism of subject versus object. And Derrida seems to offer us something that escapes this dualism. *Différance*, and the temporality that it gives, is neither subjective nor objective, but transcends the distinction. If we insist on a more positive formulation, perhaps we can say that temporality, insofar as it is given by *différance*, is textual.

David Wood, in his critical extension of Derrida, offers a description of temporality as textual, in the sense that the temporal structure of language is generalized to time itself, so that "language (understood in its widest sense as significant articulation) is seen as the very source of... temporal structures."[10]

> The claim is, of course, that the correspondence goes beyond mere analogy, and that "lived" experience is already impregnated with those very reflective structures elaborated in textuality in general and narrative in particular. (*Deconstruction of Time*, hereafter DT 358–59)

This is a complex claim. But insofar as Wood contends that language structures time (DT 336) rather than time structures language, and insofar as language transcends the structures of time-consciousness and, for precisely that reason, expands the possibilities of consciousness (DT, 336), then perhaps time has a reality independent of consciousness. Time is written into consciousness by a linguisticality that transcends subjective intentionality. Time is not something we read into the textuality of the world; it is produced by a mechanism in the writing that writes itself.

Time, then, is something more than consciousness; it is to be found in the infrastructural effects that give/produce consciousness and the world. But does this mean that time has the status of reality? There is at least one reading of Derrida's writing that would prevent us from drawing this conclusion.

Richard Rorty, for example, reads Derrida as propounding a form of textualism that he views "as the contemporary counterpart of idealism."[11] On this view, just as an idealist might argue that the mind perceives only its own ideas, and reality itself is nothing more than an idea, a product of thought, so a textualist would argue that reality, like every other metaphysical concept, is simply another text, a trace product of the operations of *différance*. Thus, just as McTaggart would conclude that time is not real because it is entirely a matter of consciousness, so a textualist might conclude that time is not real because it is entirely a matter of textuality. In this way it would be quite possible to view time as lacking translinguistic reality.[12] Wood's own criticism of Derrida is directly relevant to this point. For Derrida, he claims, *différance* is anterior to time; in some way "*différance* is a 'movement' that makes time possible. But it is not itself temporal" (DT 273). Thus, time seems relegated to a metaphysical status dependent on arche-writing, and would have no ontological status outside of textuality. On this reading, Derrida takes up a position in some ways similar to the views of Husserl and McTaggart, albeit with an important difference. Notwithstanding the difference, time would remain unreal, unless in some other way we could give it flesh.

2. TIME À L'ÉCART

Although Merleau-Ponty, in his *Phenomenology of Perception,* begins to develop a critique of the traditional view of time, he still remains, in some respects, caught within Husserl's phenomenological and metaphysical framework. Yet, his expressed position, that "we must understand time as the subject and the subject as time,"[13] differs substantially from both Husserl's transcendentalism and McTaggart's idealism. For even if he suggests that time is not a real process, and that it "arises from *my* relation to things" (PhP 411–12), the subjectivity at stake is an embodied subjectivity rather than a transcendental consciousness or a set of cognitive functions. "In every focusing movement my body unites present, past and future, it secretes time. . . . My body takes possession of time; it brings into existence a past and a future for a present; it is not a thing, but creates time instead of submitting to it" (PhP 239–40).

In his later writings, Merleau-Ponty moves away from the Husserlian emphasis on the constitutive powers of subjectivity. Indeed, his later analysis, posed in terms of his concept of *écart,* is similar to Derrida's account of *différance,* and yet, in an important way, suggests the possibility of a quite different answer to McTaggart's question. In this sense Merleau-Ponty not only develops an answer of his own but also provides a way to read Derrida differently.

In his critique of Husserl's analysis of time-consciousness, Merleau-Ponty questions the phenomenological reflective procedure in a way not unlike Derrida's later questioning. A certain distortion and reification enters into the flux by way of phenomenological reflection. Reflection reads into experience the origins of experience that it discovers only retrospectively, after the fact. In effect, as Husserl himself notes, only *after* the present phase of consciousness is already past does reflection intuit it as present. As Merleau-Ponty remarks, reflection is not installed within the flux; it is posterior to the flux and from that position finds "a massive presence to self, the Retention's *Noch im Griff,* and through it the *Urimpression,* and the absolute flux which animates them."[14] Reflection thus leads us to the wrong starting point. "Husserl's error is to have described the interlocking [of pasts by retention] starting from a *Präsensfeld* considered as without thickness, as immanent consciousness" (*The Visible and the Invisible*, hereafter VI, 173).

Every view of time that takes its starting point in reflective detachment is insufficient for an analysis of time (VI 184). In reflection, "even while I am installing myself at this zero point of Being [or presence], I know very well that it has a mysterious tie with locality and temporality" (VI 113). Reflection requires me to do the impossible: placing myself in the present, I would have to detach myself from the flow, that is, from myself. I would have to "soar over my field," suspend "all the sedimented thoughts with which it is surrounded, first of all my time, my body—which is not only impossible for me to do in fact but would deprive me of that very cohesion in depth [*en épaisseur*] of the world and of Being without which the essence is subjective folly and arrogance" (VI 112).

Merleau-Ponty, thus motivated to ask whether a temporality that is essentially variation, change, or flux can be eidetically reduced to an invariable, unchanging presence, suggests that time eludes this fixation in presence (VI 46). Such reflective fixation leads us away from a certain facticity that cannot be reduced to presence. Reflection requires that I forget or repress the "non-knowing of the beginning which is not nothing, and which is not the reflective truth either, and which also must be accounted for" (VI 49). What is the facticity, the beginning which is not nothing, that gets eclipsed in Husserl's analysis?

The reflecting phenomenologist is already differentiated in a localized and temporalized factical existence. What appears to be the presence of absolute subjectivity is what it is only by an "immense latent content of the past, [and] the future," which it both announces and conceals. Husserl fails to consider "the influence of the 'contents' on time which passes 'more quickly' or 'less quickly,' [the influence] of *Zeitmaterie* on *Zeitform*" (VI 184).

How can the material of time (temporal content) have an influence on the form of time? Merleau-Ponty here appeals to the notion of *écart*. In *The Visible and the Invisible*, this term is first introduced in the context of seeing. When I see something, physiological processes and their products do not interfere with or disrupt the visual field. For example, most of us suffer from a condition called physiological diplopia, but most of us do not notice its effects in normal vision, because it *is* normal vision (see PhP 230ff).

If we focus on something in the distance, an object near our eyes appears double; if we focus on the near object, objects in the distance appear double. The physiological condition does not interfere with clear vision because it is edited out on the level of perception. In a related discussion of binocular vision, Merleau-Ponty indicates that two-dimensional retinal images do not interfere with vision but operate as effaced sketches that are transformed in perception. The physiological images "are only a certain divergence (*écart*) from the imminent true vision . . . drafts for or residues of the true vision, which accomplishes them by reabsorbing them" (VI 7–8). The difference between the physiological process and perception cannot be summarized as a founding relation, as an addition, or even as a synthesis. *Écart* signifies an irreducible difference of order; an incompossibility at the very heart of the visual process that nonetheless must be held together in a relation of *écart*. Merleau-Ponty characterizes *écart* as "originating presentation of the unpresentable" (VI 203). Vision, then, is binocular only by its dependence on monocular elements, yet can be so only by effacing them, diverging from them, leaving them unpresented, unreflected, invisible.

The effacement is accomplished by the body: perception maintains in its cohesive depth its corporeal ties and the "decidedly singular" relations that exist between things and the body (VI 8). The experiential fact, or more precisely, the fact that remains just short of experience, namely, that the body remains normally unpresented, operating outside of intentional presence in a prenoetic fashion, is an essential aspect of bodily relations to things that makes perception possible.[15]

> The moment perception comes my body effaces itself before it and never does the perception grasp the body in the act of perceiving. . . . my body does not perceive, but it is as if it were built around the perception that dawns through it; through its whole internal arrangement, its sensory-motor circuits, the return ways that control and release movements, it is, as it were, prepared for a self-perception, even though it is never itself that is perceived nor itself that perceives. (VI 9)

In a related way temporality, also, involves *écart*. What is the primal impression, the source point of the living present in Husserl's model of time-consciousness? Merleau-Ponty gives his answer in one of his working notes: it is neither coincidence nor fusion; neither conscious act nor *Auffasung*; "it is *écart*" (VI 191). To think temporality as *écart*, Merleau-Ponty, in contrast to Derrida, does not appeal to writing or textuality; he reverts to embodiment. The corporeal schema, "which is the foundation of space *and of time*," makes *écart* comprehensible. "It is a perception-imperception, i.e., an operative and not thematized meaning (this is at bottom what Husserl means when he considers retention to be fundamental: that means that the absolute present which I am is as if it were not)—" (VI 191). Merleau-Ponty's suggestion, in his last writings, that embodiment is the foundation of time is not, as we have seen, for him a new one; nor is it a new idea in the metaphysical tradition.[16] Yet, the precise way in which he constructs this idea is new and important and provides a unique answer to the metaphysical question concerning the status of time.

3. PRE-NOETIC REALITY

Husserl's analysis ignores the "time of the body, taxi-meter time of the corporeal schema" (VI 173). For phenomenology, the time of the body is something that necessarily exceeds the framework of intentionality. Husserl construes the past as an intentional content, constituted in retention or through an act of recollection. This view of the past, which reduces it to the past-in-view, robs the past of its extra-intentional reality and its power to have an anterior effect on conscious experience. Once we think of time in terms of *écart* and embodiment, without which, Merleau-Ponty says, "the past would fall to zero" (VI 124), we must think of the past as having an effect on intentionality similar to the effect that physiology has on perception. Thus, Merleau-Ponty can say of this extra-intentional past that it is no longer

> a "modification" or modalization of the *Bewusstsein von....* Conversely it is the *Bewusstsein von*, the having perceived that is borne by the past as massive Being.... The whole Husserlian analysis is blocked by the framework of *acts* which imposes upon it the philosophy of *consciousness*. (VI 244)

Husserl's focus on the noetic act of consciousness misses the latent, anterior, pre-noetic dimension eclipsed by experience. For Merleau-Ponty "it is necessary to take as primary, not the consciousness and its *Ablaufsphänomen* with its distinct intentional threads, but the vortex which this *Ablaufsphänomen* schematizes, the spatializing-temporalizing vortex (which is flesh and not consciousness facing a noema)" (VI 244).

In the vortex of the body schema, in its "operative but not thematized meaning," in its effaced performance, one can find the facticity, the beginning which is not nothing, the *Zeitmaterie* that has an influence, a real and anterior effect on temporal form. With respect to the past, for example, the body in its habitual schemas retains a past that falls short of explicit, intentional memory; yet this is a past that helps to define the present. This past falls short of an explicit act of remembering in the sense that I am not required to have a conscious act of recollection in order for this past to be operative in the present. Edward Casey provides an example of this keeping of the past in the body:

> Consider only the way the body keeps the past in a veiled and yet entirely efficacious form in its continuing ability to perform certain skilled actions: I may not remember just how, or even when I first learned the breaststroke, but I can keep on doing it successfully—remembering how to do it—without any representational activity on my part whatsoever.[17]

In a case like this, that is, in cases of bodily schematic operations and habitual behaviors such as swimming, walking, maintaining posture, and so forth, experience does not recede on a train of retentions into a remote past. Rather, the present is built upon a past that remains unconsciously, pre-noetically, in play and efficacious.

This pre-noetic effect of the past operates as an *écart*. That is, in a way similar to the case of seeing, there is a necessary relation between intentional and pre-noetic dimensions, the necessary difference of irreducible, incompossible orders that nonetheless intrude upon one another. In the order of intentionality, the "to be conscious" of the primal impression is, Merleau-Ponty says in his working notes, "an incontestable, but derived, characteristic: it is the culmination of *écart* in *differentiation*..." (VI 191). The pre-noetic force of the past encroaches upon the primal impression. This encroachment is neither the frontal imposition of an objective time nor the trailing along of a retentional train; it is an intrusion *a tergo*. Time transcends consciousness, not in the direction of the objective world. It transcends consciousness in the direction of the pre-noetic dimension.

Human posture and gait, as well as the possibilities that are built into them—possibilities that include human reason—are not my own personal accomplishments, although my personal experiences modify the general possibilities. Body schemas are in some respects innate and in some respects the product of an ancient evolution.[18] They operate with a past that is not under noetic control, a past so far beyond the reach of memory that our reconstruction of it is confined to theory. Yet, this is a past that is still operative in a significant way in every step we take, in every action we perform, in every perception we participate in. The ordering of consciousness into an intentional temporalizing structure geared into the surrounding world depends on an embodied and continually effective past, operating in a pre-noetic fashion.

Folk psychology suggests that places are often full of memories. The habitual memory of the body is supplemented by pasts that are kept in the things that surround us, in places and landscapes.[19] The fact that intentionality always takes place in a place, the fact that consciousness is always situated, provides convenient storage for such pasts. These pasts, however, are not there in an objective fashion; they are not necessarily intentional objects of consciousness, retained or remembered in overt presence. Rather, they are there only insofar as they have a real, and often covert, effect on intentional consciousness—a trace effect that, in some instances, "comes over" us, an effect that we have no option but to suffer or cope with. A place can do this. So can a song, a phrase, a practice. So can another person.[20]

The content of present experience elicits effects whose origins are long since past, well beyond the reach of retention, recollection, or phenomenological reflection. Such effects, irreducible to retention or recollection, are in an order different from the intentional. Some of these effects are a matter of forgotten autobiography, others are more a matter of common cultural practices. The pre-noetic force of such temporal dimensions affects intentionality while remaining effaced in the form of the perceiver's body schema, in the environment, in language, in social custom, and so forth.[21]

So this is a temporality that is real, a time not limited to the irreality of consciousness or of textuality. Real, not in the sense of an objective reality, set over against subjective ideality or summarized in the intentional noema; but real in the sense that it is capable of a pre-noetic effect. Capable of such effect, not because time is something *in itself*, anterior to everything there is, like Newton's *tempus quod equabiliter fluit*, but because it is operative, anterior to time-consciousness, in the *écart* relations between the body and environments that are both social and physical.

According to Derrida, in our considerations of time we are all unavoidably metaphysicians. On one reading it would seem that Derrida's textualist proposals, if pressed to say something in response to the question of the ontological status of time, lead to a conclusion similar to ones found in McTaggart's idealistic metaphysics and Husserl's transcendental phenomenology of consciousness: time is not real. It is psychological (McTaggart), transcendental (Husserl), or linguistic (Derrida), but not something that has an extra-intentional effect.[22] Merleau-Ponty offers us a way to think about time as having a real effect, but not in the traditional metaphysical sense of being something *in itself*, objective, on the *far* side of phenomena. The temporality that he associates with the body's *écart* has the status of a pre-noetic reality. Anterior to intentionality, the facticity of the body, in its *écart*, in its effaced but nonetheless effective operation as a pre-noetic force, contributes to the institution of an inordinate temporality, the "flesh of time" (VI 111) that remains unreflected in phenomenological reflection, yet nonetheless has a refractory effect on intentional life.

Merleau-Ponty's notion of *écart* not only provides a different way to think about the reality of time, it also suggests a different reading of Derrida. The pre-noetic reality of time is not confined to the operations of the body. Language also has a pre-noetic role to play in this regard. Rather than interpreting Derrida's concept of textuality as a linguistic idealism, as Rorty does, we can understand it as an attempt to express the pre-noetic force of language. The facticity of language, which effaces itself in the same manner as the body, which holds within itself a past that cannot be reduced to noetic structure or noematic content, has an effect on conscious experience—a trace-effect that disrupts the living present of intentionality. The temporality of language, like the temporality of the body, is not reducible to an irreal form or formal structure. Rather, it has a pre-noetic reality that transcends both memory and retention, yet a reality that nonetheless encroaches on intentional experience by introducing a *Zeitmaterie* of sedimented (or surplus) meanings into the very heart of primal impression.

Notes

1. J. Ellis McTaggart, "The Unreality of Time," *Mind* 68 (1908), 457–74.
2. See Jacques Derrida, "Ousia and Gramme: A Note to a Footnote in *Being and Time*," trans. Edward Casey, in *Phenomenology in Perspective*, ed. F. J. Smith (The Hague: Nijhoff, 1970), pp. 88–89.
3. Edmund Husserl, *On the Phenomenology of the Consciousness of Internal Time* (1893–1917), *Collected Works I*, trans. John Brough (Dordrecht: Kluwer Academic, 1991), 84–86.

4. See my "The Theater of Personal Identity: From Hume to Derrida," *The Personalist Forum* 8 (1992) 21–30.

5. Jacques Derrida, *Speech and Phenomena and Other Essays on Husserl's Theory of Signs*, trans. David B. Allison (Evanston: Northwestern University Press, 1973), p. 64; hereafter cited as SP.

6. Jacques Derrida, *Of Grammatology*, trans. Gayatri Chakrovorty Spivak (Baltimore: Johns Hopkins University Press, 1976), p. 62.

7. Ibid., pp. 68–69.

8. Jacques Derrida, *Positions*, trans. Alan Bass (Chicago: University of Chicago Press, 1981), pp. 28–29.

9. Jacques Derrida, *Writing and Difference*, trans. Alan Bass (Chicago: University of Chicago Press, 1978), p. 227

10. David Wood, *The Deconstruction of Time* (Atlantic Highlands: Humanities Press International, 1989), pp. 267ff; hereafter cited as DT.

11. Richard Rorty, "Nineteenth-Century Idealism and Twentieth-Century Textualism," in *Consequences of Pragmatism: Essays: 1972–1980* (Minneapolis: University of Minnesota Press, 1982), p. 140.

12. M. C. Dillon suggests that for Derrida time is an ideality, since "the being of time is relational and relations are held to be ideal" ("Temporality: Merleau-Ponty and Derrida," in *Merleau-Ponty, Hermeneutics, and Postmodernism*, ed. Thomas W. Busch and Shaun Gallagher [Albany: SUNY, 1992], p. 204).

13. Merleau-Ponty, *Phenomenology of Perception*, trans. Colin Smith (London: Routledge and Kegan Paul, 1962), p. 422; hereafter cited as PhP.

14. Merleau-Ponty, *The Visible and the Invisible*, trans. Alphonso Lingis (Evanston: Northwestern University Press, 1968), p. 49n; hereafter cited as VI.

15. See my "Body Schema and Intentionality," in *The Body and the Self*, ed. Jose Bermudez, Naomi Eilan, and Anthony Marcel (Cambridge: MIT Press/Bradford Books, 1995), pp. 225–44.

16. Although time is closely associated with the soul in both Neoplatonic and Aristotelian traditions, still, human nature is temporal, and the soul must deal with time, indeed is trapped in time, primarily because it is embodied. For Aquinas, the temporality of human nature is closely tied to human embodiment understood as an underlying potentiality. As embodied creatures, we necessarily seek perfection only according to the order of succession (see, e.g., *Scriptum super Libros Sententiarum*, I. d19. q2). For Spinoza, the experience of temporal objects is due to physiological changes in the sensing body (see *Ethics*, II. props. XVII and XXVI).

17. Edward Casey, "Keeping the Past in Mind," *Review of Metaphysics* 37 (1983), p. 80.

18. On the innateness of the body schema, see Shaun Gallagher and Andrew Meltzoff, "The Earliest Sense of Self and Others: Merleau-Ponty and Recent Developmental Studies," *Philosophical Psychology* (forthcoming); concerning evolution and the body's role in cognition, see Maxine Sheets-Johnstone, *The Roots of Thinking* (Philadelphia: Temple University Press, 1990).

19. See Casey, "Keeping the Past in Mind." This idea is also expressed in literature. Milan Kundera, for example, in *The Book of Laughter and*

Forgetting, writes: "We will never remember anything by sitting in one place waiting for the memories to come back to us of their own accord! Memories are scattered all over the world. We must travel if we want to find them *and flush them out from their hiding places*" (trans. Michael Henry Heim [London: Penguin Books, 1983], p. 167).

20. On the social aspects, as well as aspects pertaining to bodily practices, see Paul Connerton, *How Societies Remember* (Cambridge: Cambridge Press, 1989).

21. In *Signs* (trans. Richard C. McCleary [Evanston: Northwestern University Press, 1964]), Merleau-Ponty writes: "It is asked '*Where* is history made? Who makes it? What is this movement which traces out and leaves behind the figures of the wake?'.... Everywhere there are meanings, dimensions, and forms in excess of what each consciousness could have produced; and yet it is men who speak and think and see. We are in the field of history as we are in the field of language or existence" (p. 20).

22. Dillon suggests: "Derrida has not freed himself completely from the ontology and methodology of his primary mentor, Husserl.... Derrida's deconstruction of Husserl's language theory operates from within the Husserlian conceptual matrix. It is my contention that, although Derrida challenges and alters that matrix, he does so within the overriding standpoint of transcendental methodology and idealistic ontology" ("Temporality," p. 201).

9

Reconstructive Time: *Écart, Différance,* Fundamental Obscurity

Dennis T. O'Connor

PROLOGUE: BEING SITUATED

I am thankful for the invitation to participate with you and my fellow authors writing and written about herein. Deeply grateful indeed to Maurice Merleau-Ponty and Jacques Derrida, neither of whom I've ever met. My acquaintance with them has been limited in at least that way; irremediably in the case of Merleau-Ponty. I have been moved and touched, indeed struck, by each and by both as they were by each other. What follows is largely a series of grateful gestures.

FORSAKING FORESEEING

It would be interesting to see what this writing does, can do, will do; to see and see now and knowingly what we are doing or will do with *it*.

Would I change, regulate, modulate it if I could so see/know now? I have to suppose so. This writing will change regardless.

I know I cannot see thus and so. I would have to cease being an I for that to happen. Even so it is not my intention to write or appear here as a specific, unchanging I in any case.

I know or feel that such a now would be odious. If my writing makes a difference, I do not and cannot know what it is—nor, of course, for whom. I am neither able nor desirous to be able to control the difference. I'm thankful for that.

These are working notes: not because I am dead—though I may be by the time you come across them. I hope you find them somehow helpful, that your collaborative effort of reading will be somehow enriching. I am finding this way of working instructive. And painful. I am not sure where or how this is proceeding. So thus far we are together in at least that! No one, certainly not I, knows where this is going.

For a time, nearly twenty years it seems, I have failed or refused to write: commit *écriture*. I am doing so now as a response to a kind and timely invitation.[1] I cannot conceive of any more appropriate conditions or terms of such objection: addressing Merleau-Ponty and Derrida together.

Keeping company with them for the past decades has been enriching, intimidating, and fun. I have kept myself in their company and, I suppose, become myself and lived, as it were, in a certain odd neighborhood. The *sense* as well as *being* of being-and-meaning-being-as-a-self is not fundamentally auto-affection but being-gifted. Donative. Hence thankfulness. That is the condition of this commencement, which is a recommencement.

COMING ACROSS DERRIDA

There was a time[2] when I perceived or felt a profound philosophical affinity between Merleau-Ponty and Derrida, which I hope to indicate in what follows. The affinity was "about" their treatments of Husserl: their work on his late work—specifically his essay entitled "The Origin of Geometry."[3]

Having completed a thesis on *The Structure of Behavior*, I was attempting slowly and unconfidently to understand *Phenomenology of Perception*: to understand meant to get through the whole thing and discern its unity and what was fundamental to it as a unity; or at least as an entirety. That, increasingly, took the form of correlating and seeing correspondences between three chapters: "The Body as Expression and Speech," "The Cogito," and "Temporality." The last two being contiguous forced me to treat them as a doublet and a progression. The chapter on "The Body" seemed to me precursive of the doublet. It seemed to me that the reflective work on the *Cogito* led to and was deepened by the reflections on temporality.

What I could not do was "link up" the earlier chapter with the later ones. I recognized that I needed to deepen my understanding of Husserl, because it became increasingly apparent to me that the earlier chapter was an intensive reworking of Husserl's *Crisis* and "Origin."[4] In this project of correlating the late Husserl with the Merleau-Ponty of 1945, I came across the Derrida of 1962: which is to say I read more or less carefully his *Introduction* and translation *as an access to* someone else—Husserl—and *on the way to* the "depth problem" (roughly,[5] the manner of being of meaning in history). Attentiveness to Derrida's texts, thought, etc., in its "ownness," in its commencement-exercise-like dimension, evaded me entirely—or almost entirely.[6] I retained merely his name and the sense he was a serious, disciplined Husserl scholar. I still retain those senses, sort of.

I was seeking a precise and determinate understanding of what Merleau-Ponty was saying—in fact, had long since written—*therefore* reading Husserl *and* using Derrida's introduction. In part what Merleau-Ponty was saying was that:

> The precise and entirely determinate world is still posited in the first place, no longer perhaps as the cause of our perceptions, but as their immanent end.[7]

I was progressively getting lost in a "world" of inter-textual, polylinguistic immanences "bearing on" Kant's "transcendental deduction" and Husserl's "transcendental reduction."[8]

The polylinguisticality had several different *dimensions*. First, the axis German-French-American-English. Second, the axis Kant's-vs-Husserl's-German insofar as there was a kind of different hyperspecificity and evolving technicity proper to each, where the latter is informed and tempered by the former. Third, Merleau-Ponty is not only thematizing the difference between original and constituted speech, he is writing differently—and very appreciably and necessarily differently—than he did in *The Structure*. Fourth, Merleau-Ponty is trying to deal with, work through, a series of questions bearing on transcendental language.[9]

What became clear to me, then, was that for both Merleau-Ponty and Derrida there was a *fundamental* problem in Husserl's discursiveness—that the nature of the problem required careful, albeit perhaps paradoxical, specification. Further, that Merleau-Ponty and Derrida judged that Eugen Fink's insights on the issue of Husserl and language were invaluable.[10]

TELEONOMIES

I was seeking . . . interrogating . . . trying to link up . . . trace passages. What? A precise and determinate understanding of what Merleau-Ponty was saying/had written. I thought there were laws operative—*opérant*—and I sought in the ways I did because I found it fecund. (The thematics of *poros-penia* are perhaps irreducible.) I worked in the wake of Merleau-Ponty, took bearings from his gestures,

not to get to know him nor to agree with him nor to repro-
duce him or his results but because I just kind of came to find it
imperative.

When we live—and I am addressing *living* here—interrogatively,
I suspect we follow (almost entirely unnoticingly) imperatives. When
I say/write this (this being the imprecise but specific sentence which
immediately precedes the one you are reading) I am not speaking
about "us," "the world," "philosophy," save insofar as these indicate an inseparable relational unity whose destiny is . . . shall we
say, precarious. I do not think it makes much sense, frankly, for
me or you to interpret what is going on in this paragraph intro-
spectively or introspectingly.

Directedness came from only tenuously specifiable quests: To "link"
"The Body As . . ." with "The Cogito" and "Temporality." To trace
the passage from phenomenology to ontology: three curiosities 1)
the retro-spective destiny of the *cogito-tacite*; 2) the thesis regarding theses and their relation with perceptual faith; 3) philosophical labor. To get real, better, approximatively. We do ontology living
carnally. That, I think, is important to somehow say and to do so
thankfully. Ontology is soulful, mindful, carnal collaboration.

What follows is what is left of those quests and curiosities.

What is Seemingly Instructive Worth trying to see, share, say—
perhaps sing!

THE BODY AS . . . EXPRESSION AND SPEECH

If we are to understand being embodied in such a way as to be
able to speak, hear, read, listen, write meaningfully and communicatively, we must recognize that speech is an originating realm.
This recognition *naturally comes* late, if at all, and in its wake we
undergo an experience of *fundamental* obscurity vis-à-vis *our* own
individual and cultural ontogenesis and maturation. Our being thus-
and-so-embodied manifests, reveals, and renders only possible but
really possible an intimate complicity with the world and fellow
humans. Thinking this manner of being ontically in a tradition
somehow Cartesian means seeking and experiencing clarity, con-
fusedness, distinct and in-distinctness in a pre-delineated stylistics.

When we affirm *that* it is the body that speaks, points out, and
affirms; *that* I am *and* have my/a body; *that the* body is not an
object; *that* my *awareness* of it is not a thought; *that* its unity is
implicit and vague; *that* I *know* it only by living and taking up on
my own account the drama we are playing *out* and getting lost

and found in. . . . When we do all this we experience "as an ultimate fact," within a regime of factuality, an enigmatically open
and indefinite power of giving and receiving meaning which is
creative and collaborative.

This *re*-discovery (*redécouverte*) of "the body" is an experience
of obscurity and necessarily broken familiarities, which spreads to
or seeps into the entirety of the world as we normally-naturally-
culturally live it.

To assess, gauge speaking's/language's power we have to exploit,
deploy, employ openings, dimensions, landscapes, operations which
are *almost* as obscure for the adult as for the child. The little boy
who puts on his granny's glasses and *is* chagrined and *shouts* "what
a fraud!"—that little boy is instructive. There *is* enigma and obscurity here—for the boy, for us readers—even though we'd be hard
put, as it were, to say definitively what the character of the enigma
is. The story of the little boy indicates the "theme of linguistic
incantation" with its "reliefs"; the story works differently and necessarily differently for those who have successfully worked through
or emerged from the gap. Some of us smile backward more or less
fondly when we come across the story of the little boy who helps
us understand the *cogito tacite*'s precarious presence to itself, *its*
inarticulate gasps likened to an infant's breath. This *is* linked with
Balzac's *Peau de chagrin*, where there came into being "a white
tablecloth like a covering of snow newly fallen"; a tablecloth Cézanne
tells us he spent his youth trying to paint.[11]

We experience, express, think, undergo likenesses of different
but related dimensionalities only insofar as we are carnal creatures. This is what the body and the chapter on "The Body as . . ."
insist on. They insist on reawakenings, rediscoveries, reflective
reappropriation: intensive interrogation.

What the chapter does not do is situate its results, its affirmations,
within the framework of intentional analyses,[12] constitutive levels,
and validities. The carnal process of signification is registered as
"factuality," as fundamentally obscure and entirely elusive within
a Cartesian reversion to transcendental immanence. In this sense
the chapter is a remarkable prelude to "The Cogito," as well, I
think, as Merleau-Ponty's earliest and most inchoate articulation
of perceptual faith.

Merleau-Ponty's efforts "to situate" these results take the forms,
first, of a reflective critique of the Cartesian *cogito* for its timelessness[13]
(*Phenomenology of Perception*, hereafter PP, 372–74, 410–30) and
verbal character (PP 400–402[14]); and, second, a reflection on ultimate

subjectivity (PP 404–409).[15] In his thematic development of "time as the subject and the subject as time" (PP 422) we have the clearest early formulation of *écart*.

By 1945, Merleau-Ponty concluded that it is through an analysis of primordial temporality that we gain *access* to: the concrete structure of subjectivity (PP 410); the presence-field as originary experience, the privileged sphere of absolute self-evidence (PP 416); the most precise notion of consciousness of which we are capable (PP 426); a correct formulation of the problem of rationality; a deeper understanding of the *problems* of passivity, genesis and acquisition (PP 427–30).

This analysis allows us to *say*, speak, determine, both positively and negatively, something like the following. *Positively* regarding ultimate subjectivity we may affirm: it is ek-static, explosive, dehiscent, transitional ipseity. Its essence is to make visible, manifest itself to itself, express significance: to encounter, live, and undergo as well as intend, posit, and create meaning. It is not so much a plenary being as a presence, a finite, non-self-originating presence which, while personal, never has the density of an absolute individual. As an operative carnal presence it co-inhabits a pre-objective world with an art hidden in its own depths—an art known only through its productions. It dwells within the thickness of a pre-objective present which is a non-successive, non-intratemporal temporalization, whose best formula is perhaps "as future-which-lapses-into-the-past-by-coming-into-the-present" (PP 420–33).

What we must say *negatively*: It is neither a thing, nor a consciousness, nor a subject, nor a substance or absolute individual; it is neither an empirical self nor a Cartesian *cogito*; neither a Kantian nor Husserlian transcendental ego, nor a Heideggerian spontaneity. It is neither self-creating nor self-constituting nor even self-identical. Nor, of course, does it dwell in a fully determinate time or place.[16]

These affirmations and negations *mean*, if we follow their direction, their polarization toward what they are not, while refusing to be oblivious to what they are—utterances. They are indices of a philosophical vision glimpsing itself glimpsing—of a dehiscent auto-affection achieved necessarily, ambiguously, transgressively. These indices point to, without explaining or grounding, *how* we mean—*a specifically human manner of existing*—as a sentient being coming to itself in return; a return which is in a sense a self-begetting, yet a return which is neither an activity nor a passivity but *both*, and with a bearing that must be born (begotten by and through others' bodies) and sustained, nurtured, naturally—culturally.

> Our analysis of time has confirmed . . . that it has meaning for us only because it is "what we are." . . . It is literally the tenor of our life. . . . It is through time that being is conceived. . . . What is true . . . is that our open and personal existence rests upon an initial foundation of acquired and stabilized existence . . . it could not be otherwise if *we are temporality.* . . . (PP 431–32)[17]

These affirmations and negations have for me the indeterminate status of utterances, forced recognitions, which are no longer and not yet cognitions. They are neither theses[18] nor propositions nor truths but rather faithful work sites; relatively stable specific designations for being unsettled; precursive[19] for ontology: they are to be lived in the interrogative mode. Their merit is gauged by the questions they open and the listening they require.[20]

> We have with our body, our senses, our look, our power to understand speech and to speak, *measurants* for Being, dimensions to which we can refer it, but not a relation of adequation or or immanence . . . we ourselves are one sole continued question, a perpetual enterprise of taking our bearings. (*The Visible and the Invisible*, hereafter VI, 103)

In dialogue or in monologue the essence is always a certain vanishing point, a certain newly won silence.

Along these lines, perhaps we can see what motivated Merleau-Ponty to ask: What sees (VI 131–33)? What wishes (VI 133–45)? What possesses (VI 151–52)? What speaks (VI 154–55)? Now we have arrived at the chiasm. The issue here is living wakefully in what Husserl called history—the vital movement of the coexistence and the interweaving of original formations and sedimentations of meaning—living bondedly.

By 1945, Merleau-Ponty had taken Husserl's kinesthetically living body back to what is originary—speech and seeing and temporalizing of/as flesh and blood existence; traditionality; a subject trying irremediably to understand itself as an intra-ontic occurrence; a functioning concealing itself in its psychic acts, in its objectifications. At these limits he discovered *fundamental* obscurity. Thereafter he turned to history—the history of our time, the Cold War—to the prose of the world, to political freedom, to language and painting, to expression direct and indirect. He did this for a decade, then felt compelled "to do ontology." We have his working notes. We live and see and touch and breathe, I think, along lines he made palpable, visible, tangibly explorable, in accordance with what is fundamental—flesh laboring and interrogating expressively. With flesh as elemental, elusive, allusive, dehiscent but cohesive. Merleau-Ponty's "flesh" is not a concept; it is barely even a word or notion. He did not *construct* an ontology.

DERRIDA 1962

In what follows I would like to proffer two moments discernible in Derrida's Introduction to his translation[21] of Fink's transcript of Husserl's "The Origin of Geometry." The first moment puts in relief a series of reflections on phenomenological language; the second marks a distinctively Derridean conclusiveness regarding Destiny, Delay, *Différance*, Dehiscence, Disquietude.

This manner of presentation runs the risk of suggesting that the Introduction is a critique or dismissal of Husserl, which would be a grotesque misreading. Derrida states his ambition "to recognize and situate one stage of Husserl's thought with its specific presuppositions and its particular unfinished state" (*Edmund Husserl's Origin of Geometry: An Introduction*, hereafter I, 27), and this is more or less what he does with considerable care and scholarship. His relatedness to "The Origin" is close, faithful, and informed. The voice listened to is preeminently Husserl's.

Derrida situates Husserl's text, thought, and practice in a series of rather deft ways: (1) Husserl's *works* in their multi-ordered relations with each other—chronological, architectonic (*arché*-telic); (2) Hussel's *thought* in what is essential and fundamental in its relationship with itself—its unity, promises, hopes, privileges, delays, deferrals, consistency, novelty, tentativeness, procession; (3) Husserl's thought *about and within* traditionality—European, philosophic; Kantianism, phenomenology, transcendentality; (4) the dialogical-empirical *historicality* of Husserl vs. Kant, vs. Fichte, vs. Heidegger, vs. Frege, vs. Dilthey, complicity with Heidegger vis-à-vis what is primordial, essential, and definitive; (5) Husserl's already rich French *legacy* of translators, commentators, philosophers[22]; and (6) Husserl's *ethic* of radical finitude, prudence, rigor, and critical humility. Manifest in this treatment is Derrida's disciplined philosophical engagement; his scholarly—archival, exegetic, explicative, thematic-analytic skill and care are remarkable in a man barely thirty years old. Remarkable as well is his conclusiveness.

Derrida's efforts to analyze what Husserl meant/recognized in treating history as institutive—"to specify the subtle and specific character of the Husserlian question"—led him to a series of reflections on, and within, phenomenological language and speech. I would like to indicate, albeit briefly, how Derrida's effort proceeded to trace Husserl's "strange procession of '*Rückfrage*' sketched in "Origin." Having indicated this, I will try to specify a kind of summing gesturing[23] and conclusiveness[24] on Derrida's part. This way of treating Derrida's efforts is motivated by a desire to see clearly, early on as it were, the origins of *Derrida's* project as points of departure from a relatively specific work site: Husserl's "Origin." Its specificity is, of course, deeply problematic not least because of its being meant and situated in a tradition which it narrates transcendentally.

SPECIFYING THE QUESTION

Husserl's procession—a movement called *Rückfrage*, a return to the originary, the origin in its firstness—marks a zigzag way of movement. With the recognition of history as *institutive* Husserl recognizes the necessity of a *historical reduction as reactivating and noetic*; of reawakening an inaugural act—an institutive act— now concealed under secondary passivities and millennia of sedimentations. For Derrida, the doctrine of tradition faces a double necessity with respect to origins—eidetic prescriptiveness and a priori normativity. The unity of geometry's sense is that of *a* tradition, *a* history—but of a unity still to come, ongoingly worked out on the basis of what was announced in its origin. Secondly, the ground of this unity has the character of a primordial sense-fashioning (*Sinnbildung*) grounded in "the-world-itself as the horizon of the infinite totality of possible experiences in space in general" (I 47–55).

It is important here to note—if we are to grasp the full exemplarity of "Origin"—the duality of Husserl's treatment of geometry. For the most part, geometry is simply one specific form of culture— world traditionality: meanings come into being through spiritual accomplishments, inscribed, passed on or transmitted—retained in and through a process analogous to that of the internal time—consciousness described, noematically, as early as the 1904–10 lectures (I 57). Referring to this scheme, Derrida writes:

> Sedimentary retention is not only the condition for the possibility of protention; it also belongs to the general form of protention,

which is itself conceived under the absolutely unique and universal form of the Living Present. The latter, which is the primordial absolute of temporality, is only the maintenance of what indeed must be called the *dialectic* of protention and retention, despite Husserl's repugnance for that word. (I 57–58)

The point here is that without this "always renewed originality of an absolute primordiality, always present and lived as such," *history* in its unity and coherent totality would not be possible. The "idea of geometry" as a historical totality is a cultural structure, has a project character, like any other archetypal form of traditionality.

On the other hand, science and perhaps particularly the geometrical disciplines have an essentially privileged status:

The idea of science is the index of pure culture in general, it designates culture's *eidos par excellence* ... "exemplary" in the double sense of this word eidetic and teleological: it is the particular example which guides the eidetic reduction and intuition, but it is also the example and model which must orient culture as its ideal. (I 58)

Derrida's point here is that for Husserl the *ideality* of this type of non-descriptive pure science is *absolutely* normative. The validity of this science's ideality—of that which does not exist as something personal, whose existence is objective if there is absolute identity and self-sameness for everyone, omni- or super-temporally for all peoples, all ages, identically the same in "the original language" of Euclid and in all "translations," this objectivity is peculiar to the objective, pure sciences (I 57–59). As Derrida states it, the tradition of truth (this form of truth intending) is the most profound and purest history (I 59); only a communal subjectivity could produce and be wholly responsible for and to such a historical system of truth, recurrently fruitfully (I 60) in such a way that at every present stage a total acquisition is, so to speak, the total premise for the acquisitions of a new level (I 60; "Origin" 355).

It is through these themes—that a sense production must have *first* presented itself as evidence in the personal consciousness of the inventor, thereafter and *subsequently* reactivated in intersubjective circulation for everyone, for all future possible actual geometers— that Husserl elicits a kind of fiction of "before" and "after" which must be neutralized in its factuality and ontic meaing. Husserl's narrative account cannot be understood as having been meant as a factual historical account of the genesis and reactivation of concrete acts and interconnections of "what really happened" (I 65). The "before" and "after" have been neutralized *de jure* at the outset (I 51).

> *Pure-interconnections-of* history, *a priori-thought-of* history, does this not mean that these possibilities are not in themselves historical? Not at all, for they are *nothing but* the possibility *of* the appearance *of* history as such, outside which there is nothing. History itself establishes the possibility of its own appearing. (I 66)

Now we can see the general thematic question posed repeatedly by Husserl—"How can the subjective egological evidence of sense become objective and intersubjective? How can it give rise to an ideal and true object?" (I 63)—as the matrix within which Husserl poses the specific question of geometry's sense of ideal objectivity: How is ideal Objectivity possible? This question receives "its sharpest . . ., most adequate" and most difficult form in the "Origin" (I 67).

The question is how to reveal, respect, and show the *historicity of the ideal object itself*—the seeing and experiencing of the geometrical essence itself as instituted, meant, sedimented, retained, reactivated.[25] Husserl's response, Derrida tells us, is direct, quick, and surprising: "Ideality come to its Objectivity by means of language, through which it receives, so to speak, its linguistic living body" (I 76).[26] Language, we are told, is thoroughly made up of ideal objectivities[27]—ideal identities of sense freed from any and all factual connections with their empirical, phonetic, or graphic materialization, which evoke worldiness no less than factual linguistic subjectivity (I 67).

What is decisive here for Derrida is that

> despite the constant interest it bears (from the *Logical Investigations* to the *Origin*), the specific problem of language—its origin and its usage in a transcendental phenomenology—has always been excluded or deferred. (I 68 n65)

Precisely here Derrida rehearses the now familiar warnings of Fink and Bachelard concerning natural language, the natural function of language, ordinary sense's embeddedness in and hold to the natural attitude.[28] The question seems to become one of the possibility of settling accounts where what counts is the possibility of an account at all: the unitary ground from which this diffraction of sense is *permitted* and *intelligible*. We are calculating here, Derrida

states, "how difficult is every attempt to reduce (in some ultimate
and radical transcendental regression) a phenomenology of historicity" (I 69).

> It is rather significant that every critical enterprise, juridical or
> transcendental, is made vulnerable by the irreducible factuality
> and the natural naiveté of its language. We become conscious of
> this vulnerability or of this vocation to silence in a second re-
> flection or the possibility of the juridico-transcendental regres-
> sion itself . . . an irreducible proximity of language to primordial
> thought is signified in a zone which eludes by nature every phe-
> nomenal or thematic actuality. (I 69–70)

Derrida continues with a question and a declaration: "Is this immediacy the nearness of thought to itself?" "We would have to
show why that cannot be decided" (I 70).[29]

What is it to know, to think, the ideal Objectivity of geometry in
its absolutely objective, infinitely translatable and traditional ideal
identity, untainted by factual contingency, subjectivity, eventuality? This is the question which the Husserlian search for a space
for a transcendental historicity prescribes (I 75–77). Husserl's re-
descent toward language, parenthesizing constituted language, allows us to recognize that:

> At bottom, the problem of geometry's origin puts the problem of
> the constitution of intersubjectivity on par with that of the
> phenomenological origin of language. Husserl is very conscious
> of this. But he will not attempt this difficult regression with the
> *Origin*, although he says it "arises here." (I 79)[30]

What is decisive in this connection, for Derrida, is that speech as
opposed to writing is incapable of *absolutely grounding* the ideal
objectivities of sense. Speech leaves sense tied to the synchrony of
an exchange within an institutive community; written expression
assures absolute traditionalization, creates a kind of autonomous
and subjectless transcendental field of pure intentional idealities
(I 87–92). These formations of pure geometric idealities, based on
the "bound idealities"[31] (morphological pre-geometrical
determinations still tied to sensible and imaginative intuitiveness),
are attributed not to the "real praxis" of perfecting, of pressing
toward the horizon of conceivable perfecting "again and again,"
but of an *ideal* praxis of pure thinking.[32] What is discernible here,
decisively for Derrida, is:

> The privileged position of the protential dimension of
> intentionality and that of the future . . . a transcendence that es-

sentially can never be mastered, the idealized space of mathematics[,] allows us to go immediately to the infinite limit of what is in fact an unfinished movement. Thus, the transcendence of every lived future can be absolutely appropriated and reduced in the very gesture which frees that future. (I 135–36)

What is fundamental to the Husserlian project is the *Idea* of an ethico-teleological prescription of an infinite practical-theoretical task, grounded in the movement of primordial phenomenological temporalization,

> in which the Living Present of consciousness holds itself as the primordial Absolute only in an indefinite protention, animated and unified by the Idea . . . of the total flux of lived experience. (I 136)

The unity of this movement is given as indefinite; this thought-unity can never phenomenalize itself, can never be made itself the theme of a phenomenological description, can maintain itself only in tension with the principle of all principles (I 137–38).[33] This phenomenological non-thematization, Derrida observes, "obeys a profound and irreducible necessity":

> Phenomenology cannot be reflected in a phenomenology of phenomenology . . . *its logos can never appear as such*, can never be given in a philosophy of seeing, *but (like all speech) can only be heard or understood through the visible.* (I 141, emphasis added)

At its greatest depth, Derrida tells us, this is what Husserl has disclosed; intentionality is the root of historicity: *historicity is sense*, that is, history's *appearing* and the *possibility* of its appearing. This marks the limit, Derrida states, of phenomenology as the propaedeutic for the passage from the question *how* sense proceeds to the question *why*. Knowing what sense is as historicity, we stand in the precarious openness of a question: the question of the origin of being as history, for

> that historicity is prescribed for Being; that delay is the destiny of thought itself as Discourse—only phenomenology can *say* this and make philosophy equal to it. For phenomenology alone can make infinite historicity appear. . . . Delay is the philosophical absolute . . . this *alterity* of the absolute origin[34] structurally appears in *my* Living Present[35] . . . the Absolute is *present* only in being deferred-delayed [*différent*] without respite.[36] (I 152)

This impotence and this impossibility[37] are given in a primordial and pure consciousness of Difference.[38] (I 153)

Such a consciousness, with its strange style of unity, must be able to be restored to its own light. Without such a consciousness, without its own proper *dehiscence* [emphasis mine],[39] nothing would appear.

Difference would be transcendental. The *pure and interminable disquietude of thought striving to "reduce" Difference* [emphasis mine] . . . while maintaining Difference—that disquietude would be transcendental.

What this means is unimaginable—erase your imaginative schemes of noumenal substance. The sense of the above is as an articulation of a movement of an ought-to-be-seen-and-said. Difference cannot, I think, be properly analyzed from any stable *point de départ*. I have tried, however, to indicate where and how and why it began to appear in Derridian apophantics. I have tried to do this by almost entirely failing to appear and shoulder the burden of meaning what I write. That was a thoughtful decision or perhaps a cowardly response to too much noise. I have tried to return, recall, evoke others' limits, beginnings as they appeared at the end of an introduction. This is a clumsy way of proceeding to follow a strange *series* of moves that have not and cannot have unity: Derrida avows, I think, many points of departure, none of which are points or commencements. He proffers them with extraordinary generosity and a singular dexterity, for which I am grateful.

Epilogue

Writing is not really like dying, it just seems like it. You have just got to get a handle on it.

Écart and *Différance* are abyssal—at the limits of being in-definite: where we speak of or about gaps, tears, incohesion without warrant or propriety. What is fundamental is that often what we hold together here is held together with a fisted hand, trying to clutch onto and strike out. We employ ready-to-hand "things" (hammers, essays, books, languages, *begriffes*). In so doing we run the risks of being banal, idiosyncratic, dishonorably and naively factitious, scary, elusive, too principledly for-or-against the current. Beliefs *appear as* "constructs," usually, I suppose, only too late, when they have started to appear to have come from somewhere else or just come apart. Avowals count even in the face of ferocious alpha-bets.

We construct verbal constructs (articles, books, archives) because we have learned to rely on, depend on, lean on, learn from, live according to them/each other. All this doing is collaborative and in the world historically ongoing—hence we *feel* the current rather than know it. Its velocity and force are unmeasurable. We are exposed to the elements as we say and we seek the elegance of elementarity. That is difficult when we are crawling or being swept away.

The flesh that Merleau-Ponty left us with is not a concept; it is nothing precise at all; it is absurd to say precisely what he indicated with that word at the abyss—to do justice to his work there without working there. The incised flesh Derrida circumfesses about, tearfully and obscenely, should scare us, make our skin crawl, seek the solace of others' lips. The work site of this settling of accounts is fearful in its dimensions.

These ways of working *hurt*; that is what is reassuring about them—our way of registering that they work, of being instructed.

If my rather goofy way of constructing this *essai* in this workbook is somehow helpful I am thankful for that. The abyss is a remarkably untidy site—that should be registered. I am grateful for the opportunity to work with my colleagues here in this effort.

Notes

1. Correspondence regarding this volume dated 15 November 1993: "Your essay should specifically address the theme of the book—*Écart* and *Différance: Merleau-Ponty and Derrida on Seeing and Writing.* That is the *only constraint....* Sincerely, M. C. Dillon."
2. The past tense evoked here is provisional and fictive but no less necessary, for now. Marking time is crucial *de jure*: for retelling, re- and de- construction, recapitulation, recognition, remembrance; repetition retains the presumptive *petition* through differences. Writing is always in addition to thinking; as interment, if it takes place, is in addition to living.
3. Edmund Husserl, "The Origin of Geometry," Appendix 6 to *The Crisis of European Sciences and Transcendental Phenomenology*, trans. David Carr (Evanston: Northwestern University Press, 1970). Hereafter cited as "Origin."
4. My copy of Merleau-Ponty's "The Body as ..." was rapidly, and almost entirely, defaced with notes correlating it with "The Origin," notwithstanding the fact that the former makes only one explicit reference to the latter.
5. "Roughly" hardly covers the degrees of inchoateness I had yet to undergo vis-à-vis "depth," "being of meaning," meaning of "geometry," specifically "history," "historicality," "historicity," *a priority*, "passivity." Reawakening became the *name* of a series of problems more or less articulatable if and only if it could cease to be the name of a

solution or, still worse, as I came to recognize, merely a virtuosity employed traditionally. We must face *our* unreflective life, history, etc.

6. Today my motive is to be differently attentive. Hence, what needs to be said/written is different. Obviously.

7. Merleau-Ponty, *Phenomenology of Perception*, trans. Colin Smith (London: Routledge and Kegan Paul, 1962), p. 31. Hereafter cited as PP. The issues here are motivation and attention; certainly not intro-spection.

8. The title as well as the preface to John Barth's *Lost in the Funhouse* comes to mind here. Try to follow its instructions.

9. To see and grasp the world as properly paradoxical we must break certain familiarities; we must recognize and constantly reexamine the possibility of the transcendental reduction and our dependence on linguistic virtualities in carrying it out or forward; we must recognize our reflections are enacted in a temporal flux; that primordial silence is an achievement; that this can barely be said written, glimpsed, evoked, indicated.

10. The number of times and ways Fink is cited by both authors deserves careful attention. Fink figures not only as author of the transcription of the Husserl manuscript but also as its elaborator, interpreter, respondent—critic for both Merleau-Ponty and Derrida.

11. This paragraph correlates the anecdote regarding a small boy (PP 401), a young Cézanne (PP 198), and a Balzacian image. Only flesh can undergo and enact such linguistic incantation.

12. Merleau-Ponty is clearly *indebted to* three Husserlian themes: (1) the kinesthetically functioning living body—cf. *Crisis* III, A 28, 47, and III, B 62; (2) the "inseparable relational unity man-world-language-of "Ursprung", p. 359; (3) the warnings about ontic certainties—cf. *Crisis* III, A 55, and their relation to the problem of the essential modality of the social—cf. *Crisis* III, A 53 and 546.

13. This critique culminates in his treatment of primordial temporality.

14. This critique culminates in the famous *cogito tacite*. Ibid., 404.

15. Ibid., 404–409. Cf. Husserl's "Ich als Ur-Ich." *Crisis* III, A 546.

16. The tradition of thought here delineated is not being negated but avowed, retrieved and resumed.

17. These affirmations are neither ontology nor anthropology. The "body proper" and "ultimate subjectivity" are not "flesh." If we cease overlooking the interrogative (PP 446) we find a being which is in pursuit of itself outside (PP 451). I am from the start outside myself. . . . But what is required here is silence (PP 456).

18. This anticipates Merleau-Ponty's remarks about converting the convictions of perceptual faith into theses or propositions—cf. *The Visible and the Invisible*, ed. Claude Lefort, trans. Alphonso Lingis (Evanston: Northwestern University Press, 1968) pp. 8–11; and Chapter 2, pp. 92–93. Hereafter cited as VI.

19. This anticipates his remarks re "the dialectic without synthesis," which leads neither to skepticism nor relativism nor the reign of the ineffable but to surpassings, which are concrete, partial, encumbered with remnant, saddled with deficits. . . . Cf. VI 95.

20. This anticipates Merleau-Ponty's remarks concerning the listening,

witnessing, questioning consonant with the porous being it questions, Cf. VI 101–102.

21. Edmund Husserl's *Origine de la Géométrie, traduction et introduction*. (Paris: Presses Universitaires de France, 1962). My citations will be to the Leavey translation of Derrida's second, revised French edition of 1974, *Edmund Husserl's Origin of Geometry: An Introduction* (Stony Brook, N.Y.: Nicholas Hays, 1978). Hereafter cited as I.

22. S. Bachelard, Berger, Blanchot, Cavaillès, Hyppolite, Levinas, Merleau-Ponty, de Muralt, Ricoeur, and Sartre in particular are Derrida's collaborators.

23. The "summing gesture" is a sentence followed by a footnote: the sentence begins, "And the latter is *grounded...*" (emphasis mine); the footnote reads, in part, "on a *deeper* level, theoretical consciousness, is nothing other, in itself and *thoroughly understood*, than a practical consciousness..." I, 136, n162.

24. Derrida's "conclusiveness" is what I take to be an effort to work out what is implicitly or explicitly necessitated as *articulations of* the summing gesture. Cf. I, 136–53.

25. How to understand this question of the how, the *quomodo*, is indeed grave since recourse to the "natural objectivity" of worldly existents is cut off, neutralized in principle, as contaminating or misleading.

26. Here Derrida quotes "Origin" 358.

27. Derrida specifies (I 71 n69) that at issue here are objectivities of the understanding whose mode of pregivenness is their production in the predicative activity of the Ego.

28. The series of Derrida's footnotes 65–80 (I 68–80) is an extraordinary massing of dimensions of the depth problem's articulation. This series is a crucial precursor to Derrida's other work of 1962, *Speech and Phenomena: And other Essays on Husserl's Theory of Sign*, trans. David Allison (Evanston: Northwestern University Press, 1973), hereafter SP, where the pen of Derrida has preeminence over the writing of Husserl.

29. In these pages I hope to have indicated a certain affinity or proximity between Merleau-Ponty and Derrida. Listen now to Merleau-Ponty in a working note dated May 1959.

> I. What is the "receptive" element of the absolute consciousness? H[usserl] is right to say that it is not I who constitute time.... But the term "receptivity" is improper precisely because it evokes a Self distinct from the present and who *receives* it—It must be understood simply by opposition to spontaneous acts....
>
> 3. What is the impressional consciousness... it is in reality not a term *effectively* untraversable.... And the "to be conscious" of this *Urerlebnis* is not coincidence, fusion with.... It is a perception—imperception, i.e., an operative and not thematized meaning (this is at bottom what Husserl means when he considers retention to be fundamental: that means that the absolute present which I am is as if it were not).
>
> 4. All this still leaves untouched the question: what is "to know," "to be conscious," "to perceive,"... A question never raised....

Self-presence *is* presence to a differentiated world—The perceptual separation [*écart*] as making up the "view" such as it is . . .
and enclosing being for itself by means of language as differentiation . . . one cannot go back any further. (VI 190–91)

30. Derrida cites the specific passage in "Origin" where Husserl recog-
    nizes this, and an earlier section in *Formal and Transcendental Logic*,
    p. 73, where the problem of constitution and expression arose with
    respect to "the idealizing presupposiitons of logic."
31. For Derrida's treatment of Husserl's developing sense of the unity of
    signification and linguistic ideality, see, in particular, I 66–76, 86–97,
    117–18, 124–34. For his treatment of idealization, see I 132–37. For
    his treatment of ideation, see I 134–35.
32. Derrida cites here *Crisis* II, 9A, p. 26.
33. "The principle of all principles: that every intuition that presents some-
    thing originarily is a source of legitimacy for knowledge, that every-
    thing presented to us originarily (in its 'flesh and blood' actuality as
    it were) in intuition is to be taken simply as that which presents it-
    self." *Ideas* 24.
34. The alterity which "structurally appears" presumably refers to the phasic
    character of auto-affection or self-temporalization experienced
    protentionally: if we think this experience impurely vis-à-vis acts.
35. The *my*, here, has to be understood *almost* purely gratuitously in this
    typicality of *structural* appearance.
36. Perhaps we must hear "The Voice That Keeps Silence" here. See SP
    82–85, esp. nn8 and 9.
37. It's unclear to me how to understand the phenomenological "function"
    of the impotence and impossible here evoked. This enunciation must
    be "correlated" with Derrida's abjured lack of lament. Cf. I 151–52,
    n184.
38. This phrase, "primordial and pure consciousness of . . . Difference"
    (ellipsis added) seems to me almost perfectly oxymoronic.
39. Derrida's deferrals, delays, differences, and disquietudes bear on
    dehiscence within the lament that "phenomenology is not an ontology."

10

Merleau-Ponty, Derrida, and Joyce's *Ulysses*: Is Derrida Really Bloom and Merleau-Ponty Dedalus, and Who Can Say "Yes" to Molly?

Glen A. Mazis

I. MERLEAU-PONTY AND DERRIDA: AN ODYSSEY'S
COMPARABLE NON-ORIGIN

Out of the cave, the mammoth Polyphemous roared in answer:
"Nobody, Nobody's tricked me, Nobody's ruined me!"
—Homer, *The Odyssey*[1]

Comparing Merleau-Ponty and Derrida is quite a formidable task, like taking on monsters or voyaging to far-off places. There seems to be lacking a common framework for comparison. Yet, Derrida uses an image from Joyce's *Ulysses* that contrasts the odysseys of its two main protagonists to contrast his writing with that of Levinas.[2] It may be even more apt to see how Merleau-Ponty and Derrida can be seen through these differing odysseys of *Ulysses'* Leopold Bloom and Stephen Dedalus. Leopold and Stephen, wanderers displaced in their personal histories—both drifting and struggling to forge relationships and to come to terms with the body, history, and writing (mirroring the dislocations within their culture)—are an uncanny supplement to Homer's Odysseus, who was portrayed as displaced already at the supposed origin of the Western tradition. Immediately, it seems as though we are in Derrida's domain, but it may even be more so Merleau-Ponty's.

Despite the fact that Merleau-Ponty and Derrida diverge on their odysseys as surely as Bloom and Dedalus do in *Ulysse*s, it is easy to forget that something about their struggle with a monstrous tradition makes a similar past appear—what Derrida would call a non-origin. Both Merleau-Ponty and Derrida take on the "metaphysics

167

of presence," which for them was like the Cyclops imprisoning Odysseus, blocking access to the fields and to wandering freely. For both Merleau-Ponty and Derrida, the Cyclops was the monocular Western philosophical tradition of Plato-to-Hegel, whose gaze was focused on seeking a truth of being and its reason. This tradition's claims for a universalizing foundation blocked access to the shifting material, historical, political, and cultural context of philosophy's articulation and to the means for unmasking the tyranny of its claims to adequation and certainty—as effectively as the boulder Cyclops put in the cave's entrance trapped Odysseus inside.

Like Odysseus, both Merleau-Ponty and Derrida answer "nobody" to the question posed to them as to the identity of the doer of deeds, which provides the key to undermining the unquestioned authority of the keepers. Like Odysseus, through this trick Merleau-Ponty and Derrida are released from remaining imprisoned. Both can no longer be kept contained within philosophy's previous bounds, and the former keepers of the cave do not know what to make of them and their words. It is as much a clash of perspectives between Odysseus and Polyphemus as it was between either Merleau-Ponty or Derrida and those of the Plato-to-Hegel tradition: Merleau-Ponty and Derrida articulated what the philosophical Cyclops prized as the crypt of truth—the inner core of knowledge and enlightenment—as a prison. Both Merleau-Ponty and Derrida demonstrate that the preservation of certain signifiers as keys of mastery against an encroaching world is a clumsy will to power. Both Merleau-Ponty and Derrida see the greedy grasping of the attempted logocentric closure of the project of knowing as yet another big bully, trying to devour wandering thinking as it passes by, or at least to capture and dominate it. The tradition's vision of a gaze as bright as the sun that would enclose all experience in a single vision is revealed by them not as the accomplishment of totality, but rather of totalitarianism.

Both Merleau-Ponty and Derrida can be seen to plunge stakes into the tradition's seeing eye, or "I," in concert with their response of "nobody" as site of perception or of writing—their response to Cyclops' question about who it is within the crypt or prison. Both Merleau-Ponty and Derrida, as surely as Odysseus did, take a burning stake and gouge it into the Cyclopean eye of the tradition, and do it irreparable violence. In Merleau-Ponty's insistence that perception does not offer universal verifiable inputs for cognition, but instead is a structuring, context-bound, power of dialogue intertwined with all other modes of understanding, implicates knowing in an indeterminacy of meaning. This undermines the notion of essence and the universality of a determinate truth, which were the organs of sight for this philosophical gaze. Equally violating to the tradition's vision, Derrida's articulation of writing as the "nobody" who responds through *différance*, in intertexuality, in the spacing of writing, and in the trace of the signifier, undermines the integrity of language as adequate description of either the doer or the deed, and gouges a hole in the tradition's ability to capture its vision and communicate truth.

The tradition misunderstood both Merleau-Ponty and Derrida in the very same way that Polyphemus misunderstood Odysseus, when he took an indication of an absence of relationship—a ploy or play of speech that deferred the direct grasping of the beings in his cave and announced they would not be revealed indubitably in their identity—as instead the straightforward name of a (reified) presence. Similarly, for the philosophical Cyclops—this monovision of the tradition—caught in dualisms, the mutilations of the means of knowing articulated by Merleau-Ponty and Derrida are taken to be foolish claims of a grasp of more immediate sources of being, whether in perception or language, that are opposed to the mental being of the detached thinker. The Cyclops can only understand an attack on its power in terms of an abstracted being of knowing versus a more immediate and effulgent presence—ready to admit that this ungraspable gap between the two will always remain, and also determined to defend the superior and exhaustive being of its choice in response to this dilemma. However, both Derrida and Merleau-Ponty mutilate the kind of vision that looked through the lens of this dualism, so that the philosophical Cyclops is utterly confused about the nature of the attack and the source of the critique of its vision. Merleau-Ponty and Derrida choose neither term of a series of traditional dualisms, but instead undermine the dichotomies. This is the utter craftiness of Merleau-Ponty and Derrida that makes either of them an Odysseus of the philosophical domain.

The Odyssean ploy can be seen in the texts of these wily thinkers. Merleau-Ponty states, "The I, really is nobody, is the anonymous. . . . is this negativity as openness, by the body, to the world."[3] Merleau-Ponty does not substitute for the traditionally identified subject—the "eye" and "I"—a "pre-reflective being," fully present but beyond the meager grasp of reflection, in the spirit of some sort of neo-Romanticism, as Sartre may well do. Instead Merleau-Ponty's "nobody" *undermines* the being/non-being, present/absent, necessary/contingent, mind/body dichotomies with their either/or

logic and background atemporal presumptions—each term is the
fiction of an opposition, where there should be an identity within
difference. This can be seen further in Merleau-Ponty's later description of a perceiving-becoming, when pointing to the place in
which the tradition had located the subject and its relationship to
its object. Instead Merleau-Ponty points to "two vortexes . . . the
one slightly decentered with respect to the other" (*The Visible and
the Invisible*, hereafter VI, 138). Neither perceiver nor perceived
stands outside of the ongoing becoming of world, so the announced
lack of a definite someone as source holds, but neither is there is
a mere void, a "hole in being" for Merleau-Ponty. In his later phrasing,
Merleau-Ponty calls this separation, which is an intertwining in
which there is a gap but also an identity within difference, *écart*.

Likewise, in Derrida's response to the Cyclops, there is a parallel in his description of *écriture* as that which points to nobody in
the place of the author: "writing" is marked by the "absence of the
signatory." For Derrida, too, there is a deconstruction of the dualism that would want to locate presence somewhere else as the ground
for this negation, but Derrida goes on to say that writing also is
"the absence of the referent," such that "writing is the name of
these two absences."[4] It is the name of two absences not as non-
being, but as a lack of a ground in which there is nevertheless a
play of differences, or, as Derrida articulates it, *différance*: "It belongs to no category of being, present or absent."[5] By undermining
the presence/absence dualism the logic of *différance* is meant to
both escape the Cyclops' prison, but also to mutilate its means of
vision: "In this way we question the authority of presence or its
simple symmetrical contrary, absence or lack. We thus interrogate
the limit that has always constrained us, that always constrains
us . . ." ("Différance," hereafter D 139). The either/or logic of the
one-eyed vision of the Plato-to-Hegel tradition is overcome for Derrida,
since "'*différance*' is neither simply active nor simply passive. . . .
it announces something like the middle voice" (D, 137). The play
of *différance* in writing—an "action" which is not an action and is
undertaken by nobody, by the inscription traced in language—also
undermines the being/non-being, present/absent and necessary/con-
tingent dichotomies of the tradition: "The concept of *play* [*jeu*]
remains beyond this opposition: on the eve and aftermath of philosophy, it designates the unity of chance and necessity in an endless calculus" (D 135).

Merleau-Ponty's evocation of the anonymous life of the body and
Derrida's response as the authorless inscription of writing were

both successful in toppling the tradition because both notions exploit the blind spot of seeing identity as sheer presence, as if the defile of sheep out of Cyclops' cave in The *Odyssey* is an adequate representation of being itself, in which time is a stage across which beings march on their way in the "now-point" of presentation. As Polyphemus, the Cyclops, became intoxicated with Odysseus' draughts of what Polyphemus called "ambrosia," so too the tradition, caught in the dichotomy of presence/eternity, was intoxicated in its quest for a transcendence of the series of temporal points, seeking the pure draught of an abiding eternal truth and essence.

One of the problems with this vision of time, for Merleau-Ponty, is its blindness to depth, which he envisions as the going together of incompossible temporalities through the unfolding-enfolding becoming of time. The body, in perception, in action, in expression, and in language, comes to articulate that which was neither not yet present, nor present but hidden, but rather was *founded* as a present *coming to be*, enacted and expressed: "It refers to an unreflective fund of experience which it presupposes, upon which it draws, and which constitutes for it a kind of original past, a past which has never been present."[6] There is no determinate arena as spatializing or temporalizing in which to be imprisoned or to which to be returned, but instead there is only a true odyssey, the working through of the body engaged in a nexus of interrelation, creating the promise of a future from a past that had not been, like the hand improvising on the keyboard—which in doing something novel makes its past become the history of that improvisation. The unfolding is also an enfolding of temporalities that brings into relation times which are not in linear or logical relation and become so in perceiving-acting.

Similarly, for Derrida, *différance* and trace are the origins of the origin, played out as having triumphantly emerged from the cave of darkness, but they were never there: "To say that *différance* is originary is simultaneously to erase the myth of a present origin. Which is why 'originary' must be understood as having been *crossed out*, without which *différance* would be derived from an original plenitude. It is a non-origin which is originary" ("Violence and Metaphysics," hereafter VM, 203). The trick against the Cyclops sets up a series of repetitions for Derrida, such that "the signifier is from the very beginning the possibility of its own repetition," (VM 91), which is the slippery course of writing, to be taken up as its play, "the presence-absence of the trace which one should not even call its ambiguity but rather its play" (VM 71). In writing, that which should have been an origin, but never was, is the play of the trace in the text. Writing as dissemination proliferates meanings in a time when repetitions differ among themselves, so always to slip away from the mythical crypt of truth of meaning of the metaphysical tradition.

The prison, or treasure-house, seen differently depending on one's position in the drama, in which captives or prizes were kept, was seen by both Merleau-Ponty and Derrida to be a construction of a castle in the air, since there was no "outside" as the keepers had believed. At the beginning of his writing, Merleau-Ponty stated that "the phenomenological world is not the bringing to explicit expression of a pre-existing being, but the laying down of being. Philosophy is not a reflection of a pre-existing truth, but, like art, the act of bringing truth into being" (*Phenomenology of Perception*, hereafter PP, xx). Yet, for Merleau-Ponty, philosophy is always this process—this "laying-down"—a continued expression of the inexhaustible. Even in his earliest formulations, Merleau-Ponty's sense of philosophy was as an articulation "never knowing where it was going," and never getting there, designated in his latest writings as "interrogation." Derrida also states of writing that "in short, the classical system's 'outside' can no longer take the form of the sort of extra-text which would arrest the concatenation of writing (i.e., that movement which situates every signified as a differential trace)."[7] For Derrida, writing does not capture the pre-existent logos. Merleau-Ponty and Derrida deny a progress toward a triumphal homecoming to a truth from which we have been exiled and to which perception or the transcendental signified of language could serve as a conveyance back to origins.

However, an *odyssey*, despite its appearance to the contrary, is not a return home, even if one does arrive in Ithaca. As the Cyclops cannot contain the one odysseying, and his efforts will become a part of the odyssey, so it is the case that the movement of the flesh as *écart* or *différance* within writing, as articulated by Merleau-Ponty and Derrida, has no beginning, end, or destination—and cannot be confined. So, both Merleau-Ponty and Derrida make philosophy into an odyssey. This is non-philosophy insofar as philosophy since Plato has been the nostalgia to regain a lost home.

For Plato, philosophers, and all inquirers know in their soul the answer that would give their soul the closure of winging back to its true abode. Merleau-Ponty and Derrida destroyed the tradition of overcoming space, time, and wandering in thought and word. Instead, Merleau-Ponty sought words most "charged with philosophy" that would "not necessarily contain what they say," but would rather "convey the life of the whole and make our habitual evidences vibrate until they disjoin" (VI 102). For Merleau-Ponty "the interrogative is not the mode derived by inversion or by reversal of the indicative and of the positive, but an original manner of aiming at something, as it were a *question-knowing*, which by principle no statement or 'answer' can go beyond" (VI 129). For Merleau-Ponty, the crypt of truth was never full. Similarly, for Derrida, writing is "another name for this structure of supplementarity" (*Of Grammatology*, hereafter GR, 245), but it is not a supplementarity which adds toward a totalization, but instead, in a field of infinite substitutions—of play—it takes the center's place in its absence. The supplement is a surplus of signification, "adds something which results in the fact that there is always more, but this addition is a floating one because it comes to perform a vicarious function, to supplement a lack on the part of the signified."[8] So, for Merleau-Ponty this "question-knowing" is not a hearkening back to what was always knowable and known in some fashion, as in some Platonic recollection, but the original grasp of truth is only presumed and kept alive by being kept open in its "gaping-open," as, for Derrida, the supplement does not add to what was signified, but rather keeps open its lack.

II. Differing Supplements in *Ulysses*: Different Philosophical Odysseys?

But this disappointment issues from that spurious fantasy which claims for itself a positivity capable of making up for its own emptiness. It is the regret of not being everything, and a rather groundless regret at that.

—Maurice Merleau-Ponty[9]

For a very long time, the question of the *yes* has mobilized or traversed everything I have been trying to think, write, teach or read.

—Jacques Derrida[10]

If Merleau-Ponty and Derrida have indeed attempted to make philosophy qua non-philosophy into an odyssey, a point of departure is presented in a remark written by Derrida in an essay considering the violence of the tradition of metaphysics, in which he responds to this Cyclops by recalling Joyce's evocation of Odysseus in the dual figures of Stephen Dedalus and Leopold Bloom in *Ulysses*: "And what is the legitimacy, what is the meaning of the *copula* in

this proposition from perhaps the most Hegelian of modern novel-
ists: 'Jewgreek is greekjew. Extremes meet'?" (VM 153). Derrida calls
Stephen "the Hellenic Jew." In Derrida's discussion, it is the Jew
who is the one for whom there is the infinitely Other. For the
Greek, there is the drive to capture transcendence within the mesh
of *logos*. It seems a fair reading of Stephen that he is the Hellenic
Jew in his long-suffering war with Catholic guilt, in his long struggle with writing as a trying to face the absent call of the still-felt,
crushingly powerful and distant Other. Stephen's odyssey across
Dublin cannot return home, because he is still called to find an
alter of this absent Other. On the other hand, Bloom wears his
identity as Jew during his long march across Dublin and through
this fateful day, 16 June 1904. He seems to be seeking the Other in
his abandonment by Molly, by his dead son, and by his absent
father (who killed himself), yet not only is he revealed not to be
Jewish in a brief aside toward the end of the book, but he has
demonstrated that he is the Greek who does articulate wonder in
his ongoing commentary to himself throughout his odyssey, and
sees wonder everywhere in a Greek, burning passion for this life
and its sensual shapes. So, Leopold is Jewgreek.

Derrida's fascinating footnote to this citation from Joyce takes
issue with Levinas's reading of *Ulysses* as a nostalgic return home
and a "closing of the circle." Derrida wonders if the return home
of *Ulysses* does not harbor some other logic, a logic which Derrida
approaches by citing Joyce's calling it a "feminine logic," where
wandering endlessly and returning home are not opposites—where
there is some copula which brings into play Bloom and Stephen,
Jewgreek and Greekjew.

The kind of voyaging that Bloom and Stephen inscribe seems to
parallel the philosophical journeys of Merleau-Ponty and Derrida—
one taken into endless meditations on perception and action in
the world in order to found the body and its felt relations as an
answer to death, while the other worries about how to write and
how writing reveals the nature of language as a response to the
presence of death from before it was born and as response to the
threat of the father. What sort of relationship between embodiment
and language do Bloom and Dedalus each articulate in the writing
of Joyce that could throw light upon the relationship of Derrida
and Merleau-Ponty? Derrida, in his contrasting himself with Levinas,
seems to cast himself as a Bloomian Ulysses. Does this also make
Merleau-Ponty a Stephen Dedalus, wandering still within the Hellenic world of logocentrism—another kind of "Saint Stephen, the

Hellenic Jew," in believing in the Otherness of the perceived world? This vision could be supported by remembering that Bloom is a wonderful trickster of language, and that Stephen could be seen to be looking into the world to find another kind of truth than the rejected Catholicism of Ireland. Or did the impossibility of Bloom's movement away from his father's suicide, his son's death, foreclosed in time, never having been put underway, open the opportunity for another space, another language, that the non-Jew Merleau-Ponty finds where Bloom found it, in the flesh—the flesh of the world? Bloom, the archetypal Jewish wanderer, revealed in passing after 700 pages of *Ulysses*'s text to not really be Jewish, is he Merleau-Ponty? Is the Jewish Derrida a Stephen Dedalus, the one who writes but can't write a book, who gives a theory of the impossibility of language being its birth, yet lives circling within language's charms—a wanderer and writer who tricks us into believing he has given an odyssey?

In the early chapters of *Ulysses*, Stephen Dedalus begins his wandering, realizing that "Thought is the thought of thought,"[11] as he ponders the Mass, his mother, and guilt; that "I fear those big words that make us so unhappy" (*Ulysses*, hereafter UL 26) as he discusses nationalism and justice; and that "History is a nightmare from which I am trying to awake" (UL 28) as he struggles to project his life. He is committed to writing and to the spell of thought in language, yet the specter of his dying mother, asking him to pray for her and his silent refusal to her last wish, still blocks his way to language years later.

The third chapter opens with Stephen's attempt to discern the nature of perception and its relation to reality:

> thought through my eyes. Signatures of all things that I am here to read, seaspawn and seawrack, the nearing tide, the rusty boot. Snotgreen, bluesilver, rust: coloured signs. Limits of the diaphane, But he adds: in bodies. Then he was aware of them bodies before them coloured. How? By knocking his sconce against them, sure. Go easy. (UL 31)

Stephen at first sets up the dyad signifier and signified, and then posits a brute facticity prior, but rejects this schema as too easy an answer for a mind as penetrating as Stephen's. He also realizes, in a passage almost identical to one from Derrida above, that time cast as linear, inexorable, will repress and fail to repress the lack of presence that the dyad of the signifier-signified was supposed to betoken Greekwise. At first, as Aristotelean, he declares, "I am,

astride in time. A very short space. A very short space of time
through very short times of space. Five, six: the *Nacheinander*."
However, he sees that if he "fell through the *Nacheinander* ineluctably" (UL 31)—there is the void, falling and death. Within this
dyadic logic there is only "Shut your eyes and see," darkness and
light, within and without, falling into the void or bumping against
"there all the time without you: and ever shall be, world without
end."

Joyce also presents the reader with another dimension when
Stephen attends to "Crush, crack, crick, crick. Wild sea money."
As Stephen takes up the movement of the sea, his experience shifts,
"Rhythm begins, you see. I hear," but Stephen cannot stay with
this Bloomian moment. Stephen, who is no phenomenologist, passes
it by, and returns to his visual, linguistic experiments.

Stephen's brilliance at articulating the lack of presence comes in
his pronouncement of his theory of language and meaning, in the
ninth chapter of this eighteen-chapter work, the chapter of this
odyssey entitled "Scylla and Charybdis"—articulated under the guise
of discussing Shakespeare. Stephen is able to admit to his inter-
locutors that the lack of presence that marks existence could betoken a kind of openness upon the world as an experience of
intertwining:

> Creation from nothing. What has she in the bag? A misbirth with
> a traveling navelcord, hushed in ruddy wool. The cords of all
> link back, strandentwining cable of all flesh. This is why mystic
> monks. Will you be as gods? Gaze in your *omphalos*. Hello! Kinch
> here. Put me on to Edenville. Alpha, alpha: nought, nought, one.
> (UL 32)

For Stephen, this intertwining of the flesh as some founding experience could only be some signification within the binary system,
presence or absence, one or nought, materialism or mysticism, and
he wisely abandons these dyads. Instead, Stephen turns to the text,
to writing, to find the opening of sense.

In his theory of language, Stephen finds the power of weaving
as unweaving (UL 157) emerging in writing, "so that through the
ghost of the unquiet father the image of the unliving son looks
forth" (UL 160). Stephen disputes the notion that father and son
reconcile in language, but instead insists it is the place of sundering, a sundering which is always repeating: "The images of other
males of his blood will repel him. He will see in them grotesque
attempts of nature to foretell or to repeat himself" (UL 161). Writing emerges as the soul has been given poison through the ears

(UL 161)—pharmakon-cure-poison—as language always turns else-where and backwards (UL 162), as language is "ravisher and rav-ished" (UL 162), and its repetitive course is one in which "no later undoing will undo the first undoing." For Stephen, this is an affirmation of the text, of writing, in its movement from the undo-ing of death, the father, and ravishment—the non-origin—to fur-ther undoing.

Shakespeare, for Stephen, is not a graced genius, is not the man who can become his own father. Shakespeare, as Stephen's inter-locutors suggest, is the power of writing. For Stephen, "A father ... is a necessary evil" (UL 170): the ghost, the promise of the origin one wishes to recapture, but cannot be found in the play of the text, as a play of time, of repetitions which never recapture, yet never start anew. One finds in writing, not identity, not author-ship, but what Stephen can only call "overplus" (UL 172):

> When Rutlandbaconsouthhamptonshakespeare or another poet of the same name in the comedy of errors wrote *Hamlet* he was not father of his own son merely but, being no more a son, he was and felt himself the father of all his race, the father of his grand-father, the father of his unborn grandson who, by the same to-ken, never was born, for nature, as Mr. Magee understands her, abhors perfection. (UL 171)

For Stephen, in the text, "we walk through ourselves," as Rutlandbaconsouthhamptonshakespeare—emblem of author—finds in the tracing of his writing the marking of his thought of thought. For Stephen, in this walking through ourselves we are "always meeting ourselves," but not in the self-recollection of self-conscious-ness—the inner voice—but in the endless proliferation of names, roles, signifiers that Stephen could probably toss off for pages, if his interlocutors had enough play in them. The latter are disap-pointed to hear this theory that Stephen admits he doesn't believe, or rather, a page later he admits he does—he "unbelieves" it. The interlocutors cannot believe "you have brought us all this way to show us a French triangle" (UL 175). Stephen/Joyce arrives at Derrida.

Writing and death. In "Freud and the Scene of Writing," Derrida writes:

> Is it not already death at the origin of life which can defend itself against death only through an economy of death, through deferment, repetition, reserve? For repetition does not happen to an initial impression; its possibility is already there, in the re-sistance offered *the first time*. . . ."[12]

Freud had demonstrated that it is the life instinct to differ/defer—
différance—through its series of productions its inevitable and
impossible return to sheer presence—death. The text, writing, is
that non-origin that accomplishes *différance*. Stephen and Derrida
odyssey to disbelieve death into life through writing. Yet, can death
be disbelieved through the "necessary evil of the father"?

   For Leopold Bloom, the odyssey across Dublin is a darkened one,
as his wife commits adultery during this day, as Bloom faces the
death of a compatriot at a funeral, as the paralysis he has felt at
the death of his young son, the suicide of his father from his own
childhood, his decade-long estrangement from Molly since their
son's death, come to be overwhelmingly palpable, comprehended
finally, and thus enter in the unfolding of his time on this wandering day. This day that he ends not by coming back home—for a
true odyssey has no homecoming, but rather comes to itself—in *its
path as wandering*. It never returns to the spot it departed from,
despite often returning to the same location in a Cartesian space-
time grid—as Bloom indeed does. For Bloom (whom Joyce honors
as "distinguished phenomenologist" in a dreamlike fantasy sequence
in "nighttown," inscribed upon a vellum scroll and presented to
him just as he had been berated as a Jew), as he wanders through
the day, "Everything speaks in its own way." However, what he
means by this is not that there is a "natural language" or a "universal language" of the senses, which Lynch and Stephen discuss
as a theory of language that would be "pornophilosophical
philotheology" (UL 353), but rather that for him there is "wealth
of the world," even on this day of odyssey, death, and peril—where
the perceptions of the street assail him and "his brain yielded.
Perfume of embraces all him assailed. With hungered flesh obscurely,
he mutely craved to adore" (UL 138). After the funeral he ponders
"the stream of life," but has no adequate name for its meaning, so
he considers his upcoming bath and its "gentle tepid stream," which
gives him his only rejoinder: "This is my body" (UL 71).

   Bloom, like Stephen, also a lover of texts, considers writing as
his deferral of death: "*Let my epitaph be*. Kraaaaaa. *Written*. I have./
Pprrpffrrppffff./*Done*" (UL 238). However, he cannot remain within
writing: sound, non-sense, the indirect voices obtrude. For Bloom,
writing always empties itself out, not just in an internal economy
of death, non-presence, *différance*, but also into silences, the hungers of the sensual-fantastic-imagined-memorial-voiced blooming of
a world of inter-course. The world as bloom, for Leopold, can come
erupting into existence—as on the day in Gibraltar decades ago—

with "Howth below us bay sleeping: sky. No sound," lying with Molly, the hill, the sky, the seedcake in their mouths. This moment is one by which the entire sensorium causes him to be "ravished," and he has become "No-one" (UL 144). The power of the moment is such that it overtakes him at lunch a decade and a half later. When Bloom and Stephen meet at the end of their odysseys, Bloom is not bothered by the lack of light, "because of the surety of the sense of touch in his firm full masculine feminine passive active hand." Bloom repeatedly seeks himself by being taken over in his perceptual, affect-riddled round of encounters, whether with breakfast delicacies or with the wood grain of the bar at the tavern.

For Bloom, the body's promise of love is not an answer to death, nor does it give an outside to language that would be redemptive, that would give a non-linguistic origin and touchstone. In wonderful counterpoint to Stephen's "thought is thought of thought," Bloom articulates that "Love loves to love love" (UL 273). Love too is non-origin, coming back to its ever non-present—casting itself as that which it never was and will never be, in attempting to become itself through itself. It too has its place in the binary opposites of naming: "Love, says Bloom, I mean the opposite of hatred." If taken as transcendental signifier, love too becomes bathetic: "You love a certain person. And this person loves that other person because everybody loves somebody but God loves everybody" (UL 273). Bloom certainly cannot stomach this, not on a day when his wife, with whom he has slept head-to-toe for a decade, is taking a lover, not on a day in which he is plagued by so many deaths. However, for Bloom, like Merleau-Ponty, there is a limit here, which speaks of another kind of truth than the tradition of one-eyed truths. After the funeral, Bloom thinks of his dead son, Rudy, of the end of the name, "Bloom," of the hatred he could feel and says, "Hate. Love. Those are names. Rudy. Soon I am old" (UL 237). It is his own impending death which cannot be textualized, that strips away this play of signifiers. There is a difference that Stephen and Derrida cannot accommodate in the economy of *différance* between all the texts of death, which do give us a face with which to face its glare; but, *acting* in the face of this outstripping, ultimate call—as Heidegger rightly calls death—breaks all economies. There is a reason why Stephen still cannot write in the face of his mother's last request: her cold flesh never will be textualized.

Bloom is quite aware of the power of the text in its non-presence: "In spite of careful and repeated reading of certain classical passages, aided by a glossary, he had derived imperfect conviction from the text, the answers not bearing in all points" (UL 554). Bloom does not say this as a nostalgic lament for clarity of grasping understanding (or actually Joyce, who is the one who says this from his omniscient perspective), for he sees that there is not even a referent for his own proper name, despite others' pretense to that effect: "From inexistence to existence he came to many and was as one received: existence with existence he was with any as any with any: from existence to nonexistence gone he would be by all as none perceived" (UL 545). Yet, Bloom knows, on this day, that this impending death can lead to an absence of the Dubliners rootless in time, and instead he undertakes the odyssey of committing to a time that transforms.

Bloom sees himself facing the riddle of Polyphemus to Odysseus:

What universal binomial denominations would be his as entity and nonentity?

Assumed by any or known to none. Everyman or Noman. (UL 599)

Bloom, like Merleau-Ponty, will not enter through Scylla and Charybdis—will not assume a universal essence nor a mere lack of identity—but rather the ambiguity he finds is in an embodied thickness of self and world in which one is called to act. Act even on a day of crisis, which can render the past decade an odyssey, or, as Merleau-Ponty would put it, a *passage*—which is neither rest or movement as seen in the binary categories of presence and absence. It is truly becoming as affirming the intertwining of flesh. For Bloom to so journey, he has to answer the riddle of the odyssey:

What would render such a return irrational?

An unsatisfactory equation between an exodus and return in time through reversible space and an exodus and return space through irreversible time. (UL 599)

Space is not reversible for beings who as flesh take up their intertwinings with the world, for it is not the same 9 Eccles Street to which Bloom returns that night. Nor is time irreversible, for in taking an odyssey that day Bloom is able to find the time of Molly's being-in-the-world of Gibraltar of decades ago, to find his son's death finally in the becoming of time, and to find the place that had never been there for them in their bed this past decade, in which they might come to lie together again. To achieve this, one would have to—in a Heideggerian sense—without any basis and being outstripped, answer that which truly has no answer, not the Sphinx, not the Cyclops, but death—one's own death and the death of those one loves.

There is no adequate response in writing to death, nor should we hold up this chimera to language, for it is a smokescreen which hides its abuses as will to power of the basest kind: for this reminder about this cruel trick, we should thank Merleau-Ponty, Derrida, Bloom, and Stephen, who all reveal it. However, the latter two meditate on this situation together in the following inverse and indicative fashion:

Did Stephen participate in his dejection?

He affirmed his significance as a conscious rational animal proceeding syllogistically from the known to the unknown and a conscious reagent between a micro and a macrocosm ineluctably constructed upon the incertitude of the void.

Was this affirmation apprehended by Bloom?

Not verbally. Substantially.

What comforted this misapprehension?

That as a competent keyless citizen he had proceeded energetically from the unknown to the known through the incertitude of the void." (UL 572)

Bloom, unlike Stephen, has emerged from the non-origin of non-presence, to a place of truth of a differing sort, of acting, of engagement, even though "keyless," without solutions or adequate responses. He understands certain aspects of his world substantially, outside of language. Bloom, as Merleau-Ponty would concur, sees language as the power of the gesture of the body. Gesture is meant to address that to which it is not adequate but is nevertheless com-pelling. Rather than the emptiness of the signifier, it is the hunger, the lived call to further action by the world, which Merleau-Ponty saw as the power of both language and the gaps within it to point beyond language. This hunger moves Leopold on, to odyssey. He is left feeling hungers, for breakfast made by Molly, for Molly's body, that he had not felt without this passage of 16 June 1904.

As Stephen leaves, Bloom has an experience that Stephen and

Derrida would see only as more text, but for Bloom it is another indirect and silent voice which is his interlocutor:

Alone, what did Bloom feel?

The cold of interstellar space, thousands of degrees below freezing point or the absolute zero of Fahrenheit, Centigrade or Reaumur: the incipient intimations of proximate dawn. (UL 578)

As embodied, Bloom and all humans are woven into a fabric of sense, a flesh wider than that of the human world, hearing a larger multivocity and pluralism. This is what Merleau-Ponty articulates:

Say that the things are structure, frameworks, the stars of our life: not before us laid out as perspective spectacles, but gravitating about us.

Such things do not presuppose man, who is made of their flesh. But yet their eminent being can be understood only by him who enters into perception, and with it keeps in distant-contact with them—.(VI 220)

This is the kind of vision and the kind of affirmation of his flesh that Leopold attains, which allows him an odyssey—a true passage—and will allow him to arrive at the non-home which, on this day, is the coming to a history that had been sedimented but never was:

Somewhere imperceptibly he would hear and somehow reluctantly, suncompelled, obey the summons of recall. Whence disappearing from the constellation of the Northern Crown he would somehow reappear above delta in the constellation of Cassiopeia. (UL 598)

Bloom is caught intertwined with the world's unfolding, which constantly remakes what was never quite there, but becomes to be. It comes to be only as still, yet caught up in the doubling-back fabric of Dublin, of innumerable crossing lives, and even of the seawrack of the tides at Dublin's beach, as well as with the constellation of Cassiopeia.

III. SAYING "YES" TO MOLLY

The eschatological final "Yes" occupies the place of the signature at the bottom right of the text. Even if one distinguishes, as one must, Molly's "Yes" from that of *Ulysses*, of which she is but a figure and a moment, even if one distinguishes, as one must also do, these two signatures (that of Molly and that of

Ulysses) from that of Joyce, they read each other and call out to each other. To be precise, they call to each other across a *yes.* . . .

—Jacques Derrida[13]

Yet there is a world of silence, the perceived world, at least, is an order where there are non-language significations—yes, non-language significations, but they are not accordingly positive. There is for example no absolute flux of singular *Erlebnisse*; there are fields and a field of fields. . . .

—Maurice Merleau-Ponty[14]

Both Merleau-Ponty and Derrida saw that the insistence on presence in the Western metaphysical tradition was an attempt to will a power over being and over others from a vantage that disallowed the mortality and vulnerability that has cast Bloom and Stephen on their weary search across Dublin. By contrast, Merleau-Ponty's notion of perceptual faith and *écart* and Derrida's of writing and *différance* are resistances to a mortality, a contingency, and a lack of foundation (or origin), which recognize and articulate it in their resistance.

To consider Derrida first, if writing is a deferral of death that also always speaks of itself, then it too is the kind of recognition that has plagued Leopold, Stephen, and Molly on 16 June 1904. Indeed, Derrida writes, "The trace is the erasure of selfhood, of one's own presence, and is constituted by the threat of anguish of its irremediable disappearance, of the disappearance of its disappearance" ("Freud and the Scene of Writing," hereafter FS, 230). In looking at Derrida's notions, one might say that language as ongoing dissemination is the death we die continually—a transposition of the Heideggerian being-unto-death into *écriture*: "This erasure is death itself" (FS 230). Yet, there is a fine line between a recognition of death—a being-unto-death—that defers in a creativity that is Eros, the life spirit, and one which becomes a blind spot, a refusal such that neither Eros nor Thanatos receives its due. Rather than odyssey, at that point of denial of death (and its ongoing lucid deferral as life) one becomes a lost wanderer, a shade wandering through a barren Dublin. This is the question that Molly poses to Derrida, by stating "Yes." Hers is an affirmation of a re-found promise of life while looking at the throes of death. Death in the guise of her lost son, her lost mother, her lost youth, and the lost bloom of love with Leopold assail her, and yet she re-finds in the past that perhaps had never been until this moment a "yes" in response.

Derrida, always writing of the *yes*, given the opportunity of opening the Ninth International James Joyce Symposium in Frankfurt in 1984, "only knew I wanted to discuss the *yes* in *Ulysses*" (FS 266), and is so fascinated with the *yes* that he counts the 222 *yeses* in the version of *Ulysses* he reads. For Derrida, "The final 'Yes,' the last word, the eschatology of the book, yields itself only to *reading*" (FS 274). In part, Derrida explains this as a function of the capital letter, "inaudible, yet visible." Yet, what *yes* is for Derrida is a matter of *reading*—and of *écriture* and *différance*. Yet, it is a question of whether grammatology can say *yes* in this way—whether Molly can be assented to as a matter of reading and writing.

Derrida sees that *Ulysses* is a call that summons a response, like a call on the telephone, but Joyce has used the gramophone. "*Ulysses*, an immense postcard" (UG 260), as Derrida calls it, sent from "the great circular return, the autobiographic-encyclopedic circumnavigation of Ulysses" ("Ulysses" Gramophone," hereafter UG, 262), is the sending of the message of "yes," which Derrida says uncharacteristically can be seen to be sent by either Joyce or Molly, and getting caught in that discussion would be "chatter" (UG 295). Derrida notes that all *yeses* are a way that "language *remarks* the language itself," or doubly affirms: "once by speaking it and saying it and once by saying it thus has been spoken" (UG 257). In this sense of the *yes*, Derrida notes that "there is a great temptation, in French but first of all in English, to double up everything with a kind of continuous *yes*" (UG 290), which would be the way in which language comments on itself, that speaking is happening, that it is written, or that you are receiving, and so forth. One says, "yes, I got it." We can see why, for Derrida, then, the *yes* would traverse everything that he's written about. As he states this sense of *yes*: "In short, *yes* would be transcendental adverbiality, the ineffaceable supplement to any verb" (UG 297).

The *yes* taken this way actually implies a requested affirmation of itself by the other as it accomplishes this for itself: "The self-affirmation of the *yes* can address itself to the other only in recalling itself to itself, in saying *yes, yes* (UG 303). As Derrida admits, this makes the *yes* a rather comic act, a sending of a dispatch to oneself and "a sending-back [*renvoi*] of self to self" that "both never leaves itself and never arrives at itself." This makes Molly's *yes* a comic gesture: "She reminds herself, that she says *yes* is asking the other to ask her to say *yes*, and she starts and finishes by saying *yes* to the other in herself, but she does so in order to say to the other that she will say *yes* if the other asks her, yes, to say *yes* (UG 303). Such a *yes*-saying could be offered as what it is: a play, a trick, a circle that can never close upon itself. Derrida hears this as one of the *yeses* of *Ulysses*, as the signature of Joyce with Molly and their readers, to enjoy this lack of closure, to laugh in saying *yes*. This makes of Joyce a trickster, that *Ulysses* is a trick played and a grand tour of laughter, that is the supplement to Odysseus, the ruse player (UG 292–93).

Derrida also articulates another *yes*, to which this yes of laughter is a response. In some (inaccurate) sense, there is the "initial" *yes*—but given the Derridian logic of *différance*, the initial *yes* already is its own response, and could match the second yes as a shared but differing laughter—and be a *yes* that came to laugh at itself, as never having been present that way but now being part of this "yes, yes" as yes-laughter. However, Derrida also states of the signature that it "requires a *yes* more 'ancient' than the question 'what is?' since this question presupposes it, a *yes* more ancient than knowledge . . . because there can be a *yes* without a word" (UG 296). Rather than this always being a self-sending that becomes comic, it could be a *yes* that Derrida attributes to Bloom as the *yes* of "an 'implicit believer' in some summons of the other." This *yes*, which will become an answer that it is not yet (to a question to be posed) in another's *yes*, "sometimes has the force of an originary and unconditional commitment" (UG 265). Of course, Derrida does not develop this *yes*. However, it may be that when as Derrida says, "Bloom is always waiting for an answer, for someone to say 'hello, yes,' for someone to say, 'Yes, yes,'" that he receives his response from Molly in a way that the joke is on Derrida, and is a matter of commitment for them.

Derrida acknowledges that there is a *yes* as an interjection, as "the perfume of discourse" (UG 297). He admits that Leopold, voyager of the body and the senses as source of writing and thinking, is the person who follows Molly's perfume on his wanderings, and follows the world as dimension of perfumes. Unlike the performative yes, which is a promise, an intention, a comment upon itself and what is being said, there is a *yes* in this Bloomian realm that is "neither tautological nor narcissistic, it is not egological even if it initiates the movement of circular reappropriation, the odyssey that can give rise to all these determined modalities. It holds open the circle that it institutes" (UG 392). He calls this *yes* "preontological," but states that it exists only in the supplementarity of the *yes* of yes-laughter. This other Blooomian *yes*, which we might call with a Derridian flourish *perfumative*, can only be within the yoked *yes* of the performative—the response that comments on its articulation in a playful way. For Derrida, the *yeses* are twins, the one is the gramophony of the other.

We must say that Derrida cannot say "yes" to Molly. The best he can do is answer "yes, yes." He warns us, too, that "the *yes* keeps restarting itself, an infinite number of times" (UG 309). So one wonders, in response to Molly, if Derrida could even limit himself to "yes, yes." Derrida, at best, remains with laughter, the comedy of the text, but that does not really answer the *no* to which Molly and Leopold have found a response—*no* of death.[15] Derrida derides Bloom for being on call in a Heideggerian being-toward-death as a Bloomian being-at-the-telephone awaiting a *yes* (UG 272), but language itself can be towards-death if written in its own *yes*, rather than being caught in its circle of "yes, yes"—only commenting on itself. Derrida sees himself following Nietzsche's laughter of *yes, yes* (UG 287), but for Nietzsche this Derridian double-yes laughter would be the laughter of ice. Nietzsche's laughter always has a subterranean seriousness, which includes both a recognition of "going under" (death) and above all remains faithful to the earth.

Perception, for Merleau-Ponty, is an awareness that each articulation is a groping that never reaches closure, that believes it will find sense; but as *écart*, as the sensing sensible, it is both separate and inseparable from its perceived world—always on "this side" of itself, despite coming back to itself from depths beyond it. Yet, in perception, there is a rent or tearing of being part of tides of existence that carry one away. Molly in bed that night feels herself mired in herself and her slide toward death, and at the same time is pulled into other landscapes and other people, and especially into the bloom that was and is still there with Leopold. For Merleau-Ponty, there is this unending reversibility with the world, the long circle of coming back to oneself, the odyssey of differing lengths in space and time which interweave in the fabric of our lives, but it is not reciprocal, and in the end must face the silence of death, the body caught up in a world of other forces whose voices reach us indirectly.

In one of the rare passages in which Merleau-Ponty speaks of sensing one's death, he locates this sense in the fact "that every sensation carries within it the germ of a dream or a depersonalization such as we experience in the quasi-stupor to which we are reduced when we really try to live at the level of sensation." When we allow ourselves to feel most fully this nobody of the body through whom the tides of the world run as flow of sensations, we reach a

state like Molly in bed on that night in Dublin. Merleau-Ponty states
that we experience that "this activity takes place on the periphery
of my being." From this vantage, he states, "I can, then, apprehend myself only as 'already born' and 'still alive'—I can apprehend my birth and my death only as prepersonal horizons"—as
the nobody who odysseys through a foreign world. As with Molly,
in this state I am carried beyond myself to an openness to the
world, where landscapes like that of Gibraltar in its flowering richness
and damp leaking away speak to the anonymous one of the body.
Merleau-Ponty says we are in doubt about death as knowers, but
at this level of sensation, at the heart of perception, another indirect voice speaks to us from the world:

> Each sensation, being strictly speaking, the first, last and only
> one of its kind, is a birth and a death. The subject who experi-
> ences it begins and ends with it, and as he can neither precede
> nor survive himself, sensation necessarily appears to itself in a
> setting of generality, its origin anterior to itself, it arises from
> *sensibility* which has preceded it and will outlive it, just as my
> birth and my death belong to a natality and a mortality which
> are anonymous. By means of sensation I am able to grasp on the
> fringe of my personal life and acts, a life of given consciousness
> from which the latter emerge, the life of my eyes, hands and
> ears, which are so many natural selves. Each time I experience a
> sensation, I feel it concerns not my own being, not the one for
> which I am responsible and for which I make decisions, but another
> self which has already sided with the world, which is already
> open to certain of its aspects and synchronized with them.
> (PP 216)

In the end, it is in giving oneself over to the anonymous core of
perception, as artists have often done, that one experiences both
the power of death that runs through our lives, but also the very
buoyancy of tides, not of our own making, that ripple with life's
own power, which carries us inexorably to the end of our personal
existence. This calls for a different sort of *yes* than Derrida speaks
of in distinguishing at least ten different senses of *yes* in Ulysses,
but the closest is that unexplored Bloomian *yes*.

The Cyclopean tradition fled from the body as this perceptual
enmeshment in the world—as flesh of the world—because of the
threat of facticity: that we were part of a becoming which meant
our personal extinction, and tried to extract from it the certainty
of a presence captured by the word which named essence. The
Derridian opposite strategy of denying presence, and again retreating

to disembodiment and language, is still the same retreat from the body as enmeshed in a world ambiguously, reversibly, and shiftingly present. The traditional insistence on an underlying foundation of absolute presence, outside of time and represented by language, and the opposing claim that language is caught in itself in the self-devouring of a timing and spacing which slips away from presenting itself, are both retreats from a time in which there is a becoming, always transforming, but having the ability to present us with a face to which we must respond beyond our words.

For Leopold, for Merleau-Ponty, this return is always contained in the gaps of language, which are its hunger, not a gap between the bar of signified and signifier. For some, they can feel the palpable presence of Molly Bloom within the heart of her absence as text, deferred, chimera of *différance*, but nevertheless posing a questioning-contact that resonates within their enmeshment in the world with others. Joyce/Molly's notions are not Hegelian, as Derrida sometimes calls them, not nostalgic, nor do they lead to the closure of the Western metaphysics.

Of the two who set out on an odyssey—Merleau-Ponty and Derrida—only Merleau-Ponty can say "yes" to Molly, because the yes *that* is adequate to her question is the one delivered in silence, "outside" of language. It is not "outside" as some "untouched" or "unshaped" virgin territory, since as Merleau-Ponty puts it language "overruns" the landscape. Silence is not the opposite of language. It is found by allowing the gaps in language that call one to stand to face a world calling for the leap of commitment, since it is not graspable but only perceivable—where perception is understood equally as intertwined with feeling, imagining, dreaming, and remembering—the flesh of the world. Merleau-Ponty states this brilliantly in pointing to all of us, as embodied beings, as taking up the path of Odysseus:

> The perceiving subject, as a tacit, silent *Being-at* [*Etre-à*] which returns from the thing blindly identified, which is only a *separation* [*écart*] with respect to it—the *self* of perception as "nobody," in the sense of Ulysses, as the anonymous one buried in the world, and that has not yet traced its path. (VI 201)

For Merleau-Ponty, each perceiver must return from an odyssey through the perceptual world which always withholds, as "excess" sense, that which outstrips language and is an ongoing source for new articulation and for explorations of new paths of significance. Language and thought, as well as perception and the unfolding of one's existence, can never ultimately grasp where they are going. In the end, there is the gesture that points back to a world as witness, as "being-at"—both bound up with and torn loose. It is this gesture of affirmation, which we shape with words and also with acts that must plunge back into tides beyond our fathoming, that is the *yes* that Molly and Bloom may find again. Whether using words to show language's gaps or communicating by other means, the text of this *yes* is silence.

Molly's return home follows what Derrida shrewdly called a "feminine logic," when in comparison he derides Levinas for being trapped in a writing "impossible ... to have been written by a woman," and for displaying "an essential virility of metaphysical language" (VM 320–21). Merleau-Ponty does not seek a metaphysical solution, but neither does he limit himself to the comic "yes, yes." Molly's logic and Merleau-Ponty's logic do radically depart from the logic of metaphysics, especially in the sketching of the relationship of language and embodiment, such as to make an entry into the unfolding and circling back of time in earthly struggle a "yes"—an affirmed possibility—that both the metaphysics of presence and the repetitive play of Derrida avoid.

Notes

1. Homer, *The Odyssey*, trans. Robert Fitzgerald (Garden City: Anchor/ Doubleday & Company, 1963), p. 157.
2. Derrida claims that Levinas has not appreciated that the myth and Joyce's treatment of it operate with another logic than that of closure/ rupture or immanence/transcendence, because of Levinas's "metaphysical desire." Jacques Derrida, "Violence and Metaphysics," in *Writing and Difference*, trans. Alan Bass (Chicago: University of Chicago Press, 1978), pp. 320–21 (n92). Further references to this work will be included in the text in parentheses with "VM" and the page number.
3. Maurice Merleau-Ponty, *The Visible and the Invisible*, trans. Alphonso Lingis (Evanston: Northwestern University Press, 1968), p. 246. Further references to this work will be included in the text in parentheses with "VI" followed by the page number.
4. Jacques Derrida, *Of Grammatology*, trans. Gyatri Spivak (Baltimore: Johns Hopkins University Press, 1976), p. 41. Further references to this work will be included in the text in parentheses with "GR" followed by the page number.
5. Jacques Derrida, "Différance" in *Speech and Phenomena*, trans. David Allison (Evanston: Northwestern University Press, 1973). p. 134. Further references to this work will be included in the text in parentheses with "D" followed by the page number.

6. Maurice Merleau-Ponty, *Phenomenology of Perception*, trans. Colin Smith (New York: Humanities Press, 1962), p. 242. It is interesting that Merleau-Ponty articulates this sense of time after a discussion of how binocular vision brings together the dual spectacles of monocular vision by a coalescing of space, which is primordially a coalescing of time, such that the present stands forth on the basis of a past which has never been a present. The one-eyed vision of the tradition would have to overcome not only its series of dichotomies, but also its sense of time for a radical becoming in order to see the depth of the world, as binocular vision affords. Further references to this work will be included in the text in parentheses with "PP" followed by the page number.

7. Jacques Derrida, *Dissemination*, trans. Barbara Johnson (Chicago: University of Chicago Press, 1981), p. 5. Further references to this work will be included in the text in parentheses with "DS" followed by the page number.

8. Derrida, "Structure, Sign, and Play in the Discourse of the Human Sciences," (*Writing and Difference*), p. 289.

9. Maurice Merleau-Ponty, "Eye and Mind" (trans. Carleton Dallery) in *The Primacy of Perception*, edited by James Edie (Evanston: Northwestern University Press, 1964), p. 190.

10. Jacques Derrida, "Ulysses' Gramophone," in *Acts of Literature*, ed. Derrick Attridge (New York: Routledge, 1992), p. 287. Further references to this work will be included in the text in parentheses with "UG" followed by the page number.

11. James Joyce, *Ulysses* (New York: Random House, 1986), p. 21. Further references to this work will be included in the text in parentheses with "UL" followed by the page number.

12. Jacques Derrida, "Freud and the Scene of Writing" (*Writing and Difference*), p. 202. Further references to this work will be included in the text in parentheses with "FS" followed by the page number.

13. UG, p. 288.

14. VI, p. 171.

15. So, it is no surprise that Derrida says in an autobiographical interview that Derrida confesses that he is driven by an overarching anxiety about death. The interview ends with his last comment: "All my writing is on death. . . . If I don't reach the place where I can be reconciled with death, then I will have failed. If I have one goal, it is to accept death and dying" (*New York Sunday Times Magazine*, 23 January 1994, p. 25).

11

Blindness and Invisibility: The Ruins of Self-Portraiture (Derrida's Re-reading of Merleau-Ponty)

Robert Vallier

We are all, by now, familiar with the well-rehearsed claim that Jacques Derrida has not read the work of Maurice Merleau-Ponty, that is, not read him in the Derridian sense, not given a "reading" of him. Indeed, the few comments that Derrida has made about Merleau-Ponty, scattered here and there through his *oeuvre*, have been predominantly negative. This is perhaps most obvious in his thesis defense, wherein Derrida writes of the importance of phenomenology for his project, "but not—especially not—the versions proposed by Sartre and Merleau-Ponty, which were then dominant." On the contrary, Derrida argues that his work is to be conceived "in opposition to them or without them."[1] In *opposition* to them? *Without* them? These exclusionary caveats seem strange in light of the recent amount of secondary literature devoted to the task of explicating the proximity of Derrida's to Merleau-Ponty's work. When pressed to defend this elliptical distance, Derrida offered a suggestive equivocation: "If one might argue that *The Phenomenology of Perception* falls within the metaphysics of presence, with *The Visible and the Invisible* it is even harder to say."[2] In this paper, we argue that one of Derrida's most recent texts, *Memoirs of the Blind*, a text devoted to blindness and invisibility, inaugurates a program for saying what is "harder to say," that is, for reading Merleau-Ponty's late work.

One might ask, in anticipation, why, in the course of reflections on blindness, does Derrida see, as though he has just recovered his own sight, that Merleau-Ponty's late work, which one might provisionally characterize as an ontology of visibility, escapes or disrupts the metaphysics of presence? What is there in blindness that suddenly illuminates for Derrida a relation between his work and Merleau-Ponty's? Derrida himself suggests, by way of "just a few indications from the working notes," how one might proceed to answer these questions.[3] But in following these suggestions, we ourselves must not be blind to the dangers of intertextuality: it may be that the manner in which Derrida treats the relevant working notes is a bit hasty, or that his sudden interest in Merleau-Ponty is merely strategic. This will have to be decided. Such a decision, though, will require that we first attend to Derrida's thesis in *Memoirs of the Blind*, to locate and define therein the aspect of blindness that occasions his re-reading of Merleau-Ponty. We will then ask to what extent Derrida's interpretive gestures shed light on or are resisted by Merleau-Ponty's text. Finally, we would briefly consider Derrida's reflections on the self-portrait, which both demonstrates and organizes a reading of the later Merleau-Ponty. In all, we are less concerned with the questions of influence and intellectual debt than with a chiasmatic reading of two thinkers, brought together, intertwined, by the problematic of blindness and invisibility, and therefore by a certain necessity of thinking.

If we recall that Derrida once claimed that he neither knew what perception was nor believed that anything like it exists, then it should come as no surprise that *Memoirs of the Blind*, a text that bears the subtitle "The Self-Portrait and Other Ruins," a text therefore about (self-)perception and drawing, opens on a skeptical note. The word skepticism, from the Greek *skepsis*, "has to do with the eyes. The word refers to visual perception, to the observation, vigilance and attention of the gaze" (*Memoirs* 1). Thus, *skepsis* has to do with examination, but it delays evaluation, and therefore inscribes the difference between seeing and believing.[4] The event of this inscription marks Derrida's interest in the text. The movement of this event inscribes not only the ordinal difference between viewing and knowing, between doubt and certainty, between eye and mind; it also inscribes the phenomenological concept of "perception." That is, the event marks the *point* of view from which a perspective eventuates.[5] And "indeed," Derrida writes, "it is the point of view that will be my theme" (*Memoirs* 2). In the end, it will have been this point that is blind, and this blindness will have been that which calls "perception" into question. Our task is to unravel the logic of this future anterior.

The point of view is the organizing theme of Derrida' text, written to accompany an exhibit of drawings he curated at the Louvre.

All of the drawings around which the text is arranged have to do with blindness: Christ healing the blind, blindness as retribution for an Oedipal crime, the blind man as seer, the self-portrait. That an exhibition devoted to blindness finds as its theme the point of view suggests a relation between that which gives rise to a perspective and blindness; the task of thinking this relation is what we must now take up.

Derrida's attempt to think this relation proceeds by way of two non-methodical hypotheses that "run ahead of us, as if sent out on a reconnaissance: two antennae or two scouts to orient our wanderings, to guide us as we feel our way" along and through this blindness, much as the prosthetic and supplementary cane a blind person employs (*Memoirs* 2). *Two* hypotheses, because if Derrida were to see with only one eye, to have a monocular hypothesis, he would all too easily slip into a phenomenology of the tacit cogito that sees, as if with x-ray eyes, through the thing, in-tu-its very essence. *Two* hypotheses which "will cross paths, but without ever confirming each other, without the least bit of certainty, in a conjecture which is at once singular and general, the *hypothesis* of sight and nothing less" (*Memoirs* 2). *Two* hypotheses that intertwine to form one rhetorical figure, that of a chiasm. What then are these hypotheses?

On the one hand, there is the abocular hypothesis: "Drawing is blind, if not the draftsman or draftswoman" (*Memoirs* 2). This implies that the very operation of drawing would be performed without the eyes. Without the eyes, but with the hand. The hand rushes ahead without seeing, leaping without looking, and so is always "on the verge" of disaster.[6] The hand, holding onto and using the inscriptive instrument, explores the space ahead of it, blindly feeling its way through the darkness. The hand feels out this unknown area, trying to apprehend it. Because the abocular hypothesis is also *explorative*, Derrida relates it to a logic of *precipitation (from prae-caput*, exposing the head, head-first): "The hand ventures forth, it precipitates ... in place of the head, as if to precede, prepare, and protect it" (*Memoirs* 4). And it is *against* this verge, *against* the precipice that the precipitative explorations of the hand hopes to protect. But, the blind man with his cane, like the draftsperson whose pointed hand cuts across the canvas without actually seeing it (he is looking elsewhere, for example, at the thing), is always in danger of falling or failing. "They are apprehensive about space, they apprehend with their groping wandering hands [and their prostheses]; they draw in it at once cautiously and boldly; they calculate, they count on the visible" (*Memoirs* 5). They *count on* the invisible, in a *calculative* manner: the blind rely on the invisible, assuming that it neither deceives nor fails them. But to make of the invisible the stuff of instrumental reason, as we will see, is their failure: precipitative explorations are not enough. Nevertheless, the wandering hand, groping its way through the darkness already inscribes; the blind bodily gesture is already drawing. This means then that blindness is a theme of drawing, or rather, that drawing is a trace of the blindness that conditions its possibility, the "drawing of drawing" (*Memoirs* 41). For this reason, Derrida remarks the abocular hypothesis as *the transcendental logic of blindness*.

The second hypothesis, on the other hand, is that of the double genitive: a drawing of the *blind* is a drawing *of* the blind. But if a draftsperson is blind, if blindness is the condition of the possibility of drawing, then how is drawing possible? When the draftsperson "makes of the blind a theme of his drawing . . . he begins to represent a drawing potency atwork. . . . He *invents* drawing" (*Memoirs* 2).[7] What is meant by this? We must note that the "blindness" Derrida speaks of is no physical infirmity of the eye; rather, what is signified is the kind of blindness draftspersons suffer when they redirect their gaze from the thing to the canvas. What happens then? Between model and copy there is a spread of invisibility through which the draftsperson's gaze must pass in order to draw. Into this space where there is no sight, into this non-site, the trait-not-yet-traced retreats.[8] "The trait must proceed in the night. It escapes the field of vision . . . because it *is not yet* visible" (*Memoirs* 48).

If the draftsperson is to draw, he must somehow restitute the trait to the canvas before it is completely devoured by the invisibility that haunts this space, the same invisibility on which he thought he could rely. He does so according to a logic of *anticipation*. This logic, once again, has to do with the hand:

> To anticipate is to take the initiative, to be out in front, to take (*capere*) in advance (*ante*). . . . [This logic] protects against precipitation, it makes advances, it puts the moves on space in order to be the first to take. . . . to take part in taking hold, in making contact or apprehending. (*Memoirs* 4)

The logic of anticipation thus guards against the precipitous, vertiginous terror of the invisible. The outstretched hand boldly reaches across this space, like a blind man who implores the other—Christ, perhaps—to restore his sight. Anticipating the loss of the trait, the draftsperson relentlessly pursues it in the night and quickly traces it on the canvas, restoring it to the light of day before it fades from memory. What the blind man and the draftsperson have in common is a certain faith: faith in Christ who will restore sight, faith in memory that will restore the trait. But faith, in the moment proper to it, is also blind.

The draftsman forgets the thing and draws from memory. It is faith, then, a certain fidelity to the thing, a memory of the thing, that allows the draftsperson to inscribe the trait without actually seeing the thing. This is why he must "in-vent" drawing. But even then, "the invention of the trait does not follow, it does not conform" to the visible thing (*Memoirs* 45). This, and the prominent role of memory here, indicates that something other than faith is also at work. Because the trait is not yet visible, because it withdraws into the invisible, the "origin" of drawing, of the graphic mark, is the gift, debt, sacrifice. Not only the trait, but also perception of the thing; indeed, perception itself is sacrificed, and this sacrifice must be commemorated in writing, as inscription: drawing as giving thanks (*rendre la grace*) for the restitution of sight (*rendre la vue*). One sees, one has vision(s), because one is indebted to the "law beyond sight"; this "debt must be repaid with words on parchment, with visible signs of the invisible": drawing as monument (*Memoirs* 29).

Recall that for Merleau-Ponty, in "Eye and Mind," the painter's eye opens upon and inhabits a texture of being. The painter's respectful observance of this texture "gives visible existence to what profane vision believes to be invisible," "through the offices of an agile hand."[9] For Merleau-Ponty, this "magical theory of vision" practiced by the painter, or rather, *through* the painter, is what privileges the painter and his activity. "Painting celebrates no other enigma but that of visibility."[10] But for Derrida, drawing is in this regard different from painting, though they are both variants of writing. Drawing commemorates invisibility. What is drawn, what is commemorated in drawing, is a certain blindness, a blindness which both makes drawing possible and reflects its impossibility: drawing is drawing *of* the blind. This *sacrificial logic of blindness* will turn out to be nothing other than the fate or misfortune (*le fatalité*) of the self-portrait, for, as we discover by interrogating these two hypotheses of Derrida's, drawing is always self-portraiture, a drawing of itself: narcissistic and therefore blind.

Two hypotheses, then, about hands and eyes. It should come as no surprise that both hypotheses have more to do with hands than with eyes. The hands always orient drawings *of* the blind: they explore or implore, precipitate or anticipate. "If to draw a blind man is first of all to show hands, it is to draw attention to what one draws with help of that with which one draws, the proper body as an instrument": the body, in its movement, draws (*Memoirs* 4–5). And we need think here only of Merleau-Ponty's body, the non-coincidence of one hand touching the other, "a reversibility always imminent and never realized in fact,"[11] to conclude that Derrida is speaking here of a certain absence, a blindness, that gives place to writing and drawing. This always incomplete reversibility is the movement of the event, that is, of the *point* of view, which is, therefore, never a fixed or discrete point, never a "point" as such.

Two hypotheses, then, about eyes and hands, that orient a critical review of several drawings of the blind in the exhibition and circumscribe the point of view. These two hypotheses, about eyes and hands, are not distinct: this is neither pure transcendentality nor pure sacrifice. Indeed, that both hypotheses have to do with eyes and hands, that eyes and hands thematize Derrida's reflections, and that eyes and hands both belong to a body that, in its movement, gestures and therefore draws, indicates that the two hypotheses are intertwined. And, "between the two," Derrida writes, "in their fold [*leur pli*], the one repeating the other without being reduced to it, [there is] the *event*" (*Memoirs* 41). What is this event? What is found at the hinge of this chiasm? To pursue these questions is better to understand Derrida's point of view.

If, indeed, drawing is *of* the blind, if "draftspersons are blind, or rather, that in or by drawing they do not see," then in what does blindness consist? One could voice an even more substantial objection:

> If one can recall no blind draftsperson, that is, one deprived of sight and eyes in the literal sense, isn't it going against common sense . . . to claim exactly the opposite, i.e., that every draftsperson is blind? No one will dispute that the draftsman is prey to a devouring proliferation of the invisible, but is that enough to make him into a blind man? (*Memoirs* 44)

A considerable remonstration, no doubt. This blindness is not the result of a detached retina or damage to the optical nerve or visual cortex, but rather has to do with the re-direction of the draftsperson's gaze. That is, when the draftsperson is looking at the thing and not the canvas, her hand precipitatively explores the area on which she will draw, preparing the way for inscription. But when she looks at the canvas and not the thing, she relies on memory, in anticipation of the retreat (*retrait*) of the trait. Between these two directed gazes, "in their fold," there is a spread of invisibility that strikes her blind. The eye, as it glides through this space, suffers a powerlessness, or, rather, "three types of powerlessness ... or, let us say, three *aspects*, to underscore with a trait that which gives the experience of the gaze (*aspicere*) over to blindness" (*Memoirs* 44). The aspect is at once both sight itself and what is seen, the spectator and the spectacle; but it also has a privative dimension: the a-spect, the "without-sight." So then, this pivotal turning is the movement of the event, or, rather, the aspect of the eye turns or hinges on this pivot, and refers the gaze to the absolute night into which the trait must recede.

The first aspect is seen in the *aperspective of the graphic act*. Even if drawing is an originary, pathbreaking (*frayage*) movement, even when the trait is in-vented on the canvas, it still remains unseen. Why? Derrida answers: "Not only because it is not yet visible, but because it does not belong to the realm of the spectacle, of spectacular objectivity" (*Memoirs* 45). That is, the trait passes through the invisible and remains there—it, and with it the draftsperson, falls prey to the "unbeseen" precisely because the space of difference between the thing and its representation is and always remains abyssal: this is no possibility of return.

> The night of this abyss can be interpreted in two ways, either as the eve or memory of the day, in other words as a reserve of visibility (the draftsman does not presently see but he has see and will see again: the aperspective is the anticipating perspective or the anamnestic retrospective) or as the radically and definitively foreign to the phenomenality of the day. (*Memoirs* 45)

The draftsperson is always in danger of ruination at the "origin" of drawing, because the "heterogeneity of the invisible to the visible can haunt the visible as its very possibility." But the question here is one of memory, because the trait always risks the precipice. If, on the one hand, perception serves memory, if memory is a reserve of visibility, then one could draw from memory. This interpretation sacrifices perception and makes an act of memory: in order to draw, one must not see but rather recollect what one has already seen. One sees the thing in the mind's eye, but without seeing the thing itself, "as if seeing were forbidden in order to draw, as if one drew on the condition of not seeing" (*Memoirs* 49). If the origin of drawing lies in memory and not in perception,

then the aperspective is related to the absence of invisibility of the
model, or in other words, to a certain blindness, and one therefore
traces only the shadow of the thing.

But on the other hand, if the trait remains radically foreign to
the day, then not even memory can save it: the invisible loses its
memory. Considered as such,

> invisibility would still inhabit the visible, or rather, would haunt
> it to the point of being confused with it, ... The visible as such
> would be invisible, not as visibility, the phenomenality or es-
> sence of the visible, but as the singular body of the visible itself,
> right on [à même] the visible. (Memoirs 51)

The invisible is right on [à même] the visible: it is, as Merleau-
Ponty would say, the invisible of the visible. The trait that would
pretend to be visible is instead abysally invisible, and the visible
would produce its own blindness, so that the draftsperson doesn't
see the appearance of disappearance. Hence, in its first moment,
as aperspectival frayage, the powerlessness of the eye is intimately
bound up with invisibility. This "powerlessness is not an impotence or a failure" (Memoirs 44); rather, it confers upon the invisible a quasi-transcendental status: it is at once that which sustains
and aliments the visible, the conditions of its possibility, and that
which threatens the visible with wreck and ruination, the conditions of its impossibility. Hence, what drawing draws from in order to draw is this quasi-transcendentality.

This is a very difficult thought, but one might say in a different
idiom that it is the reason for Cézanne's doubt. Recall in Merleau-
Ponty's analysis of Cézanne, both in the essay devoted to him and
in "Eye and Mind," how in the painter's work there are always
barely perceptible disruptions or aberrations, places or spaces where
things are slightly askew. These, Merleau-Ponty argues, are marks
of Cézanne's style, and style is nothing more than "an exigency
that issues from perception . . . perception already stylizes."[12]
Cézanne's style was marked by these aberrations because for him,
as we said, the visible world always seemed to elude his brush
before he could trace the trait on his canvas. The aberrations are
necessary correctives to the inadequacies he experienced as he
interrogated the visible, testaments to the recognition that perception is not seamless or pure presencing; they are the visible marks
of the intertwining of the visible and vision, "an emblem of inhabiting the world, of a certain relationship to being" (Signs 53). That
Cézanne always had to struggle to paint, that in his paintings there
are traces of this struggle, perhaps confirms the spectral haunting

of the visible by the invisible of which Derrida speaks: style, then, can be understood as the tracing of this impossible haunting.

That we should take this detour into Merleau-Ponty here is not without reason, for it is at this point in Derrida's discussion in *Memoirs of the Blind* that he proposes an "entire re-reading of the later Merleau-Ponty" (*Memoirs* 52). But before we specify the plan of Derrida's re-reading, let us quickly summarize the remaining two aspects of the event of drawing. The first aspect, as we have seen, argues that in its originary *frayage,* before it is traced, the trait is invisible, and draftspersons fall prey to this invisibility, which renders them blind: a-perspective, then, marks the trace of blindness. The second aspect has to with the trait once it has been traced. What remains of it? Nothing. It is no longer what it is. It marks an edge of a contour and so becomes a limit of representation. "Once this limit is reached," Derrida says,

> There is nothing left to see, not even black and white, not even figure/form, and this is the trait, this is the line itself: which is thus no longer what it is, because from then on it never related to itself without dividing itself just as soon.... This limit is never presently reached, but drawing always signals toward this inaccessibility.... Nothing belongs to the trait, and thus, to drawing and to the thought of drawing, not even its own trace. (*Memoirs* 53–4)

Like the limit, the trait-traced appears and disappears constantly: it divides itself, interrupts its own identification. Hence, Derrida names this aspect the *differential in/appearance of the trait.* This indicates the relation of drawing to the "other ruins" of the text's subtitle.

The third aspect is the *rhetoric of the trait.* The withdrawal of the line effected by the inappearance of the trait in the second aspect leaves other traces—ruins—in its wake. And

> is not the withdrawal of the line—that which draws the line back, draws it again, at the very moment when the trait is drawn, when it draws away—that which grants speech? (*Memoirs* 56)

Since there is nothing left of the trait, these remaining phantom traces—the drawn artifact—are all we have available to us. They are ruins of the self-effacing origin of drawing, runes that grant us speech, supplementary tropes or already instituted perspective. What these three aspects tell us, then, is that the point of view, the blindness at the heart of vision, withdraws with every measure of approach, leaving traces in its wake.

And so, it is the point of view, the aspect, the event, the body—
blindness itself that is found at the hinge or fold of the chiasm.
This chiasm—an intertwining of two movements or hypotheses, a
double movement, a doubling back, a crossing over and a crossing
out, a double cross—is a pivotal moment of reversal that puts into
decision the problematic of blindness and invisibility. In or through
this decision, the invisible comes to enjoy its quasi-transcendental
status, and the graphic restitution of the invisible—drawing of the
blind—becomes both innocent and dangerous. And it is here in
this non-site, that Derrida advances his hypothesis of sight: simply
put, sight is always already blind. Or, we might say, more precisely and paraphrasing another, that sight is indirect or allusive—
that it is, if you wish, blindness. This then returns us to Derrida's
program for re-reading Merleau-Ponty.

Derrida says that he would rather have followed the traces of an
"absolute invisibility" instead of the "four layers" of the invisible
Merleau-Ponty outlines in a working note. "To be the other of the
visible, absolute invisibility must neither take place elsewhere nor
constitute another visible." It must be neither past nor future, but
rather right here, right now, right on the visible: "It is a 'phenomenon' whose inappearance is of another kind" (*Memoirs* 52). To
understand this "other kind" of inappearance, Derrida refers to a
working note of January 1960:

> Principle: not to consider the invisible as an *other visible* "pos-
> sible". . . . The invisible is *there* without being an *object*, it is
> pure transcendence, without an ontic mask. And the "visibles"
> themselves, in the last analysis . . . are only centered on a nu-
> cleus of absence—(*The Visible and the Invisible*, henceforth VI,
> 229/*Memoirs* 52)

Derrida then explicitly relates this nucleus of absence to what
Merleau-Ponty calls the *punctum caecum* in two working notes of
May 1960. First:

> When I say that every visible is an invisible, that perception is
> imperception, that consciousness has a "punctum caecum," that
> to see is always to see more than one sees—this must not be
> understood in the sense of a contradiction—it must be imagined
> that I add to the visible . . . a non-visible . . .—One has to under-
> stand that it is the visibility itself that involves a non-visible. . . .—
> The invisible of the visible. (VI 247/*Memoirs* 52)

The *punctum caecum* refers to the anatomical physio-pathology of
the eye, the blind spot on the retina where the fibrous fleshy

membranes both connect to the optic nerve (and thereby to the neurology of the visual cortex) and spread out to "prepare the vision for the rest." Derrida notes that the disappointment of the pathological definition of the *punctum* is that the ophthalmologist, seeking to discover the origin of vision, looking to see seeing, finds only fleshy material and not sight. The *punctum* cannot see itself, cannot be reflected or thought, but nevertheless allows for reflection and thought, prepares them as (the rhetoric of) vision. And,

> *What* it does not see it does not see for reasons of principle, it is because it is consciousness that it does not see. *What* it does not see is what in it prepares the vision of the rest.... *What* it does not see is what makes it see, is its tie to Being, is its corporeity, are the existentials by which the world becomes visible. (VI 248/ *Memoirs* 53)

Derrida thus links the *punctum caecum* with his theme of the point of view, not only because it is "blinded at the very point where it sees itself looking," but also because it marks that nuclear absence around which the visibles are arranged. The *punctum* is that *point* that moves Merleau-Ponty to

> raise the question: the invisible life, the invisible community, the invisible other, the invisible culture.... [and to] Elaborate a phenomenology of "the other world." (VI 229/*Memoirs* 52)

The *punctum*, like the point of view, is the aperspectival blindness at the heart of sight. This would mean, in the end, that the visible world is always doomed to ash, for is not the movement of pure transcendence also conflagration, the sacrifice of the visible? Painting, then, which celebrates visibility, needs to be remarked as drawing, that is, as commemorating the invisible of the visible, as commemorating the cinders of this movement before they burn themselves out.

Now, some might argue that Derrida has selected but a few instances from Merleau-Ponty's notes that all too easily fit into Derrida's schematic, that in fact Merleau-Ponty's interrogative ontology of visibility resists this conflagration of the absolutely invisible. There is, indeed, some validity to this claim: Merleau-Ponty himself says, in the closing pages of *The Visible and the Invisible*, that the invisible he intends to speak of is "the invisible of this world, that which inhabits this world, sustains it, and renders it visible," and as such is "not an absolute invisible which would have nothing to do with the visible" (VI 151). In light of this, one could argue that Derrida's interpretive gesture should be and is resisted by Merleau-

Ponty's text. We think that to a greater extent, however, Merleau-Ponty's text works against this objection.

Merleau-Ponty writes that an interrogation of the punctum is important

> precisely in order to know how it opens us to what is not ourselves [the invisible dimension]. *This does not even exclude the possibility that we find in our experience a movement toward what could not in any event be present to us in the original and whose irremediable absence would thus count among our originating experiences.* (VI, 159, italics original)

Derrida would argue that the *punctum* opens us to the invisible community precisely because it rests "right on" the visible, that in fact we are always open to the invisible. The irremediable absence that both opens us to the other dimension and gives rise to perspective would count as an origination experience. What, then, is this irremediable absence? For Derrida, it is the *punctum caecum* or point of view, the blindness at the heart of vision. Merleau-Ponty would no doubt agree, but would add that this absence, despite the fact that it itself is not seen, is nevertheless part of perception, which therefore is never purely present.

Moreover, this irremediable absence that counts among our "originating experience" would be, for Merleau-Ponty, more than a tear or *punctum* in/on consciousness. If what consciousness does not see is "its tie to Being, its corporeity . . . the existentials by which the world becomes visible," then for Merleau-Ponty this absence must also be the body. The many metaphors Merleau-Ponty deploys to describe the body articulate this absence as "hole," "cavity," "hiatus," "hollow" (*creux*), and "divergence" (*écart*). The body "defines a vision in general and a constant style of vision from which I cannot detach myself," and is therefore never proper, never clean (*propre*): it is "as though the visible body remained incomplete, gaping open" (VI 147). As such, Merleau-Ponty writes in another working note of this absence that

> it is to be open to oneself, destined to oneself (narcissism)—Nor, therefore, is it to reach oneself, it is on the contrary to escape oneself . . . the self in question is by divergence [*d'écart*]. (VI 249/*Memoirs* 53)

And as a *creux* or crucible—as the holy cup in which sacrificial offerings are burned and thereby become spiritual—the body is understood as the site of transcendence without an ontic mask, a site that nevertheless is forever caught in brute, wild being. The body allows for visibility and at the same time is "a certain absence, a negativity that is not nothing" (VI 151). The *punctum caecum*, that anatomical mark of blindness within the physiology of the body, by virtue of its being bodily, constitutes the irremediable absence. Hence, it is the body that is the *point* of view, and, therefore, the body that is blind. The body, the point, the *punctum*—all always slip away.

What originating experience does this give rise to? A relationship to the visible, a perspective. This relationship, or "constant style of visibility," would be, qua style, an interrogation, that is, a writing and reading of the flesh. Writing, or better, styling weaves a fabric, a text. And,

> like the weaver, the writer works on the wrong side of his material. He has to do only with language, and it is thus that he suddenly finds himself surrounded by meaning. (*Signs* 45)

The writer does not merely use entombed signs, nor does she reorganize signs like a craftsman does his tools. Rather, the writer "gropes around a significative intention which is not guided by any text, and which is precisely in the process of writing the text" (*Signs* 46). The writer stylizes. But how is it that the body gives rise to writing? Precisely because when it moves, when it gestures, the body is already a stylus; what the body writes "bears the meaning of thought as a footprint signifies the movement and effort of the body" (*Signs* 44). In this way, the body creates new meaning, writes a text that is nothing other than the visible world, and so draws. As Merleau-Ponty writes, "it is characteristic of every human gesture to signify beyond its simple existence, to inaugurate a meaning" (*Signs* 68). This gestural inauguration is an interrogation of the invisible, its in-vention, its becoming-visible.

But what precisely is a gesture? What does it mean to have a hand that holds a pen or gropes blindly in the night? What does a gesture do when it signifies beyond itself? The hand that points, the eye that moves is

> devoted to the inspection of the world, capable of leaping over distances, piercing the perceptual future and outlining ... a meaning in the conceivable flatness of being.... Already in its gestures, the body not only flows over into a world whose schema it bears within itself but possesses this world at a distance rather than being possessed by it.... The gesture of expression which undertakes through expression to delineate what it intends, ... retrieves the world. (*Signs* 67)

The gesture that writes is also the gesture that reads. Perhaps this is what Merleau-Ponty means when he remarks the body as a "Visibility sometimes wandering and sometimes reassembled" (VI 138).[13] The body both reads and writes the Carnal Word, "the silent logos that pronounces itself in each visible," it inscribes it as the more rarified flesh of language. But the body itself can never be read or written; it is irremediably absent.

The gesture—pointing—like painting, stylizes. And what is written in this stylizing is irremediable absence—the silence of language, the blindness of vision, the *punctum* of the body, the point of view. Derrida's program for re-reading suggests that the whole of Merleau-Ponty's last text, and the evolution of his thought, is arranged around these nuclear *puncta*. Such a reading would be consonant with Derrida's latest gestures, according to which we can say that these absences which give place to the visible, vision, and language are all testaments to and wreckage of the invisible. Consider what Merleau-Ponty says of the invisibility of meanings that lie behind the materiality of the signifier in language:

> It is not only that we would find in that carnal experience the occasion to think them; it is that they owe their authority, their fascinating indestructible power, precisely to the fact that they are in transparency behind the sensible, or in its heart. Each time we want to get at it, or lay our hands on it, or circumscribe it, or see it unveiled, we do in fact feel that our attempt is misconceived, that it retreats in the measure that we approach. The explication does not give us the idea itself, it is but a second version of it, a more manageable derivative.... We do not possess ... the ideas precisely because they are negativity or absence circumscribed; they possess us. (VI 150–51)

Is this description of invisibility as negativity not akin to the absolute invisibility Derrida prefers to find in Merleau-Ponty? Are these "more manageable derivatives" not traces of, monuments to, this negativity? Do these signs or tombs of wreckage not speak to us, all the time, of the blindness, the silence, that constitute them? Derrida's rhetoric of blindness is the commemoration of this wreckage. What follows this commemorative rhetoric in Derrida's text is a discussion of the self-portrait, which we suspect "performs" this rhetoric, and organizes in an exemplary manner the program for re-reading Merleau-Ponty. But because a full discussion of this performance falls outside the scope of this presentation, let us suffice with just a few indications and conclude.[14]

What we are accustomed to calling a self-portrait is in fact—if

Derrida is right that all drawing is a self-showing of blindness, that is, if drawing draws (from) itself its own blindness—a self-portrait of the self-portrait. Hence, what is drawn in a self-portrait is not the signatory-artist (who is also the model), but rather the source point, the eye and the hand, the body. The draftsperson attends to his image in the mirror and tries to draw it on the canvas. But as Merleau-Ponty understood well, not even the mirror will allow one to see oneself fully. Why? First, because the image one sees in the mirror is a reversal. More importantly, though, because when one looks at one's reversed image in the mirror, one does not see oneself full face; rather, one focuses on the focal point, where the gaze from the two eyes meets, where the two eyes cross. The effect of these crossed eyes is a sort of monstration: to look at oneself, even at one point on oneself, one must have monocular vision, one must become cycloptic. All self-portraits, all self-showings of blindness, must negotiate this monstrosity. Hence, in the mirror, as in the self-portrait, "invisibility is shared out between the eyes" (*Memoirs* 57). That is, one eye stares directly at itself—fixated, fascinated—seeing only itself, seeing itself blind, while the other eye remains withdrawn in the dark. Thus, one always remains blind to—or blinded by—one's own self-presentation. One can only see one's self as an other—one is destined to oneself, but this destination is always eluded or evaded—the "self" *is* only "by divergence": this is what Merleau-Ponty means by narcissism, and what Derrida describes as the monstrous logic of the self-portrait. What the self-portrait shows—and Derrida's *Memoirs of the Blind* catalogues—is the inability of the source point or *punctum* to be thematized or drawn, that it is instead always drawn away from its destiny, destination, or fatality. Its logic de-monstrates the specter of the invisible, lets it be seen without ever appearing. The logic of the self-portrait is Cézanne's doubt, and for this reason, and always already, the self-portrait is, like all drawing, ruinance and ruins, the wreckage of and testament to the invisible. This logic clearly merits further investigation.

In the end, then, it will have been the point of view that places the problematic of blindness and invisibility, shared by these two thinkers, into decision. One can see that Derrida is shadowed in his text by a more or less invisible Merleau-Ponty, a clandestine companion who demands restitutions of the truth in painting, pointing, and puncting; and in this restitution, the problematic of blindness and invisibility is thought as ruin, wreckage, testament, commemoration. *Il y a la cendre.*

Notes

1. Jacques Derrida, "Punctuations: The Time of the Thesis," in *Philosophy in France Today*, ed. Alan Montefiore (Cambridge: Cambridge University Press, 1983), p. 38. See also *Introduction to Husserl's Origin of Geometry*, pp. 77, 111–13, 116; *Of Grammatology*, pp. 106, 335; "Violence and Metaphysics," pp. 103–104, for some of Derrida's comments on Merleau-Ponty.
2. The comment was made in Hubert Dreyfus's seminar on Merleau-Ponty and is represented by one of the students, Nancy J. Holland, in her "Merleau-Ponty on Presence: A Derridean Reading," *Research in Phenomenology*, Vol. XVI (1986), 111.
3. Jacques Derrida, *Memoirs of the Blind*, trans. Pascale-Anne Brault and Michael B. Naas (Chicago: University of Chicago Press, 1993), p. 52. Hereafter all citations of this text will appear parenthetically in the essay as *Memoirs*.
4. The theme of *skepsis*, belief, is announced in the first line of the text: "Vous croyez?" Moreover, this theme links Derrida's texts to the questions of Cartesian doubt and the Husserlian *epoche*, both of which are also at stake in Merleau-Ponty's "Cézanne's Doubt," trans. H. L. Dreyfus and P. A. Dreyfus in *Sense and Non-sense* (Evanston: Northwestern University Press, 1964), pp. 9–26.
5. One should emphasize again, by forcing the reader to refer from one point in a text to another by way of a footnote, that this event is a movement, and as such the point of view is decidedly *not* a determinate point fixed in space and time.
6. On the "verge," and of memory, see David Farrell Krell, *Of Memory, Reminiscence, and Writing: On the Verge* (Bloomington: Indiana University Press, 1990), especially the Introduction.
7. On "in-vention," see Jacques Derrida, "Psyche: Inventions of the Other," trans. Catherine Porter, in *Reading DeMan Reading*, ed. L. Waters and W. Godzich (Minneapolis: University of Minnesota Press, 1989), pp. 25–65.
8. This formula suggests another, perhaps: the opening where not to see. In French, it would be rendered, or restituted, as *L'ouvre ou ne pas voir*, which is in fact the theme Derrida initially settled on as the organizing motif for the exhibition mounted at the homonymically evoked *Louvre*.
9. Maurice Merleau-Ponty, "Eye and Mind," trans. Carleton Dallery, in *The Primacy of Perception*, ed. James Edie (Evanston: Northwestern University Press, 1964), pp. 165–66.
10. M. Merleau-Ponty, "Eye and Mind," pp. 166.
11. Maurice Merleau-Ponty, *The Visible and the Invisible*, ed. Claude Lefort, trans. Alphonso Lingis (Evanston: Northwestern University Press, 1968), p. 147. Hereafter citations of this text will appear parenthetically and in abbreviated form (VI) in the essay.
12. Maurice Merleau-Ponty, "Indirect Language and the Voices of Silence," in *Signs*, ed. and trans. Richard C. McCleary (Evanston: Northwestern University Press, 1964), p. 54. Hereafter, references to this text will appear parenthetically in the essay.

13. We suppose this is what Derrida means when he tells us that "reading proceeds in no other way: it listens in watching" (*Memoirs* 2). Moreover, we are certain that this is the sense of narcissism for Merleau-Ponty: to be destined to oneself, but never to realize this destiny, never to reach this destination.

14. The subtle and detailed analyses of the self-portrait in *Memoirs* (57–95), repay careful study; Michael Fried's wonderful discussion in his *Courbet's Realism* (Chicago: University of Chicago Press, 1990), pp. 53ff, and in his forthcoming *Between Mannerisms*, which examines Derrida's *Memoirs*, are highly recommended.

12

Reading Postmodernism as Interruption (between Merleau-Ponty and Derrida)

Hugh J. Silverman

I shall call modern the art that devotes its "trivial technique," as Diderot calls it, to presenting the existence of something unpresentable. Showing that there is something we can conceive of which we can neither see nor show—this is the stake of modern painting. But how do we show something that cannot be seen?

The postmodern would be that which in the modern invokes the unpresentable in presentation itself, that which refuses the consensus of taste permitting a common experience of nostalgia for the impossible, and inquires into new presentations—not to take pleasure in them, but to better produce the feeling that there is something unpresentable. The postmodern artist or writer is in the position of a philosopher: the text he writes of the work he creates is not in principle governed by preestablished rules and cannot be judged according to a determinant judgment, by the application of given categories to this text or work. Such rules and categories are what the work or text is investigating. The artist and the writer therefore work without rules and in order to establish the rules for what *will have been made*. This is why the work and the text can take on the properties of an event; it is also why they would arrive too late for their author, or, in what amounts to the same thing, why the work of making them would always begin too soon. *Postmodern* would be understanding according to the paradox of the future (*post*) anterior (*modo*).

—Jean-François Lyotard[1]

I. POSTMODERNISM AS INTERRUPTION

The postmodern marks interruptions. The postmodern is not concerned with what does the interrupting nor with what is interrupted. The postmodern identifies and elaborates the interruptions themselves. In the modern, what is presented is evident to vision, to examination, to scrutiny, to explanation, to interpretation. . . . In the modern, the task is to identify what is not presented—the unpresentable. The unpresentable—the *je ne sais quoi*, the ineffable, the consciousness—is inaccessible to everyday vision, examination, analysis, scrutiny, interpretation. Yet the modern wants to make it clear that the unpresentable does nevertheless exist, that the latent, the sub rosa, the deep structure does indeed subtend the presentable. The modern wants to make it evident that the unpresentable is there, somewhere, we just need to look more closely, more attentively, more analytically.

The postmodern is inscribed in the modern. In the modern, there are breaks, ruptures, fissures between the presentable and the unpresentable. The postmodern does not seek to articulate the unpresentable—that has already been the task of the modern. The postmodern does not seek to give names, shapes, identities to the unpresentable. The postmodern is interested in what marks the differences between the presentable and the unpresentable, between what is given and what is not given, between what is manifest and what is latent. The postmodern relies on the modern to identify the unpresentable, to invoke it, to depend on it, to ever seek after it as novelty, as other, as exquisite. Between the presentable and the unpresentable is an interruption—an inscription of difference. This inscription of differences is the moment of textuality, the place of the postmodern.

As in a conversation, when one speaker holds forth, there is a presentation of views, ideas, accounts, and narratives. When the speaker is interrupted by another speaker, the presentation is interrupted and a new presentation begins. Of course, the first interlocutor can interrupt back and regain the terrain of discourse. As a figure of the modern, the interruption of the first speaker by the second permits of novelty, alterity, a shift in perspective. The narrative of the second speaker takes the place of the first. While the first was speaking, the discourse of the second remained unpresentable—the first was speaking. When the second takes over, in replacing the first, something new enters the scene. The avant-garde is the replacement of previous art practices with a new style, new set of forms, a new movement. The avant-garde is like the second speaker who interrupts the first. It is always possible for the first to reassert his or her position, to deny the avantgardist interruption, to hold to the established, traditional, accepted set of

art forms. But if the avant-gardist interruption prevails, then that
which it replaces becomes *passée*, outmoded, obsolete. In other
words, history. The avant-garde as the forerunner of the modern,
the advance scout, the prophet of the new modern, takes the replacement model as primary. There is no interest in repetition, in
return, in retrieval, unless these modes are something new in themselves. The reintroduction of the classical has no place in the modern
as such. Of course, the modern would not be modern without the
classical, but the classical cannot ever interrupt the modern definitively. Yet, in the modern the reinscription of the classical along
with the modern can occur—but only as postmodern.

The postmodern is not afraid of the outmoded, obsolete, time-
honored modes of expression. The postmodern does not reject the
historically admired, traditionally appreciated forms. Yet the postmodern has no interest in reaffirming the classical against the modern
either. The postmodern comes after the modern only in the sense
that it inscribes itself in the modern, which is already there. But
the postmodern does not refuse, reject, or replace the modern—
this is the modern speaking against itself. The postmodern does
not interrupt the modern or any of its expressions. The postmodern
identifies the places of interruption, of fissure, of break, of rupture
in the modern itself—and if these places of break are also with the
classical, they are also of interest to the postmodern.

The postmodern is not a new mode of expression. The postmodern is not avant-garde. The postmodern is not a new style that
comes after the modern. After the modern is still the modern in
new shape, new guise, new articulation. The postmodern has its
place only in the modern itself. The postmodern marks the places
of interruption, of fissure, of difference, of break between one
form and the next. When the modern interrupted the classical,
when the modern refused to apply and reapply the classical rules
of poetics, of performance, of representation in favor of an endless series of breaks with the rules, ruptures with the tradition,
refusals to remain constrained by the established conditions of
acceptability, it wanted (and still does want) the whole pie.
Each act of artistic usurpation, each revolutionary enterprise, each
call for a new manifesto has as its goal or end the complete
and total replacement (interruption) of what preceded it. The
avant-garde is ruthless. The avant-garde does not want to share.
The avant-garde does not want to incorporate. The avant-garde has
no interest in cooperation. The avant-garde is interested only in a
complete take over, a coup d'état that will give no quarter to the

previous regime. The postmodern is hardly traditional, hardly conservative, hardly reactionary, but it is also not ruthless, reckless, and totalizing. The postmodern wants the modern to go on producing novelties.

Like the new Europe, the postmodern wants new alliances but it does not want to repress the lines of difference either. Indeed, the lines of difference mark, animate, and legitimate the postmodern. If Germany, for instance, were to monetarily take over the whole new Europe, if the Bundesbank were to become the chief (and only) economic principle of European unity—as the Bundesrepublik did when the Berlin wall came down—then modernity will have prevailed, the continuity of the old *Aufklärung* will have taken over Europe, will have, in its avant-gardist zeal, replaced all alterity, all prior discourses, all previous modes of expression, all national traditions, all cultural identities. The German ideals of the 1930s will have been accomplished silently and without a single shot— Europe will have been purchased by Germany, bought up without anyone noticing. The new Europe will be the new "modern," "enlightened" Europe, that is, the new Germany, the new Empire. The return of the Empire will have been the interruption of prior modernisms, but also of differences. The postmodern wants to recognize differences—national differences, political differences, artistic differences, cultural differences.

If it is not Germany but a European Parliament that will prevail, then the question rests as to whether this Parliament will submerge all national differences under a judiciary and a set of standards that apply equally to all nations. The project of bringing all nations under one standard—monetary system, metric system, judicial system, political system, diplomatic system, and so forth—would be an unrealizable extreme. Yet, the Enlightenment conception of the unification of all differences, of all national identities under the guise of one transcendental model of communicative competence—which remains unpresentable in the context of one "European" presentation or representation—will have been the achievement of the modern over the postmodern. The interruption of differences will not be tolerated, only minority rights will be tolerated (at the discretion of the majority), and the interruption of differences as the presentation of the unpresentable will have been banished from the European frame. While, if differences are presented, if differences overlap, even contradictions between European nations are presented in their unpresentability, then the traces of a postmodern formulation of Europe will have their place.

The paintings of Rene Magritte came before their time: threshold markings of the postmodern. Officially surrealist—of the avant-gardist movements along with Salvador Dali, Luis Buñuel, Max Ernst, André Delvaux, et al.—Magritte played with realist objects, placing them in a surrealist context. But also inscribed within these paintings are impossible juxtapositions—as in Escher—where the track of continuity cannot follow through to its end. These juxtapositions mark alternative spaces which interrupt one another. The syncope of the two spaces nevertheless operates in concert, one with another. The interruption of the one does not eliminate, overshadow, exclude, or terrorize the other. Magritte's paintings are typically two alternative (binary) spaces which come into contact and overlap each other. The overlap cancels a simple jigsaw juxtaposition, the pieces do not fit, they interrupt each other in the painting. In 1939, Magritte painted a number of canvases in which these conflicting binary systems come into play. *Le Poison* (Edward James Foundation, Chichester, Sussex), for instance, presents a room with a central door. The door opens inward. The door frame centers the painting surrounded by brown walls and a wood-grained floor. Outside is something like a beach of sand with the sea beyond and beyond that: a blue sky. This would all constitute an ordered world: inside room, outside beach, sea, and sky. But coming through the door—from the outside—is a cloud. The cloud enters the room halfway, it even casts a shadow on the inside wall. But clouds do not come inside a room. Clouds do not cast a shadow inside. If one is inside, the oneiric world of sand, sea, and sky with a cloud or two remains other. For a cloud to come inside is for it to poison the exclusive—separate—peace of the inside. But it is not just the cloud that comes in—half of the door is a clear sky blue as if it were continuous with the sky above the sea. The outside world, which in principle is in conflict with the inside world, does not designate a clear line of demarcation. The interruption of the one by the other is not complete—and it is not at all clear which interrupts which. What makes the painting avant-garde is how the two are brought together, what designates a postmodern moment is the interruption itself, the jagged non-edge between the outside world and the inside world. Which poisons which? Who knows? It cannot be interpreted, and yet the two—not as two but as one—coexist. Is it psychoanalyzable—the phallic cloud coming through the door? Is it a depiction of the chiasmatic moment of an *Ereignis* as the cloud and light ecstatically illuminate the room? Is it the visible inside energized by the largely invisible outside? Whichever, the juxtaposition of differences marks an indecidable difference in-between.

In the spring of 1994, a new bookstore opened up on the Ringstraße side of the Vienna MAK (Museum für angewandte Kunst/Museum for Applied Arts). The late nineteenth-century museum (by Heinrich von Ferstel in 1871; and enlarged by Ludwig Bauman in 1906–08) itself had been significantly reconstructed in the early 1990s—keeping the basic brick-walled building with its Italianate (Palladian-type) arches, its frescoes, its large, grey, nineteenth-century corner and foundation bricks. The bookstore (*Buchhandlung*) occupies a small corner of the large building. As a sculpture/store sign/marker of the Minerva Bookstore there appeared a piece which looks like a stage prop in the shape of a window/door, removed from an inner corner of the building facade. The window is consistent with several other windows on the front facade of the building: rounded arch, iron grill-barred. Underneath are the same style gray bricks that surround the bottom of the whole building, and inscribed on the upper layer in block letters: *BUCHHANDLUNG*. In the upper corner of the window is a red neon sign: Minerva. From a distance the "sign" looks as though it were simply cut out of the wall of the building and moved out in front at an angle. At the bottom is a grill like those along the whole front of the building. In the hole or space vacated by the piece is the entrance door to the bookstore. As one walks toward the opening, one is inclined to look at the back of the statue-sign. Curiously, an iron radiator is attached. The whole piece was commissioned by a Los Angeles group, and a postcard advertising the store has a photo of the statue-sign with the fragment of the building behind. The postcard photo was taken at a time of day such that the sign casts a shadow on the side of the building, almost leading the piece into its place in the building—at the store entrance. The shadow is not unlike the one cast by the Magritte cloud inside the room of *Le Poison*. This postmodern piece designates an interruption of the wall of the building, an interruption of the writing-less brick wall, of the iron grill with a red neon sign inside the non-window, of a functional radiator behind an outdoor sculpture. Here there is a gap between the statue-sign as window-door and the doorway to the bookstore itself. The shadow designates a distance, a gap, a space of difference, it marks an interruption of the line of the building, and it cuts across the convention of the typical museum bookstore located inside the museum—only rarely (as in some Italian museums, such as Parma) is the bookstore marked on the outside of the building. The jigsaw

FIGURE 1

puzzle conception of continuity is interrupted here by the statue-sign, which both belongs to the wall and is entirely independent from it. The postmodern interest, then, lies in the place of difference.

The postmodern interest, then, is not in the presentation of the Museum für angewandte Kunst, not in the sign-statue itself, but in the unpresentable as it resides in the two presentations. The event of relation, of juxtaposition, of difference between the building and the sign-statue is the text as unpresentable, and as given in the presentation of the two in concert. Similarly, the Magritte painting—as a postmodern inscription—marks not the inner room nor the outer sand, sea, and sky, but the impossible juxtaposition of the two, of the interruption of the one by the other—just as the Minerva Buchhandlung statue-sign interrupts the MAK building and is interrupted by it as well.

What links the new Europe, Magritte's *Poison*, and the Minerva sign-statue is in the reading of them. None is in itself postmodern. Each is marked with interruptions that can be ignored in favor of the unities, syncopes that can easily be overlooked in favor of the continuities, epistemological breaks that are turned into transcendental perspectives. The postmodern occurs in the modern. It is not opposed to the modern. Hence the postmodern can be overrun in and by the modern in favor of enlightenment, unity, and totality. To deny the postmodern in the modern is to deny modernity its life, its energy, and its future.

II. The End of the (Modern) Presentation of the Invisible

In 1946, a conference entitled "Crisis in European Consciousness" took place. Maurice Merleau-Ponty offered the following comments: "I believe that were all Europeans to say to themselves 'We are Europeans,' they would be conceiving of Europe and themselves in opposition to something else. This is the kind of image one forms of Europe when wishing to oppose Europe to the United States or the USSR, for example, and I wonder whether, on the contrary, there is not a completely different type of European unity—a sort of Europe in act and not in representation. . . . It seems to me that a European spirit should be defined less by an idea or a representation . . . than by a certain kind of relation between humans and nature or between an individual and others. For example, it seems to me that if we consider efforts as diverse as Hegel's lectures on the philosophy of history, certain writings on Chinese civilization, or even Malraux's first novels, we might find something typically European."[2] Europe as a performance or act rather than an idea or representation is a concept that has been lost in the mire of European history since 1946. Yet, even today, as Merleau-Ponty suggests, Europe is not a set of boundaries, a determinate number of countries or nations which constitute the European Union, but an enactment of Europeanization, of participation in a unity called Europe. What signifies here is a concept that Merleau-Ponty was also beginning to develop in phenomenological terms: that the perception or experience of Europe was more critical than a particular gestalt of it. Europe would not be the figure of a flag (as it is today) nor the deconstitution of border controls within the confines of Europe but a certain way of asking about Europe, a certain perception and interrogation of participation in Europe.

Europe in 1946—fifty years ago now—was searching to establish its modernity, to overcome a crisis of modernity that wrenched it apart in war and strife. But as Merleau-Ponty suggests, Europe was not the prevalence of a totality that ensued after the defeat of German aggression and occupation. Europe was a performance between—at the time—the U.S. and the USSR.

But what constitutes Modern Europe after 1946? Europe became a search for the reaffirmation of nation-states, national cultures, national identities, national languages. Modern Europe in the 1990s is a turn toward abolishing the differences, overcoming multiple standards of production, measurement, and exchange in favor of a single standard. Postmodern Europe calls for many different interruptions of continuity and unity, which occur in the context of the unpresentable. As Merleau-Ponty suggested in 1946, Europe cannot be represented. Europe, then, he thought needed to focus on overcoming the crisis in the ideas of truth and objectivity, respect for freedom, and the status of work (*Texts and Dialogues*, hereafter TD, 15). Europe is the unpresentable. Europe is the interruption of nationalisms in their identities and in their furious demand for authority. Europe is not visible. Only performances and acts matter. These performances and acts are what Merleau-Ponty later called "visibility," how the modern accounts for its gaps, fissures, and alterities.

Merleau-Ponty's notion of visibility is based in a metaphysics of presence and absence, visible and invisible. Merleau-Ponty took the model of the ruin—a castle left in a shambles on the top of a hill. The ruin is visible. What is invisible is the whole castle, as it was, as it could be in the future. Its visibility is the intertwining of the visible and the invisible. But the invisible is not just the castle as it once was or as it could be. The invisible is also the seeing of the visible castle as it now is. This seeing, this vision, of the castle as it now is marks a chiasm between the seeing and the seen, between the invisible and the visible. This seeing which incorporates a vision of the castle as it once was or as it could be is what Merleau-Ponty calls visibility. In a modern perspective, Europe is the castle as it once was or as it could be. Europe is also as the nations perform themselves now in concert with one another. A postmodern Europe will be the performance of Europe as visibility, Europe not as invisible but as visibility. Europe not as it is conceived but as it links up the invisible conception with how it is, how it is visible now.

The visible is presented. The visible is what is presented. The invisible is the presentation, the conception of Europe, of Magritte's inside room and his outside sand, sea, and sky, of the MAK sign-statue as other than the MAK and as part of the MAK. But the presentation of the invisible in relation to the visible—the nations, the opposition of inside and outside interrupted by the cloud, the polarity of the commercial sign and the participation in the architectural presence of the MAK—these are the visibility of Europe, the Magritte painting, the MAK with its Minerva Buchhandlung and its trappings. The visibility of Europe is the presentation of the unpresentable conception of Europe in an act of presentation, in a performance of unity and difference, of standardization and often contradictory, independent practice. The visibility of the Magritte painting is the competing inside and outside understood (in one interrogation) psychoanalytically as the penetration of the cloud and the illumination of the room, and (in another) as the interruption of the peace of Europe. The visibility of the MAK Minerva sign-statue is the event of a commercial-architectural-artistic performance, a linking of different pieces in an impossible puzzle, as is the sublime Europe of today.

III.   THE (POSTMODERN) INSCRIPTION OF DIFFERANCES

In *The Other Heading* (*L'Autre Cap*) (1991), Derrida cites François Mitterrand (President of the French Republic) as saying, "Europe is returning in its history and its geography like one who is returning home [*chez soi*]."[3] Derrida inquires about the meaning of such a Ulysses-like statement that is both a return and an expression of self-identity. If it is a return, it would imply that it was separate from itself, that it was not identical with itself, that it was in some way *interrupted* from itself. As the President, Mitterrand speaks *for* France, for a *part* of Europe, for a part that wants to be a part of Europe—or at least the European Community.

Derrida offers an axiom for this part/whole relation. He says:

> What is proper to a culture is to not be identical to itself. Not to not have an identity, but not to be able to identify itself, to be able to say "me" or "we"; to be able to take the form of a subject only in the non-identity to itself or, if you prefer, only in the difference *with itself* [*avec soi*]. There is no culture or cultural activity without this difference *with itself*. A strange and slightly violent syntax: "with itself" [*avec soi*] also means "at home (with itself)" [*chez soi*] (with, *avec*, is *chez*, *apud hoc*). In this case, self-difference, difference to itself [*difference a soi*], a difference at once internal and irreducible to the "at home (with itself)" [*chez soi*]. It would go there and divide just as irreducibly the center or hearth [*foyer*] of the "at home" (with itself). (*The Other Heading*, henceforth OH, 9)

The part-whole relation—parts of Europe to Europe as a whole, the countries of Europe in relation to Europe as a whole may be the principle of the European Community, but is it the way to read Europe today?

Merleau-Ponty spoke of the difference between Europe as *representation* and Europe as *act*. Yes, the countries of the European Community will seek to represent themselves and be represented in the European Community. But in reading Derrida, Europe is also not pure act either. Where Merleau-Ponty sees an *écart* between Europe as representation and Europe as act, where Europe as act becomes the *écart* in its representations, Derrida is concerned with the sense in which Europe cannot be fully reunited with itself, its limits and borders cannot be fully identical with itself: "What is proper to a culture," Derrida writes, "is to not be identical to itself" (OH 9). Multiplicity interrupts self-identity. The postmodern interruption marks multiplicity and non-identity, non-homogeneity. A culture which is multiple, a culture marked by alterity, heterogeneity, and cultural differences is not identity to itself—France with its Algerian, Moroccan, Polish, Russian, and Italian (among so many other) citizens—how can it be fully self-identical? And yet it will be called Europe, and it will have been a postmodern Europe.

And who is the "we" of Europe? As an American, I am not a European, and yet I have spent a significant part of the last thirty

Reading Post-Modernism as Interruption

years in "parts" of Europe. Derrida, born in Algeria but a French citizen, lives most of the year in France but spends much time in the United States. "We" are not Europeans. He is, I am not. The question of identity is a question of difference. Europe as different from itself. Europe is at home (*chez soi*) with itself, and yet some Germans want to throw out some of its Turkish *Ausländer*, who are in many cases already citizens. The "British" have problems with "their" Pakistanis and "their" East Indians, many of whom are citizens. Are they *all* Europeans?

Derrida asks about the "Europe of today." He asks: "Is one more faithful to the heritage of a culture by cultivating the difference-to-oneself (*with oneself*) that constitutes identity or by confining one-self to an identity wherein this difference remains *gathered*? (OH 11). The same question could be asked of the MAK sign-sculpture. Is its self-identity more important than its difference to itself? As Derrida wrote in *Of Grammatology* (1967), and in his reading of that itinerant European Jean-Jacques Rousseau: "Difference does not *resist* appropriation, it does not impose an exterior limit upon it. Différance began by *broaching* alienation and it ends by leaving reappropriation *breached*. . . . *Différance* produces what it forbids, makes possible the very thing that it makes impossible."[4] Was Derrida speaking of Europe? Or will he have been speaking of the postmodern interruption, of postmodernism as interruption, of Europe as the *écart* between act and representation, of Europe as the inscription of differences, of Europe as the presentation of the unpresentable in the presentation of Europe itself?

Notes

1. Jean-François Lyotard, "An Answer to the Question, What Is the Postmodern?" in *Postmodernism Explained*, trans. and ed. Julian Pefanis and Morgan Thomas (Minneapolis: University of Minnesota Press, 1992), pp. 11, 15.
2. Maurice Merleau-Ponty, *Texts and Dialogues*, ed. Hugh J. Silverman and James Barry, Jr. (Atlantic Highlands, N.J.: Humanities Press, 1992), p. 15. Henceforth cited as TD.
3. Jacques Derrida, *The Other Heading: Reflections on Today's Europe,* trans. Pascale-Anne Brault and Michael B. Naas (Bloomington: Indiana University Press, 1992), p. 8. Henceforth cited as OH.
4. Jacques Derrida, *Of Grammatology*, trans. Gayatri Chakravorty Spivak (Baltimore: Johns Hopkins University Press, 1974), p. 143.

13

Merleau-Ponty and Derrida: Difference/Identity

Bernard Flynn

Mindful of Oscar Wilde's injunction, "Quote yourself often, it adds spice to the conversation," I begin by giving a brief summation of, followed by a reflection upon, some thoughts about the relationship between the work of Merleau-Ponty and that of Derrida which I developed in my 1984 article "Textuality and the Flesh: Derrida and Merleau-Ponty."[1] In this article, I viewed both thinkers as effecting a deconstruction of the metaphysical privileging of presence. I pursued Derrida's claim that it was ultimately impossible for Husserl to maintain the distinction, which he argued for in the *Logical Investigations*, between an indicative and an expressive sign. At the present time, I shall not rehearse the now familiar details of this argument, nor deal with Claude Evans's contention that it is grossly inaccurate. I considered Derrida's problemization of this distinction to be emblematic of an effort to show that any philosophy which proposes the primacy of presence must ultimately repress, while simultaneously employing, the intertwining of presence and absence, identity and difference. It is Derrida's contention that that which is given in presence, present in flesh and blood, is in fact constituted across a field of difference which is itself in principle incapable of ever being present. To speak of the constitution of presence is to evoke an echo of transcendental philosophy. I shall return to this later.

Let me now consider those dimensions of difference which disrupt the proposed primacy of presence and, at the same time, function as its condition of possibility. According to Husserl, the expressive sign bears its meaning, while the indicative sign refers to something other than itself. In the communicative employment of language, there is an intertwining of indication and expression, the words that I use indicate to my interlocutor the meaning present "in" my mind. In order to disengage this dimension of indication, Husserl proposes a regression, a reduction, if you prefer, to the employment of "signs" in solitary mental life, where no indicative function is involved since none is needed. Thus there is no reference to alterity. The intentional object is present to a mind which is present to itself.

Derrida argues that this privileging of presence, this pretension to an identity which is prior to difference, and in reference to which difference will be thought of in terms of privation, is disrupted from a number of directions. He contends that this disruption happens both on the side of the intentional object and on the side of the subject that intends it. Let me begin on the side of the intentional object. Can a meaning, a signification, be present? Derrida claims that it cannot, because every signifying unit is constituted in reference to its possible repetition, and thus absence. It is not just that every meaning, or ideal object, can be repeated. In fact, Husserl insists on this. Rather, it is that the possibility of repetition is what constitutes it as a signifying unit. A non-repeatable signification would not signify, it would be an event in the world.

Furthermore, and for our purposes most importantly, Derrida critically appropriates Saussure's diacritical conception of meaning, whereby the meaning of a sign may not be traced to the subjective sense-giving which bestows a meaning, but must instead be viewed in terms of its diacritical relation with other signs within the system. Whether it is used communicatively or in solitary mental life, the sign, on the level of signifier and signified, has meaning by virtue of its difference with other signifiers and signifieds. Its reference to the, in principle, absent system is essential to its identity. On the level of the subject, Derrida attempts to show that Husserl's analysis of time and the subject's self-relation introduces difference into the very heart of identity. The living present itself is engendered as an intersection of a system of retentions and protentions which veer off into an indefinite horizon. The very ipseity of the self is constituted in terms of the self's relation to itself, the auto-affection of a voice which hears itself speaking. An initial non-identity is the condition of self-consciousness, and thus of identity.

Turning to Merleau-Ponty, the guiding thread that organized my reading of his work was his critique of the notion of being as determinate. Already in *The Structure of Behavior*, he criticizes proponents of Gestalt Theory for trying to think the notion of the gestalt within an objectivist ontology, thus viewing it as determinate, as a sort of thing. In *Phenomenology of Perception*, he continues to pursue this path through his critique of the hypothesis of constancy. In this critique he shows how both objectivist and intellectualist conceptions of perception attempt to construct the perceived world from the "real world"—the "world" from the "universe." He claims that the motive is the same in both conceptions, namely, to resolve the ambiguity of the perceived world, with its horizon of indeterminacy, into the determinacy of the "real world"; relegating indeterminacy to the side of the subject and thus opening the path for its elimination, as the "confused thought" of perception becomes a clear and distinct concept. Against this he argues for the irreducibility of the ambiguity of the perceived world.

In *The Visible and the Invisible*, Merleau-Ponty presents our insertion into the *there is* of the world as a veritable labyrinth of indeterminacy. He develops the notion of flesh which is less a being than a ray of being, an element in the ancient Greek sense, which exists by a fundamental *écart*, or divergence from itself. In his analysis of the touching-touched, he tells us that the immanence of the body is indefinitely *deferred*. His late writings abound with themes of non-identity, the derived character of presence. The present, he tells us, is like a screen-memory in the psychoanalytic sense, which is to say, it is derived; its privilege, its primordial giveness, is illusory.

On the above topics one can, as I have, construct a number of points of convergence between the work of Merleau-Ponty and that of Derrida. Nevertheless, what I would like to do now is to direct our attention to their appropriations of Saussure's linguistic theory, in order to see if this does not lead us to a profound divergence in their philosophical projects. We begin with Derrida. He tells us that failing any "legitimate" beginning point for philosophical reflection, we must begin from where we are, which is to say, in a philosophical field in which the thought of difference proliferates. He evokes Nietzsche's notion of the differentiation of forces, Freud's idea of breaching, the ontological difference of Heidegger, and, of course, the role of difference in the linguistics of Saussure. As is well known, Derrida's appropriation of Saussure, and of others as well, is not uncritical. In *Of Grammatology*, he gives us a deconstructive reading of Saussure. The basic movement of this text is his claim that Saussure wishes to exclude writing from the object domain of linguistics, thereby valorizing speech and thus repeating what Derrida considers to be the founding gesture of metaphysics from Plato to Heidegger. At the same time, Saussure evokes the differential character of signs within a linguistic system, which leads him to have recourse to writing. Thus what is excluded at the level of enunciation re-enters on the level of description. This is the contradiction which provokes the deconstructive reading. Notwithstanding the deconstructive reading, in a certain sense a critique, there is nonetheless a positive appropriation, a reinscription, of Saussure's conception of difference.

Différance, with an "a" to signify the irreducibility of writing to speech, becomes, as Rodolphe Gasché argues, one of Derrida's infrastructures. It becomes part of a "system," as Gasché designates it, beyond Being. In the reinscription of Saussure's notion of difference within Derrida's own work, it is of course no longer employed in the service of the exclusion of writing. On the contrary, it is connected to writing, arche-writing. Furthermore it is "liberated" from its circumscription within a determinate system, a totalized structure. In his article, "Structure, Sign, and Play," while specifically speaking about Levi-Strauss but obviously referring to structuralism in general, Derrida argues that structures, even when viewed in a guilty and nostalgic lament for a lost center, are what limit the play of difference. He tells us that the play of difference must be thought as "prior" to Being. The first chapter of *Of Grammatology* is entitled "The End of the Book and the Beginning of Writing." The book is, of course, the "good book." Thus he writes,

> The idea of the book, which always refers to a natural totality, is profoundly alien to the sense of writing. It is the encyclopedic protection of theology and of logocentrism against the disruption of writing. . . . against difference in general.[2]

Difference, liberated from its circumscription in the structure or the book, becomes dissemination. Any attempt to re-totalize the play of difference will be viewed as a rear-guard action of logocentrism. The question that we pose here, and for the moment leave unanswered, is the following: "Is there no alternative between, on the one hand, a determinate totality—structure or book—and, on the other hand, the indefinite play of difference?"

Claude Evans contends that Derrida's reading of Saussure is inaccurate; however, when we consider Merleau-Ponty's reading of Saussure there is no question as to its accuracy. It is clearly inaccurate. As the analysts say, it is a strong misreading. In *The Prose of the World*, Merleau-Ponty makes the extraordinary claim that "Saussure has the great merit of having taken the step which liberates history from historicism. . . ."[3] In fact, Saussure meant to liberate us not from historicism, but from history entirely by conceiving

diachronic linguistics as an ancillary discipline in reference to the
real object of linguistics, which was to be synchronic and ahistorical.
Merleau-Ponty's *Humanism and Terror* is a work of radical historicism. In the *Phenomenology of Perception*, he has an expressive conception of language—*la parole parlante* expresses the
emotional essence of the world, *la parole parlée* is simply an institutionalization, an alienation, of the more original act of expression—but in the Working Notes of *The Visible and the Invisible*,
he writes, "language has us and that it is not we who have language."[4] A radical shift has taken place. Language is no longer our
expression; rather, it is we who dwell within language. Between
these two conceptions of language stands Saussure. As is well known,
Saussure distinguishes between *la parole* and *la langue*, between
the event of speech and the structure of language. In the service of
a project to think of history in such a way as to liberate us from
historicism, Merleau-Ponty transforms Saussure's distinction into
that of event and advent. In *The Prose of the World*, he writes:

> We propose, on the contrary [to Malraux's conception], to con-
> sider the order of culture or meaning as an original order of
> advent which should not be derived from the order of mere events,
> if such exist, or treated simply as the effect of unlikely
> conjunctures.[5]

The advent, unlike the structure, "does not leave time behind: it is
a promise of events."[6] The event is a datable occurrence. The advent institutes a *style*, which can be continued or transformed. It
"detaches" itself from spatial-temporal location by opening a horizon. Meaning is given not in the transparency of a concept, or a
determinate structure, but in tufts and thickets. It is neither fact
nor essence, neither event nor structure; rather, it institutes a mode
of generality. In the Preface to *Signs*, Merleau-Ponty continues to
develop this notion in his discussion of the classics. The classic,
for example, the work of Marx, Descartes, and others, does not
contain timeless truths nor is it strictly datable, rather, it "pre-
sides over a certain time" by opening horizons for further thought.
It reveals a certain dimension of Being, an indeterminate style which
bears within itself the latency for further thought, including those
thoughts which come to contest it. Even if we are not Cartesians,
we owe many of our reasons for not being so to Descartes.

Merleau-Ponty does not think the relationship between event and
advent in terms of a juxtaposition. Recall that, in his description
of the advent, he said events, "if such exist." There is between

event and advent a relation of intertwining. The French Revolution, which he evokes as an example, is indeed a datable event, which took place in 1789, but it also, like the Greek *polis* or the Roman Republic, institutes a certain vision of history. It continues to preside over an indefinite time. Indeed, it unleashes a play of significance, but one that is neither rigorously determined by a structure nor purely indeterminate. Rather it institutes a mode of generality of Being, of the *there is* in which we are irreducibly inscribed. It is neither beyond Being nor beyond history. He writes, "Acts of signification are essentially historical, the advent is event."[7] Advent is event and event is advent. For Merleau-Ponty the problematic of identity and difference is inscribed within the problematic of reversibility. Between the hand as touching and the hand as touched there is a reversibility. The identity of the body with itself is always deferred. Identity is always already marked by difference.

Nevertheless, it must be emphasized that this always deferred immanance of the body with itself does not foreclose the question of the body's unity, its identity. Merleau-Ponty's thought is far from that of Deleuze's appropriation of Artaud's notion of a "body without organs," a body become pure fluidity or flow of energy. According to Merleau-Ponty, the experience of reversibility reveals the body as a being of layers. Like the sensible world in which it is inscribed, the body is a being of surface and depth. In *The Visible and the Invisible*, he writes:

> The visible can thus fill me and occupy me only because I who see it do not see it from the depths of nothingness, but from the midst of itself; I the seer am also visible. . . . [the one who sees] feels himself emerge from the visible by a sort of coiling up or redoubling, fundamentally homogeneous with it; he feels that he is the sensible itself coming to itself and that in return the sensible is in his eyes as it were his double or an extension of his own flesh.[8]

The body is an archetype of Being; as there is a reversibility of the touching-touched, so there is a reversibilty of the seer and the seen—the narcissism of vision.

Indeed, for Merleau-Ponty, there is a problematic of difference. In his analysis of the color "red" he does not view it as an absolute sensible quality but rather as the play of difference within the field of reds, both real and imaginary. The play of difference is not circumscribed, or regulated, by a concept or structure; rather, it is engendered in terms of an initial inherence in the *there is* of the world, of language, and of history.

In *The Visible and the Invisible*, Merleau-Ponty presents a profound critique of both Husserl's practice of free variation and transcendental philosophy in general. To put it succinctly, we might say that his problem with free variation is that, in order to effect it, what is required is a subject who is capable of transforming its inherence in the world into a pure possibility. He claims that I do have the power to "give myself leeway," to move from the real to the possible, from the actual to the virtual, but what I do not have is the power to complete the cycle by transforming the real into a variant of the possible. To do so would require a subject capable of detaching itself from its inherence in the *there is* of the world.

He also shows that transcendental reflection attempts to follow backward, in a manner similar to which one can follow, in either direction, the path from Notre-Dame to Étoile, the path by which the transcendental subject constitutes the world of experience and thus arrives at the subjective conditions of the possibility of experience. Here again what is presupposed is the possibility of a subject capable of detaching itself from its inherence in the world in order to arrive at the pure conditions of its possibility. In the case of both Husserl and Kant, in different ways of course, the terminus is a worldless subject. In lieu of this form of reflection, Merleau-Ponty proposes "hyper-reflection," a reflection which is cognizant of its inherence in the world and, consequently, of the limitations of its capacity for reflection. A form of reflection that, in agreement with Kafka, could say, "The things give themselves to me not at the root but at a point somewhere in the middle."

Do we dare suggest that this critique might apply to the philosophy of difference? In one respect, obviously not: transcendental reflection terminates in the unifying power of the subject, whose unity—transcendental apperception—is the archetype of the unity of the object and of the field of experience. We are not attributing to Derrida a secret doctrine of absolute subjectivity. Rodolphe Gasché has argued that Derrida's "infrastructures"—*différance*, arche-writing, trace, supplement, and so forth—form a chain and cannot be viewed as simply different aspects of one and the same unified movement. This is crucial, for if they were aspects of one movement, not only could Derrida's thought not be viewed as "hermeneutic nihilism," anything goes, etc., but it would become a form of transcendental idealism. Gasché insists on the singularity of each of the infrastructures. He contends that they form a chain of singular and strategic interventions. But even if one grants that there is no one, unifying movement of which each infrastructure would be a moment, nonetheless there is at least a "family resemblance" between the infrastructures. May not the chain itself, even in default of any ultimate unity, play a role analogous to what the philosophy of reflection claims to achieve? Namely, that of a stratum, as Derrida himself says, "older than Being," which subtends our inherence in the *there is* of the world.

Gasché is fully aware of the proximity of Derrida's thought to the philosophy of reflection. He differentiates it from a philosophy of reflection by claiming that it is more *radical* (a term he says that he uses only for convenience). It is more radical in the sense that, in the classical philosophy of reflection, including Hegel's doctrine of absolute reflection, alterity is thought only in the form of opposition, or negation; here negation is "put to work" in the service of identity, through the dialecticizing of alterity, whereas in Derrida's work alterity is thought in a manner different from that of dialectical negation. The chain of infrastructures does not have the structure of opposition, nor do the infrastructures present an essence, nor can they be totalized. The chain of infrastructures is both more and less than a ground. It is more in that it inscribes the entire oppositional discourse of philosophy in a "more" original relation to alterity; or, in the language of Bataille, it inscribes the restricted economy within a general economy. It constitutes a "reduction of the phenomenological reduction."[9] It is less than a ground in that it reaches no unique point of origin. The origin and its constitutive operation are themselves "situated within a syntax without origin."[10] Unlike a ground, the chain of infrastructures does not command, or regulate, the play of difference, but rather inscribes the structure of command itself within a non-oppositional and unregulated relationship to alterity.

My point is not, arguing against Gasché, to claim that the chain of infrastructures does in fact constitute a ground in the traditional sense, thus reducing deconstruction to an esoteric form of transcendental philosophy. Rather, I wish to pose the question as to whether their proximity to the notion of a non-phenomenal ground does not render them subject to the type of critique that Merleau-Ponty directed against transcendental philosophy, namely, seeking a level beneath, or even on the side of, the phenomena of the world—the *there is* of the world—which in some way accounts for its phenomenalization. A similar point was made by Gasché in his 1978 article, "Deconstruction as Criticism," but with a completely opposite valence. After speaking about Merleau-Ponty's conception of hyper-refection and its insertion into the *there is* of the world, into being, Gasché writes:

> The desire for such a pre-reflective *being* keeps hyper-dialectics in the bonds of philosophy. . . . Nonetheless, *hyper-reflection* came close to anticipating the *strictly speaking* no longer philosophical operation of deconstruction.[11]

I am suggesting that the failure to "take the next step" is perhaps Merleau-Ponty's virtue.

My point is that both Merleau-Ponty and Derrida reject an ultimate grounding in the notion of a constituting subject. But Derrida takes the "next step" in seeking a non-oppositional relation to alterity—a system of infrastructures "older than Being," an unregulated play of difference. Whereas for Merleau-Ponty, our assertion into the *there is* of the world is that beyond which no next step is possible. The identity of the body is both deferred and achieved, not by its submission to a non-phenomenal, unregulated play of difference, but by its divergence from itself—*écart*. Its insertion into the *there is* of the world is an "advent" in the sense referred to above. It is my contention that in the thought of Merleau-Ponty one can think difference as divergence, *écart*, and identity, whereas in the thought of Derrida one can think difference, but identity is either thought of as a rear-guard action of logocentrism, and thus subject to a deconstructive critique, or as completely indeterminate.

What consequence might this have for, for example, political philosophy? Let me now turn to Derrida's attempt to think the identity of Europe in his book *The Other Heading*. And then let me, all too briefly, compare it with a similar project in the work of a thinker inspired by the philosophy of Merleau-Ponty, Claude Lefort. My reading of Derrida is something of a test, but not a trial, much less an inquisition. His intentions are clearly admirable: an attempt to respond to the question of European identity, while avoiding racism, Eurocentrism, and xenophobia. The question is whether or not his philosophy has within itself the resources necessary to do so satisfactorily.

In *The Other Heading* one meets, but not for the first time, another member of the family of infrastructures, namely, exemplarity. A large part of Derrida's text concerns itself with a critical reading of the conception of the notion of European identity as advanced in the work of Husserl, Heidegger, and, most importantly, Paul Valéry. I will abstract from the differences between them, which are quite considerable, in order to focus on what Derrida sees as

their commonality. None of them proposes to define Europe's identity
with itself, and thus its difference from other cultures, in terms of
the presence of some empirical determination—for example, we
are smarter than they—thereby removing the discussion from a simple
racist discourse. Rather Europe is defined as an *example* of humanity, but this exemplarity is elaborated in such a way that Europe becomes not just any example, but the good example—the
leading example, the head example—thus the title of the book. As
we have seen above, in Derrida's thought there is no simple identity. Identity is always constituted through internal differentiation.
The self *is* a relation to self. Internal difference does not befall the
self, it *is* the self. Metaphysics both recognizes and represses difference in identity, absence at the heart of presence. From Husserl,
Derrida takes up the anti-metaphysical insight that meaning does
not depend on intuition, on presence, since empty intuitions are
meaningful. But then, according to Derrida, Husserl represses this
insight by claiming that empty intuitions are finalized toward
fulfillment, and thus conceived of privatively as "empty" until they
are fulfilled. Teleology, or finality, renders provisional the difference that troubles identity.

According to Derrida, the metaphysical concept of finality is found
to be operative in Europe's thought of its own identity. On the one
hand, Europe is one society among others; it is an example of
humanity. But on the other hand, it is *the* example in which the
idea of which it is an example becomes visible. *Après coup* all
other cultures are also visible as examples of humanity, however,
their exemplarity can only be read off the leading exemplarity of
Europe. Paradoxically, the uniqueness of Europe is that it embod-
ies the universal idea of humanity. Conceived empirically, it is
one particular society; but in terms of its idea of itself, it is universal. Its modesty is also its hubris. "The value of universality
here capitalizes all the antinomies, for it must be linked to the
value of *exemplarity* that inscribes the universal in the proper body
of a singularity. . . ."[12] There is a deconstructive instability in the
logic of exemplarity; it tries to assert two incompatible positions
at the same time. On the one hand, it is particular, only an example; on the other hand, the fact that it perceives itself as an example institutes a complicity with the universal. Derrida writes:

> Whether it takes a national form or not, a refined, hospitable
> or aggressively xenophobic form or not, the self-affirmation of
> an identity always claims to be responding to the call or assig-
> nation of the universal. There are no exceptions to this law. No

cultural identity presents itself as the opaque body of an untranslatable idiom, but always, on the contrary, as the irreplaceable *inscription* of the universal in the singular, the *unique testimony* to the human essence and to what is proper to man.[13]

The instability between the singularity of the example and the universality of the idea of which it is the example is resolved through the notion of finality, thus laying the deep philosophical foundation for what Charles Taylor has called "a cultural minus position," that is to say: after other societies shed the finite dimension of their culture—after a "cultural meltdown" provoked by modernization, market relations, universalization of proletarian class consciousness, or some universal solvent—they will, if not become like us, at least head in the same direction. Needless to say, such a conception can legitimate considerable violence against others. Derrida cites a document from the French Ministry of Foreign Affairs which states that, "French cultural identity would thus be *responsible* for the European *today* and, thus, as always, for the trans-European . . . *today*. It would be responsible for the universe: and for human rights and international law. . . ."[14] What has happened, and not only once, is that "what is proper to a particular nation or idiom would be a heading for Europe; and what is proper for Europe would be, analogously, to advance itself as a heading for the universal essence of humanity."[15]

After a critique of such conceptions, how to respond responsibly? The bearer of the heading is the head man. The bearer of the cap, thus the French title *L'Autre Cap*, is *le capitaine*. Derrida invokes the ship in Plato's *Republic*; heading also denotes direction—where are we heading? Thus, what to do? Seek another heading; that is, change direction—seek a "completely other heading."[16] But how characterize this other heading? According to Derrida, it is impossible; for any positive characterization would fall back into the logic of exemplarity. We are submitted to a double bind: while retaining the idea of the universality of the old Europe, at the same time we must *invent*, I emphasize, another heading, a heading of the other, a heading "to come," as in "democracy to come." Derrida explicitly avows and defends this impossibility, arguing that to think it as other than impossible would be to finitize the infinity of responsibility. It would be to turn it into a technology, "the simple application of knowledge or know-how."[17] This is, for me, the problem. After having deconstructed a certain conception of European identity, Derrida ends by saying that any positive characterization of it is impossible. His conclusion justifies some of my worst suspicions about his ability to think identity.

Now let us shift our attention to another possibility, one elaborated by Lefort and inspired by certain aspects of the ontology of Merleau-Ponty. Our insertion into the *there is* of the world is, for Merleau-Ponty, an irreducible contingency. Hyper-reflection acknowledges its inability to go to the root of things; it is always, as Kafka put it, at a point somewhere in the middle. Let me begin by noting certain similarities in Derrida's and Lefort's conception of Europe. Both see an unstable interplay between particularity and universality. Nevertheless, for Lefort this interplay is not explicable by a "law of exemplarity," but rather by the particular historical nature of the European monarchy and its relation to Christianity. Lefort views the self-representation, the *mise-en-scene*, of the monarchy as being drawn from the figure of the mystical body of Christ. The double nature of Christ, both human and divine, serves as the *imago* through which the European monarchy was constituted. As Christ was both human and divine, likewise the Church constituted a mystical body, both visible and invisible, with the Pope as a figure of mediation between the temporal and the eternal, between the faithful and Christ. The secularization of this notion issues in the figure of the kingdom, the realm, unified as a quasi-mystical body, with the king as its head, and in like manner, as a point of mediation between God and man. In virtue of this role of mediation, the king has two bodies: body of nature and body of grace. Lefort draws from the brilliant analysis of Kantorowicz in his book *The King's Two Bodies: A Study in Medieval Political Theology*.[18] The body of the king is the point of intersection between the visible and the invisible. The king represents, at the same time, the unity of the realm and the intersection with the divine, through which operations of power have their legitimacy. For Lefort, this representation is not an ideology, a mystification of power; rather, it exists within the symbolic dimension of society. The symbolic order is, for Lefort, as it was for Lacan, a marker of radical finitude, of society's non-identity with itself.[19] Lacan writes, "of the symbolic order, no metalanguage can be spoken, or, more aphoristically, there is no Other of the Other."[20]

In a prolonged meditation on Dante's *The Monarchy*,[21] which Lefort contends is a fundamental document for the formation of the European monarchy, he claims that Dante lays the foundation for a secular politics by elaborating the idea of a universal monarchy, which would be ruled over by a universal king and would unify mankind politically. He credits Dante with being the first to make the concept of humanity—a concept which, of course, precedes him—a political concept. The universal king draws his legitimacy directly from God and not from the Pope. The symbolic *place* of legitimacy is *another place*—a massively affirmed invisible. The king is not deified, but the doubling of his body situates his body of grace in the place of transcendence. The figure of the monarch represents the unity of mankind. Thus Dante installs a certain ambiguity concerning the limits of sovereignty.

Marx said, against Prudhon, that history always moves on its bad side. According to Lefort, the good and the bad sides are profoundly intertwined. The phantasm of the One, representing the political unity of mankind, on the one hand, fuels messianic dreams of world conquest, but, on the other hand, ultimately gives rise to the notion of the rights of man. For Lefort, our political modernity consists in the disincarnation of the figure of the king. In a monarchy, at the time of the death of a king, one said: "The king is dead, long live the king." But after the beheading of Louis XVI, one could only say: "The king is dead." The place of sovereignty remains, but it must remain as an *empty place*. It can be filled only provisionally; no one can again claim to incarnate the realm, or humanity. The attempt to do so is the totalitarian phantasm.

The ambiguity concerning particularity, singularity, and universality that Derrida has noted remains, but not because of the "law of exemplarity," to which there is no exception, but because of a historical contingency due to our insertion into the *there is* of the flesh of history. Hyper-reflection recognizes the contingency of its own origin. It rejects as illusory the attempt to find the non-phenomenal system of infrastructures older than Being. In the Working Notes of *The Visible and the Invisible*, Merleau-Ponty tells us: "No idea without a geography." Lefort thinks the identity of the European monarchy, not by seeking a concept, or structure, that would circumscribe internal differentiation, but in terms of the disincarnation of the figure of the sovereign, which retains its place as an empty place.

Is Europe a leading example? For Lefort, it is not an example at all, since there is no idea of which it would be an example. Its internal differentiation is not that of singularity to universality, but rather that of the flesh of history that exists as divergence, as non-identity with itself.

Notes

1. Bernard Flynn, "Textuality and the Flesh: Derrida and Merleau-Ponty," *Journal of the British Society for Phenomenology*, Vol. 15: 2 (May 1984), pp. 164–17.
2. Jacques Derrida, *Of Grammatology*, trans. Gayatri Chakravorty Spivak (Baltimore: The John Hopkins University Press, 1976), p. 18.
3. Maurice Merleau-Ponty, *The Prose of the World*, trans. John O'Neill (Evanston: Northwestern University Press, 1973), p. 23.
4. Maurice Merleau-Ponty, *The Visible and the Invisible*, trans. Alphonso Lingis (Evanston: Northwestern University Press, 1968), p. 194.
5. Merleau-Ponty, *The Prose of the World*, p. 79.
6. Ibid., p. 82.
7. Ibid., p. 81.
8. Merleau-Ponty, *The Visible and the Invisible*, pp. 113–14.
9. Rodolphe Gasché, *The Tain of the Mirror* (Cambridge: Harvard University Press, 1986), p. 159.
10. Derrida, *Of Grammatology*, p. 243.
11. Rodolphe Gasché, "Deconstruction as Criticism," *Glyph*, No. 6 (1979), p. 188.
12. Jacques Derrida, *The Other Heading*, trans. Brault and Naas (Bloomington: Indiana University Press, 1992) p. 72.
13. Ibid., pp. 73–73.
14. Ibid., pp. 51–52.
15. Ibid., p. 48.
16. Ibid., p. 30.
17. Ibid., p. 45.
18. Ernst Kantorowicz, *The King's Two Bodies: A Study in Medieval Political Theology* (Princeton: Princeton University Press, 1957).
19. For a further elaboration of this see the chapter on Lefort in my book, *Political Philosophy at the Closure of Metaphysics* (New Jersey/London: Humanities Press, 1992).
20. Jacques Lacan, *Ecrits*, trans. Alan Sheridan (New York: Norton & Co., 1977), pp. 310–11.
21. Dante, *La Monarchie*, trans. Michele Gally, preface by Claude Lefort, *La Modernité de Dante* (Paris: Belin, 1993).

14

... wild being/*écart*/capital ...

Wilhelm S. Wurzer

To dare the impossible: let the signature of our *Zeit/Geist* be read as uncanny divergence, indeed, as capital beyond conventional references. This signature begins to surface in the textual double of Merleau-Ponty's *écart* and Derrida's *différance*. Clearly *écart* and *différance* are not the same. We are merely recalling one to another, both for and against a twofold relation to capital. There are always divergences within the textual rhythms of these relations. Irreducible dispersions, *écart* and *différance* are very much the markings of our time. Thus each in its own way provides a curious echo of the subject, giving freely of the double—flesh/text. Oscillating between these two "graphic" dimensions, a split occurs (*kommt*)—capital, the madness of the clearest reference of all ready-to-hand beings. Now, taking to heart this "higher split," the textual double of *écart* and *différance* explodes, playing (out) the ends of textuality.

These ends begin with virtual flesh, marking the transcendence Merleau-Ponty names *écart*. Decentering the subject, this kind of *Selbsterscheinung*[1] points to presence beyond a coincidence with itself. Such presence is the new carnality, capital, a culmination of *écart*. "Here is the common tissue of which we are made" (*The Visible and the Invisible*, hereafter VI 203). A postmodern divergence is given precisely as pure auto-apparition.[2] No longer nature nor the beauty thereof, no longer subject nor its object, capital signifies the divergence of all beings, always at a distance from "the *Selbstgegeben-heit* of the exterior thing" (VI 191).

A free play, capital is no longer simply a concept but rather what Derrida calls "the other heading" of presence, the possibility of a postmodern *Urerlebnis*, yet always other than a primal referent. Derrida elucidates:

> From this paradox of the paradox, through the propagation of a fission reaction, all the propositions and injunctions are divided,

234

the heading splits, the capital is deidentified: it is related to itself not only in gathering itself in the difference *with itself* and
with the other heading, with the other shore of the heading, but
in opening itself without being able any longer to gather itself.[3]

For Derrida, the other heading of *différance*, or capital, marks a
certain renunciation of presence without giving in to a Marxist
intimidation. Diverging from the left and the right, capital indicates the site of the impossible. A rhythmic alterity, a specular
libido, capital blurs the thematics of Being.

> To say it all too quickly, I am thinking about the necessity for a
> new culture, one that would invent another way of reading and
> analyzing *Capital*, both Marx's book and capital in general. . . .[4]

What links capital to the theme of *écart* and *différance* is precisely what Merleau-Ponty calls "wild being" (VI 204). *Wild because being is capital rather than concept, historical rather than
transcendental.* Wild being, then, is that milieu without which
nothing is thinkable. Without always naming capital per se, Merleau-
Ponty proposes the question of *le capital* from the perspectives of
a certain spread between being and the abyss, "a wild perception"
(VI 212), a silent divergence. This entails a desire to see philosophy advance toward a certain separation from textuality. Thus, while
Derrida is certainly more postmodern in his renunciation of presence and in his affirmation of capital, he remains seemingly more
conservative than Merleau-Ponty in reading *différance* typographi-
cally. A certain theoreticism, therefore, remains in Derrida's philosophy. For Merleau-Ponty, however, *écart* is always already a
kind of *Vorhabe* of Being, in short, "wild Being"—a meta-textual,
post-textual, exceedingly out-of-textual, untraversable, in-visible
échappement (leakage). There is no textual immanence in *écart/*
capital, so that, as Merleau-Ponty writes, "the conception of history one will come to, will be nowise *ethical* like that of Sartre"
(VI 275).

> It will be much closer to that of Marx: Capital as a *thing* (not as
> a partial object of a partial empirical inquiry as Sartre presents
> it), as 'mystery' of history, expressing the 'speculative mysteries'
> of the Hegelian logic . . . . Work-over-matter-men=*chiasm.*"[5]

As concerns Derrida, capital is not wild being but rather another
heading for the inevitable paradox of the impossible. Unbridled
textuality beyond figurability, capital comes on the scene resem-
bling *différance.* A silent absence of the carnal leads to an apparitional

textuality. For Merleau-Ponty, on the other hand, "there is no other meaning than carnal, figure and ground" (VI 265). Indeed, *le Capital comme chose*, quite different from anything in particular, is the visible as in-visible, a new historical corporeity. By virtue of this (wild) dislocation of being comes all verticality. A unique *Erfüllung*, then, capital unfolds the world in divergences. "*Now*, this moment of the unfolding, is how the world senses itself across the multitudes of its individual sensors in the present phase of its becoming" (*Merleau-Ponty Vivant*, hereafter MPV, xxviii). In other words, capital shows itself as free play darkly in-between language and being, presence and absence beyond ontological differences.

Wild being marks difference as the *visible comme in-visible* (*Le Visible et l'invisible*, henceforth VI-F, 295). Because Merleau-Ponty takes into account a corporeal presence, capital cannot be merely theorized. It cannot be merely inscribed into *différance* if the same is taken to be writing. Merleau-Ponty is still working with the notes on history, namely, the history of the body. "My body is to the greatest extent what everything is" (VI 260). Accordingly, my body touches the universal thing, wild being/capital. And flesh of the world, while distinct from my flesh, touches me as intra-corporeal capital. This historical touching does not install another architecture of noeses-noemata but opens up the very possibilities of *écart*. Ultimately, there are multiple entries into wild being enveloped in the visible. The touch-divergences which Merleau-Ponty introduces are to be understood as "a community of verbal *Wesen*," "*eine Art der Reflexion*" (VI 256). Here we encounter an ineluctable return to a carnal assignment, a presence on the verge of de-presencing, perhaps, even multiple attempts to exit the textual logic of *différance*. In his later work, Merleau-Ponty does not show, as D. M. Levin claims, that he was as much an enemy of the "metaphysics of presence" as Derrida has been (MPV 67). Philosophy is not ever a question of being an enemy of metaphysics. If anything, it is a sad friend after a certain separation (*écart*), wild as it may seem. To touch oneself is not to see according to a narrow auto-apparition but to touch the wild thing, the unpresentable, invariably decentering the body. This is not a question of narcissism but rather a communal mirroring, a self-showing of capital as inter-corporeality. This intertwining remains ontological in the Heideggerian sense for Merleau-Ponty. Philosophy, therefore, is still a question of *phainesthai*, not of the flesh per se, but rather of a wilder presence, that of multiple inter-corporealities, consistently in-different to a phenomenology of narcissism. Surely, Merleau-Ponty thinks beyond the point of a new form of subjectivity. Indeed, with regard to this self-showing of capital divergences he goes beyond Derrida's narrative of "another heading." For Merleau-Ponty, capital is more than a kind of philosophy-writing-about-its-textual-ends. It is a wild phenomenon, wild, even in Nietzsche's sense of Dionysian wisdom. However, unlike Nietzsche, and partially like Derrida, Merleau-Ponty regards the divergence from eternity as a kind of *Überschreiten* (VI 259), an exceeding of presence rooted in the sovereignty of inscriptions.

It is not clear to me whether Derrida desires post-textual divergences. It appears that *différance* belongs to the order of a certain textuality, yet escapes the auto-textualities of metaphysics. In coming years it remains to be seen whether Derrida will be irresistibly drawn to throw off the yoke of pure textual surging and to open *différance* a step beyond Merleau-Ponty's *écart*. For now, it appears that Merleau-Ponty's thought is a step ahead of Derrida's insofar as he does not confine capital to the question of Capital under another heading. This is obvious when one thinks of *écart* as the other being, wild while being capital.

Thus, Merleau-Ponty does not slide into the void of a new dimension but opens philosophy to non-philosophy, to divergences without an absolutely pure philosophical word. This does not reduce history to the visible, but it touches philosophy on both sides— the visible *and* the in-visible. This wildly open intimacy remains a divergence, yet always historical from the very beginning. Derrida recognizes this without difficulty. Still, he carries his reading of capital as far as possible toward the tenor of a textual resistance, advising that there is still a neo-capitalist exploitation. Regardless of the validity of this claim, Derrida views the divergences from the standpoint of linguistic difference rather than that of a possible "imaginary" onto-historical *écart*. He disregards the exemplary power in capital in its always-already-other-than-its-own showing. These divergent showings are not mere indications or expressions of non-philosophy. They are disruptions and disturbances within and without philosophy. "Whence carnal relations, from below, no less than from above and the fine point ... Entwining" (VI 269)— wild capital/vertical being, doubtless the *Horizonthaftigkeit* of inevitable differences. In any case, Merleau-Ponty's visible may be seen today in a radical displacement of one of Spinoza's leading propositions, which may now be read differently: "Whatever is, is in capital, and nothing can be or be conceived without capital."[6] Apart from capital, no visible dwelling can be illuminated within the in-visible. Consequently, Merleau-Ponty's philosophy, that is,

nonphilosophy, is not an anthropology but a distinct reading of
history rooted in capital folding over upon itself, becoming paradoxically its own *écart*.

Contrarily, to some extent at least, Derrida moves from Text to
texts, beyond metaphysics to a grammatological "time." There is
certainly discontinuity, a post-figurable *écart*, a textual homeless-
ness, a *glissement* in-different to history as well as to the concrete
philosophy of wild being. Regarding being as a nostalgic preference, Derrida exceeds the Heideggerian configurations of *Denken*.
Merleau-Ponty, on the other hand, does not seek refuge from the
draft of ontological presence. On the contrary, *écart* is merely the
difference between *phainesthai* and *logos*, between capital's self-
showing and its letting be seen at a distance from itself. A de-
monic in-between, this erotic shift from philosophy to non-philosophy
back to philosophy does not turn away from a certain figurability
of *work*. Merleau-Ponty listens to the silence following Diotima's
discourse, which, more pointedly, unfolds an erotic stillness in
work, capital's wild performance:

> After all, everything that is responsible for creating something
> out of nothing is a kind of poetry; and so all the creations of
> every craft and profession are themselves a kind of poetry.[7]

Between philosophy and non-philosophy lies capital's symposium, a commemorative gathering of scenes from life. For us, this
life descends to a concrete, dynamic work-world (*Werkwelt*).[8] Such
is the fictioning power of capital, *poiesis* of world. Here there is
still too much figurability for Derrida, precisely because he believes *différance*, as if she were beyond it/id, eludes wild being.
Wild being, then, presents a distinct, non-imaginal tracing of the
in-visible to the visible. Still, writing and capital are not one and
the same. There is always an inter-shadowing of references, which,
in fact, does not proceed from an assimilation of textuality to history. In its continuous dissimulation, capital as *écart* is more wildly
differential than *différance*, more primordially free (and open) than
écriture.

We can see that the relationship between Merleau-Ponty and
Derrida is not a simple one, even if *écart* shows a certain alliance
with *différance*. This alliance, however, becomes questionable when
we encounter Merleau-Ponty's irreversible desire for historical presence, more clearly, for the figurability of work, more strenuously,
the work-over-matter-men=chiasm=capital. *Écart* is always separation from the "sunny places of thought,"[9] invariably desistance of

any typography beyond presence. Here *écart* strays from the *jouissance* of a general text. In a strange manner, philosophy is destined to provide a reason for the great pain in life. With regard to this, Merleau-Ponty quotes Nietzsche:

> We are not thinking frogs, nor are we objective and registering mechanisms with their innards in refrigeration. We constantly give birth to our thoughts out of pain, and, like mothers, endow them with all we have of blood, heart, ardor, joy, passion, agony, conscience, fatality. For us, life consists in continually transforming all that we are into clarity and flame, just as it transforms everything that we touch. (*Continental Philosophy*, hereafter CP, 10)

For Merleau-Ponty, philosophy, therefore, presupposes an *écart* between ourselves and capital, between my visible and invisible being. This separation marks a necessary *Weltthesis* of work/pain/history. Nonetheless, *écart* is also more complex. It involves a series of divergences as well as identities within difference. It is necessary that somewhere *écart* and capital be brought together and that this curious constellation be seen as gift. Under this name it is, not surprisingly, time-that-is-given in the historical figurability of work (*ergon*), which, however, is not drawn into a Derridian parergonality. The juncture of capital and flesh does not negate the divergences which manifest themselves even, and perhaps especially, within the disclosure of work (*Werk*). The alliance with work is simultaneously a separation from it. And this *écart* signifies wild capital, now regarded beyond its infrastructure as the chiasm, the intertwining of visible and invisible, of flesh and *phainesthai*. Note the different type of filiation, the kind that is not merely another heading for being but is organized around the historical work-to-be—a new naturality. Thus, Merleau-Ponty's *écart* signifies a phenomenological how, a mysterious who, as in Heidegger saying: "Der Mensch ist und ist doch nicht."[10] So, capital, too, looks like being and then it does not. And so it is with *écart*. At once pre-textual, textual, post-textual, *écart* happens notably in the kind of understanding we are, while remaining always at a distance.

Derrida is aware of this *écart*, which he records under the heading of *signature*, more precisely, *signature evenement*.[11] For him, this means that presence yields to style rather than to history. One might even read such an abdication of presence as rigorous intensification of a new interiority. Merleau-Ponty, on the other hand, concedes presence without installing it into a supplementary philosophical in-scription. Presence marks the bringing-forth of capital, unveiling "the worked-over-matter," being's turbulent chiasm without need for protection. For Derrida, however, "style uses its spur as a means of protection against the terrifying, blinding, mortal threat [of that] which *presents* itself, which obstinately thrusts itself into view."[12] Clearly this shows not only that Derrida proceeds from a rather refined philosophical view of protection, but also that this view is another beginning of academic guarding. *Différance* serves as an "unintended" shield for a spatiality otherwise known as everydayness. While Derrida would probably deny this claim, it is clear that *différance* does not speak to "the global conversation," notably the current information revolution, precisely another heading for capital.[13] Nor does he seem to address the urgent question regarding the relation of *différance* and the "electronic text," in particular "digitization."[14] Instead, on Derrida's view, style becomes a protective event. Protection from presence is accomplished by graphic effacement, leaving behind a mark, a trace, a signature, to be sure, a communicative event beyond the deed. What Derrida conveys and provides is always a presentation of beings, yet never the event of presence. Which means—if we sharpen the contours of *différance*— that philosophy is more or less a matter of style, a dispersed network of signatures. Merely exposed to these markings, philosophy is essentially no longer concerned with capital in its chiasmatic signification. At least for Derrida there are always only traces of the "worked-over-matter." Therefore, we do not encounter humans but signatures, perhaps a wilder capitalism than even Merleau-Ponty imagined. Silverman makes this clear when he defines marking the difference as marking the marking, which, he writes, "does not amount to anything contentful, anything upon which to base anything else."[15] Derrida's implacable fidelity of style to *différance* presents philosophy as virtual incorporations of an economy of meta-philosophy, differentially more philosophical, less metaphysical, yet undoubtedly more professorial. While Merleau-Ponty understands philosophy as providing a global, primordial cohesion, Derrida finds it to be a matter of the advent of style. The difference between these two philosophers cannot be marked so easily. The case of *écart* seems still very complicated. Nothing is won by saying *écart* means this and *différance* means that, especially when there is also an *écart* between the former and the latter. Nonetheless, Merleau-Ponty pushes the reader into an exemplary probity when he calls for a philosophy beyond a subject without history, undoubtedly beyond "the mark of a scriptive textuality," advancing always toward the art of signifying how the word is yet to be, how style may return, more properly, to become a re-writing of the "worked-over-matter."

While Merleau-Ponty and Derrida manifest openings that reflect the un-timely com-posure of capital colliding with spirit, they do not consider capital's own divergences, its rhythmic renunciations of presence and style. Both seem to overlook capital's wild obliteration of cultures and metaphysical closures as well as its ability to expose divergent fissures beyond the ideological tool of emancipation. Straying from waves of political images to instants of self-apparition, capital, freed from the commodified metaphysics of technology, yields an *écart* of spirit without the former alliance of dialectic and hermeneutic responses to questions. As it strays from the pure script of metaphysical textuality, roaming beyond a postmodern image-system, capital is more than a cursory glance at the ecstatic obscenity of capitalism. Disengaged from mirroring a particular cultural/textual space, capital sketches time as a sublime straying from presence *and* simulation, in turn pointing away from the logocentric signal of spirit to a disseminal constellation of free play and experimentation.

Capital's sublime play of *écart* separates *Zeit* from *Geist*, abandoning the solemnity of old cultures as well as the current repetitive culturing that may be seen fading into a "new enlightenment." Straying from the power of presence, capital will not be secured by the presence of any power. Indeed power *is* capital, at most an erosion of culture, at least the beginning of wild being. This obliteration of the West exposes the *écart* in capital as that of spirit (*Geist*) and com-posure (*Gelassenheit*). There is no awakening of the feeling of the supersensible here: only free play within experimentations, within digressions that have yet to be studied. What is most notable in these digressions is precisely the separation of culture from being, a wild working-over-the matter of the West. In view of the collapse of presence, capital persists. This new eccentricity brings about a disruption of *écart*, what might be called *sur-flections*.[16] Sur-flections are operations within *écart* which raise capital beyond the speculum of *Zeitgeist*, forward to a wild a-specificity that effaces the universal while dispersing the particular.

More pointedly, sur-flections are transcultural *Verständnisse* (understandings) of capital, in which *écart* is shown to be the free play of unlimited possibilities—a post-aesthetic convergence of satellites, television, fax, cellular telephones, and global computer networks. A new mood sets in motion the collision of these sur-flections: It is the mood of Merleau-Ponty's carnal art of swaying. Although intertwined, art and capital are not the same. Arguably, art (*Kunst*) is what capital does (*können*) and what is anticipated in *écart*. As being's wild play, art turns capital from a commodified presence to a rapidly passing event. In the wake of its self-appari-tion, capital opens into an immense field of post-aesthetic experimentations. Without vanishing from the scene, it withdraws from aesthetics, being drawn "onto-electronically" into the "worked-over-matter" of *écart*. The art work of *écart* remains a narrative, to be sure, a dis-course (*discurrere*, Lat. "to run about"). As idiom of capital, this dis-course accounts for the differentiated art of digital rhetoric within the post-textual twilight of Derridian sovereignties. Surflection, therefore, is replete with capital's most diverse opera-tional dispositions. Its discourse echoes a baffling economy, sway-ing ever so openly from "book to screen," from text to filming, from capitalism to the self-apparition of wild being.

More concretely, and in sum, capital signifies an *écart* that is for the most part other than its former *Dublette*. A peculiar *Zeig-Zeug*,[17] it indicates neither the other nor the self. Nor does it signify a triumph of privatization. As heir of Prometheus, capital marks an *Ereignis*, a *dis-appropriation*, always properly private, yet frequently open to "visible-invisible" divergences. In short, the thoughts of both Merleau-Ponty and Derrida regarding *écart/différance* neces-sitate a certain "postmodern" transformation of Heidegger's account of readiness-to-hand. However we do this, within or beyond phi-losophy, we cannot separate *écart* from world (*Weltlichkeit*). World allows us to understand what no thinker today can deny: the unassignable assignment, the *mimesis* of all ready-to-hand beings, the extraordinary convergences, quite simply, capital transforming world. Within this operation, the question of being-wild gets im-mediately underway. Hence, it is not abusive to suggest that capi-tal's status is more than the sovereignty of a certain textuality. In effect, it is the sovereignty of all textualities. In the long run it might insidiously lead us to the twilight of all sovereignties be-yond pure textual surging altogether. Or, if you prefer, as Graeme Nicholson does, more hopefully, capital may illustrate being less wildly by letting *dis-appropriation* be.

> It would (then) be the absolute disappearance of the property relation; it would continue a change in our relations, not only to one another but to the animals and things that constitute our environment.[18]

Notes

1. Maurice Merleau-Ponty, *The Visible and the Invisible*, trans. A. Lingis (Evanston: Northwestern University Press, 1968), p. 190; henceforth cited as VI. *Le Visible et l'Invisible* (Paris: Gallimard, 1964); Henceforth cited as VI-F.
2. "An apparition that is pure apparition" (VI 190–91). See M. C. Dillon's intriguing essay on "Merleau-Ponty and Postmodernity," in *Merleau-Ponty Vivant*, ed. M. C. Dillon (Albany: SUNY Press, 1991), p. xviii; henceforth cited as MPV.
   Also see M. C. Dillon's *Semiological Reductionism: A Critique of Deconstructionist Movement in Postmodern Thought* (Albany: SUNY Press, 1995).
3. Jacques Derrida, *The Other Heading: Reflections on Today's Europe*, trans. Pascale-Anne Brault and M. B. Naas (Bloomington: Indiana University Press, 1992), p. 75. Henceforth cited as OH.
4. OH 56. A year prior to the publication of Derrida's *L'autre cap*, I published two essays on reading capital differently in my *Filming and Judgment* (Atlantic Highlands, N.J.: Humanities Press International, 1990), pp. 81–97.
5. VI 275.
6. "Whatever is, is in God, and nothing can be or be conceived without God." Baruch Spinoza, *Ethics*, trans. Samuel Shirley (Indianapolis/Cambridge: Hackett Publishing Co., 1992), p. 40.
7. Plato, *Symposium*, trans. A. Nehamas and P. Woodruff (Indianapolis/Cambridge: Hackett Publishing Co., 1989), p. 51.
8. See Martin Heidegger, *Sein und Zeit* (Tübingen: Max Niemeyer Verlag, 1967), p. 117.
9. See Merleau-Ponty's "Philosophy and Non-Philosophy since Hegel," in *Continental Philosophy I*, ed. H. J. Silverman (New York: Routledge, 1988), p. 12. Henceforth cited as CP.
10. "Man is, yet he is not. It looks like being and it is not. And so it is with poetry." *Hölderlins Hymnen "Germanien" und "der Rhein"* (Frankfurt am Main: Klostermann, 1980), p. 36.
11. See H. J. Silverman's "Writing on Writing: Merleau-Ponty/Derrida," in his *Textualities: Between Hermeneutics and Deconstruction* (New York and London: Routledge, 1994) pp. 183–92.
12. Jacques Derrida, *Spurs, Nietzsche's Styles*, trans. Barbara Harlow (Chicago: University of Chicago, 1979), p. 39.
13. See Walter B. Wriston's *The Twilight of Sovereignty* (New York: Charles Scribner's Sons, 1992).
14. "For the deepest implication of electronic text for the teaching of literature is that literature can no longer be taught in isolation from the other arts. Digitization has made the arts interchangeable. You can change a visual signal into a musical one. You can zoom in on a letter until it changes from an alphabetic sign to an abstract pixel-painting. The digital equivalence of the arts has provided a genuinely theoretical basis for comparing the arts and for teaching them together. The new theory of prose style proves to be a general theory of style for the arts altogether." See Richard A. Lanham, *The Electronic Word*

(Chicago: University of Chicago Press, 1993), p. 130. Also see Nicholas Negroponte, *Being Digital* (New York: Knopf. 1995).

15. See G. A. Johnson and M. B. Smith, eds. *Ontology and Alterity in Merleau-Ponty* (Evanston: Northwestern University Press, 1990), p. 40.
16. See my *Filming and Judgment*, pp. 92–97.
17. See *Sein und Zeit*, p. 78.
18. Graeme Nicholson, *Illustrations of Being: Drawing Upon Heidegger and upon Metaphysics* (Atlantic Highlands, N.J.: Humanities Press International, 1992) pp. 278–79.

Selected Bibliography

Burke, Patrick, and Jan Van Der Veken, eds. *Merleau-Ponty in Contemporary Perspective*. Boston: Kluwer, 1993.

Busch, Thomas W. "Merleau-Ponty and the Problem of Origins." *Philosophy Today*, 2 (1967): pp nos 124–30.

———. *The Power of Consciousness and the Force of Circumstances in Sartre's Philosophy*. Bloomington: Indiana University Press, 1990.

Busch, Thomas W., and Shaun Gallagher, eds. *Merleau-Ponty, Hermeneutics and Postmodernism*. Albany: State University of New York Press, 1992.

Caputo, John D. *Radical Hermeneutics: Repetition, Deconstruction and the Hermeneutic Project*. Bloomington: Indiana University Press, 1987.

Culler, Jonathan. *On Deconstruction: Theory and Criticism after Structuralism*. Ithaca: Cornell University Press, 1982.

Dahllmayr, Fred. *Lifeworld, Modernity and Critique*. Amherst: University of Massachusetts Press, 1991.

Dastur, Françoise. "Perceptual Faith and the Invisible." *Journal of the British Society for Phenomenology*, 25 (1994): pp nos 44–52.

Dillon, M. C. *Merleau-Ponty's Ontology*. Bloomington: Indiana University Press, 1988.

———. *Merleau-Ponty Vivant*. Albany: State University of New York Press, 1991.

———. *Semiological Reductionism: A Critique of the Deconstructionist Movement in Postmodern Thought*. Albany: State University of New York Press, 1995.

Ferris, David. *Theory and the Evasion of History*. Baltimore: Johns Hopkins University Press, 1993.

———, ed. *Studies in Romanticism: Special Issue on Walter Benjamin and Romanticism*. Boston: Boston University, Winter 1992.

Flynn, Bernard. "Textuality and the Flesh: Derrida and Merleau-Ponty" *Journal of the British Society for Phenomenology*, 15 (1984): pp nos 164–77.

———. *Political Philosophy at the Closure of Metaphysics*. Atlantic Highlands: Humanities Press, 1992.

Gallagher, Shaun. *Hermeneutics and Education*. Albany: State University of New York Press, 1992.

———. "The Theater of Personal Identity: From Hume to Derrida." *The Personalist Forum*, 8 (1992): pp nos 21–30.

———. "Body Schema and Intentionality." *The Body and the Self*, ed. Jose Bermudez, Naomi Eilan, and Anthony Marcel. Cambridge: MIT Press/Bradford Books, 1995, pp nos 225–44.

Gasché, Rodolphe. *The Tain of the Mirror: Derrida and the Philosophy of Reflection*. Cambridge: Harvard University Press, 1986.

———. "Deconstruction as Criticism." *Glyph*, 6 (1979): pp nos 127–215.

Harvey, Irene. *Derrida and the Economy of Différance*. Bloomington: Indiana University Press, 1986.

Holland, Nancy. "Merleau-Ponty on Presence: A Derridian Reading." *Research in Phenomenology*, 16 (1986): pp nos 111–20.

Johnson, Galen, and Michael B. Smith, eds. *Ontology and Alterity in Merleau-Ponty*. Evanston: Northwestern University Press, 1990.

Lawlor, Leonard. *Imagination and Chance: The Difference between the Thought of Ricoeur and Derrida*. Albany: State University of New York Press, 1992.

Lefeuvre, Michel. *Merleau-Ponty au délà de la phénoménologie*. Paris: Klinksieck, 1976.

Lefort, Claude. *The Political Forms of Modern Society: Bureaucracy, Democracy, Totalitarianism*. Ed. John Thompson. Cambridge: The MIT Press, 1986.

———. *Democracy and Political Theory*. Trans. David Macey. Minneapolis: University of Minnesota Press, 1988.

Levin, David Michael. *The Opening of Vision: Nihilism and the Postmodern Situation*. London: Routledge, 1989.

———, ed. *Pathologies of the Modern Self: Postmodern Studies on Narcissism, Schizophrenia and Depression*. New York: New York University Press, 1987.

———, ed. *Modernity and the Hegemony of Vision*. New York: New York University Press, 1994.

Lingis, Alphonso. *Libido: The French Existentialist Theories*. Bloomington: Indiana University Press, 1985.

Madison, Gary B. *The Phenomenology of Merleau-Ponty*. Athens: Ohio University Press, 1979.

———. *The Hermeneutics of Postmodernity: Figures and Themes*. Bloomington: Indiana University Press, 1988.

———, ed. *Working through Derrida*. Evanston: Northwestern University Press, 1993.

———, ed. *The Ethics of Postmodernity: Contemporary Continental Perspectives*. Evanston: Northwestern University Press, 1995.

Margolis, Joseph. *Pragmatism without Foundations: Reconciling Realism and Relativism*. Oxford: Basil Blackwell, 1986.

———. *Science without Unity: Reconciling the Human and Natural Sciences*. Oxford: Basil Blackwell, 1987.

———. *Texts without Referents: Reconciling Science and Narrative*. Oxford: Basil Blackwell, 1988.

———. *Interpretation Radical But Not Unruly*. Berkeley: University of California Press, 1994.

Mazis, Glen. *Emotion and Embodiment: Fragile Ontology.* New York: Peter Lang, 1993.

———. *The Trickster, Magician & Grieving Man.* Santa Fe: Bear and Company, 1993.

McKenna, William, R.A. Harlan, and L.E. Winters, eds. *Apriori and World: European Contributions to Husserlian Phenomenology.* The Hague: Martinus Nijhoff, 1981.

Merleau-Ponty, Maurice. *Texts and Dialogues.* Ed. Hugh J. Silverman and James Barry Jr. Trans. Michael B. Smith et al. Atlantic Highlands: Humanities Press, 1992.

Morley, James, and Dorothea Olkowski, eds. *Merleau-Ponty, Desires and Imaginings.* Atlantic Highlands: Humanities Press, 1996.

Norris, Christopher. *Derrida.* Cambridge: Harvard University Press, 1987.

Olkowski, Dorothea. "Merleau-Ponty's Freudianism: From the Body of Consciousness to the Body of Flesh." *Review of Existential Psychology & Psychiatry*, 18 (1982–83): pp nos 97–116.

Olkowski, Dorothea, and Constantin V. Boundas, eds. *Gilles Deleuze and the Theater of Philosophy.* New York: Routledge, 1994.

Olkowski-Laetz, Dorothea. "Merleau-Ponty: The Demand for Mystery in Language." *Philosophy Today*, 31 (1987): pp nos 352–58.

Rorty, Richard. "Two Meanings of 'Logocentrism': A Reply to Norris." *Redrawing the Lines: Analytic Philosophy, Deconstruction, and Literary Theory.* Ed. Reed Way Dasenbrock. Minneapolis: University of Minnesota Press, 1989.

———. *Consequences of Pragmatism.* Minneapolis: University of Minnesota Press, 1982.

Ross, Stephen David. *Metaphysical Aporia and Philosophical Heresy.* Albany: State University of New York Press, 1989.

———. *Inexhaustibility and Human Being: An Essay on Locality.* New York: Fordham University Press, 1989.

———. *The Ring of Representation.* Albany: State University of New York Press, 1992.

Schrag, Calvin O. *Communicative Praxis and the Space of Subjectivity.* Bloomington: Indiana University Press, 1986.

———. *The Resources of Rationality: A Response to the Postmodern Challenge.* Bloomington: Indiana University Press, 1992.

———, ed. *Phenomenology in America: Origins and Developments.* Dordrecht: Kluwer, 1989.

Shapiro, Gary. *Alcyone: Nietzsche on Gifts, Noise and Women.* Albany: State University of New York Press, 1992.

———, ed. *After the Future: Postmodern Times and Places.* Albany: State University of New York Press, 1990.

Silverman, Hugh J. *Inscriptions: Between Phenomenology and Structuralism.* London and New York: Routledge and Kegan Paul, 1994.

———. *Textualities: Between Deconstruction and Hermeneutics.* New

York and London: Routledge and Kegan Paul, 1994.

Silverman, Hugh J., ed. *The Horizons of Continental Philosophy: Essays on Husserl, Heidegger, and Merleau-Ponty.* The Hague: Nijhoff/Kluwer, 1988.

———, ed. *Philosophy and Non-Philosophy Since Merleau-Ponty.* London: Routledge, 1988.

———, ed. *Derrida and Deconstruction.* London and New York: Routledge, 1989.

———, ed. *Writing the Politics of Difference.* Albany: State University of New York Press, 1991.

———, ed. *Questioning Foundations: Truth/Subjectivity/Culture.* New York and London: Routledge, 1993.

———, ed. *Cultural Semiosis: Tracing the Signifier.* New York and London: Routledge, 1996.

Silverman, Hugh J., and Don Ihde, eds. *Hermeneutics and Deconstruction.* Albany: State University of New York Press, 1985.

Silverman, Hugh J., and Donn Welton, eds. *Postmodernism and Continental Philosophy.* Albany: State University of New York Press, 1988.

Spanos, William V. *Repetitions: The Postmodern Occasion in Literature and Culture.* Baton Rouge: Louisiana State, 1987.

Wood, David, and Robert Bernasconi, eds. *Derrida and Différance.* Evanston: Northwestern University Press, 1988.

Wurzer, Wilhelm S. *Filming and Judgment: Between Heidegger and Adorno.* Atlantic Highlands: Humanities Press, 1990.

Wurzer, Wilhelm S., ed. *Visibility and Expressivity.* Albany: State University of New York Press, 1996.

Contributors

M. C. Dillon is Distinguished Teaching Professor of Philosophy at Binghamton University. He is author of *Merleau-Ponty's Ontology* (1988), *Semiological Reductionism: A Critique of the Deconstructionist Movement in Postmodern Thought* (1995), and essays on phenomenology, psychology, literature, and the philosophy of love and sexuality. He is editor of *Merleau-Ponty Vivant* (1991) and is writing a book on the philosophy of love. Dillon is General Secretary of the Merleau-Ponty Circle and a founding member of the International Association for Philosophy and Literature.

Patrick Burke is Associate Professor of Philosophy at Seattle University. He is author of a forthcoming volume entitled *Beyond Phenomenology, Toward an Ontology of Presence: Self-Critique and Transfiguration in the Thought of the Later Merleau-Ponty* (Phaenomenologica series of the Husserl Archives). He is coeditor of *Merleau-Ponty in Contemporary Perspective* (1993) and editor of the forthcoming English translation of Merleau-Ponty's lecture course entitled *L'Union de l'âme et du corps chez Malebranche, Biran et Bergson* (Humanities Press). He is working on a book on Merleau-Ponty's reading of Schelling.

Thomas W. Busch is Professor of Philosophy at Villanova University. He is author of *The Power of Consciousness and the Force of Circumstances in Sartre's Philosophy* (1990) and essays on contemporary continental philosophy published in a wide range of scholarly journals. He is editor of *The Participant Perspective: A Gabriel Marcel Reader* (1987) and coeditor of *Merleau-Ponty, Hermeneutics, and Postmodernism* (1992). He is writing a book on existentialism and postmodernism.

David S. Ferris is Associate Professor of Comparative Literature at Queens College and the Graduate Center, City University of New York. The author of *Theory and the Evasion of History* (1993) and the editor of *Walter Benjamin: Theoretical Questions* (1995), he is completing books on the relation of politics to aesthetics after Kant and on the aestheticization of Greek art and history within Romanticism and German Idealism.

Bernard Flynn is Professor of Philosophy at the State University of New York, Empire State College, New York City. He has taught at Southern Illinois University, Concordia University (Montreal), Skidmore College, l'École des Hautes Études (Paris), and The Institute of Philosophy (Leuven). He has written extensively in the fields of phenomenology, history of philosophy, and political philosophy. He recently published a book with Humanities Press entitled *Political Philosophy at the Closure of Metaphysics*. He is writing a book-length study on the thought of Claude Lefort.

Shaun Gallagher, Professor of Philosophy at Canisius College and recently Visiting Scholar at the MRC Applied Psychology Unit at Cambridge University, is author of *Hermeneutics and Education* (1992) and various essays on contemporary continental philosophy. He is coeditor of *Merleau-Ponty, Hermeneutics, and Postmodernism* (1992), editor of *Hegel and Hermeneutics* (forthcoming), and is completing a book entitled *The Inordinance of Time*.

Leonard Lawlor is Associate Professor of Philosophy at the University of Memphis. He is the author of *Imagination and Chance: The Difference between the Thought of Ricoeur and Derrida* (1992). He is writing a book on Derrida's interpretation of Husserl which will be called *The Basic Problem of Phenomenology*, as well as translating Jean Hyppolite's *Logique et existence*.

G. B. Madison is Professor of Philosophy at McMaster University, Hamilton, Canada, and has taught at the University of Paris and the University of Toronto (Graduate Faculty). He is author of *La phénoménologie de Merleau-Ponty: une recherche des limites de la conscience* (1973; English translation 1981), *Understanding: A Phenomenological-Pragmatic analysis* (1982), *The Logic of Liberty* (1986), and *The Hermeneutics of Postmodernity: Figures and Themes* (1988); he is also editor of *Sens et existence* (1975) and *Working Through Derrida* (1993). He is a founding member of The Canadian Society for Hermeneutics and Postmodern Thought, which he directed from 1984 to 1989.

Joseph Margolis is Professor of Philosophy at Temple University. He has recently completed a trilogy, *The Persistence of Reality*. Vol. 1, *Pragmatism without Foundations: Reconciling Realism and Relativism*; Vol. 2, *Science without Unity: Reconciling the Natural and Human Sciences*; Vol. 3, *Texts without Referents: Reconciling Science and Narrative*. The trilogy has expanded to a quartet with the appearance of Vol. 4, *Life without Principles: Reconciling Theory and Practice*. He has also recently completed a short volume, *The Truth about Relativism*, and is at work on a systematic account of metaphysics.

Glen A. Mazis is Assistant Professor of Philosophy and Humanities at Penn State Harrisburg in a senior level interdisciplinary humanities and master's program. He is author of *Emotion and Embodiment: Fragile Ontology* (1993), *The Trickster, Magician, and Grieving Man: Reconnecting Men with Earth* (1994), and many essays in journals and books on Merleau-Ponty, Sartre, Heidegger, and issues in aesthetics. Works in progress include two books, *Earthbodies* and *Moving Earth*.

Dennis T. O'Connor was born and raised in St. Louis. He completed his bachelor's and doctoral degrees at St. Louis University, where amid his studies in philosophy of science he was introduced to the work of Merleau-Ponty by Alden Fisher. The latter also introduced him to Herbert Spiegelberg by way of his phenomenological workshop. He has taught at Loyola College and Concordia University in Montreal, since 1968, and has been a member of the Merleau-Ponty Circle since 1971.

Dorothea Olkowski is Associate Professor of Philosophy and Director of Women's Studies at the University of Colorado, Colorado Springs. She is coeditor of *Gilles Deleuze and the Theatre of Philosophy* (1994) and has published widely in scholarly journals and edited collections on various topics in recent continental thought, feminism, and aesthetics.

Hugh J. Silverman is Professor of Philosophy and Comparative Literature at the State University of New York at Stony Broook. He has held visiting appointments at New York University, Duquesne, Nice (France), Warwick and Leeds (U.K.), Torino (Italy), and Vienna (Austria), and is Executive Director of the International Association for Philosophy and Literature. He is author of *Inscriptions: Between Phenomenology and Structuralism* (1987) and *Textualities: Between Hermeneutics and Deconstruction* (1994), as well as numerous articles, essays, and book chapters in continental philosophy, aesthetics, and literary theory. Silverman is editor or coeditor of eighteen volumes, including most recently *Textualität der Philosophie—Philosophie und Literatur* (1994) and *Merleau-Ponty: Texts and Dialogues* (Humanities Press, 1992), and is editor of the Humanities Press "Philosophy and Literary Theory" series, coeditor of the Humanities Press "Contemporary Studies in Philosophy and the Human Sciences" series, and editor of the Routledge "Continental Philosophy" series.

Robert Vallier is writing a dissertation entitled "The Flesh of God: The Concept of Nature in Merleau-Ponty and Schelling" at DePaul University in Chicago. His M.A. thesis was devoted to a careful reading of Derrida's *Memoirs of the Blind* and its relation to the work of Merleau-Ponty.

Wilhelm S. Wurzer, Professor of Philosophy at Duquesne University, received his doctorate from the University of Freiburg. He is author of *Nietzsche und Spinoza* (1975) and *Filming and Judgment* (1990). He has written numerous articles and chapters in books on Nietzsche, Heidegger, and Adorno. He is editing a book, *Visibility and Expressivity*, and has recently completed a critique of sigetics from Kant to Lyotard entitled *The Ends of In-Difference*.

Subject Index

106; and cognition, 126
apparition, 10
appropriation: as belonging, 2
arché-writing, 84, 99, 115, 138,
223; and *différance*, 21; and
time, 140; as unified movement,
226; infrastructure of, 226
art, ix, 104; and being, 104; and
capital, 242; and *écart*, 242
artist: as postmodern, 208
Aufklärung. See Enlightenment
auteur, 58–59; as speaker, 51; as
writer, 51; as perpetrator, 51
auteur theory, xii
authorship, 177
auto-affection, 99; and ideal
meaning, 83; and difference, 83;
and voice, 84; and pure
difference dividing self-presence,
84; as writing, 84; and
dehiscence, 154
auto-apparition, 10
autochthonous, 6
avant-garde (the), 209; and the
modern, 210; and the classical,
210; and the postmodern, 210;
as coup d'etat, 210; as
surrealism and surrealist
painting, 212
awareness: and body, 152

Bahnung (path-breaking, *frayage*),
13
becoming: and perceiving, 170;
and flesh of world, 187
beginning (the), 141
being (Being), xiii, 1–3, 13, 52, 72,
100, 122, 141, 150, 155, 221,
224–25; and history, xv; as
ground of beings, 1; house of, 1;
unity of, 2; presence of, 2; and
sameness, 2; as presence, 3–4;
as presence via appropriation, 4;
perception of, 4; and
transcendental subjectivity, 4;
and thinking, 14; and language,
14; and humanity, 14; as
diacritically structured field, 24;
field of as syntax, 24;
hiddenness of, 24; and *écart*, 26,

67; as dimensionality, 26;
reversibility of, 26; and the
invisible, 26; ecology of, 27;
consciousness as interrogative
mode of, 67; and presence to
self, 67; and self, 67; and self-
transcendence, 67; and self-
differentiation, 67; as
conditioned, 67; as condition,
67; and predication, 68; and
vision, 68; voice of, 69; as
playful logos, 69; and
consciousness, 69; as invisible
of visible, 69; *différance* as older
than truth of, 72; as flesh, 73; as
verticle, 73; and the negative,
74; and experience, 74; and
non-coincidence, 75; as not the
immediate, 75; and fusion, 76;
and partial coincidence, 76;
language as witness of, 77;
beyond of, 79, 84; and writing,
84; and form, 84–85; vs. writing,
85; and content, 86; and
possibility, 86; and art, 104; and
philosophy, 104, 122; and latent
intentionality, 125; as field, 126;
as fields, 126; and the
imaginary, 126; general manner
of emblematic as flesh, 126; in
beings, 127; and historicity, 161;
and truth, 168, 172; reason for,
168; as abstracted, 169; and
punctum caecum, 201; play of
différance as prior to, 223; chain
of infrastructures as older than,
228; and capital, 234; chiasm of,
240
being-toward-death, 186; and
writing, 183
beings, 1, 4; and being (Being), 1;
within being, 127
beliefs: as constructs, 162
believing: and seeing, 192
belonging: ontological priority of, 2
beyond, 6; as feigned reference, 7
binocular vision: and perception,
142; and vision, 142; as effaced,
142; and *écart*, 142. *See also*
physiological diplopia

constancy, hypothesis of, 222
constituting subject: rejection of shared by *écart* and *différance*, xvi
constituting subjectivity: as nonexistent, 137
constructs: as verbal, 162; of beliefs, 162
content, xi
continental philosophy, 3, 112
contingency: and societal practices, 112; and truth, 112
copula, 173
corporeal schema: as operative meaning, 143; as foundation of space and time, 143; and perception and imperception, 143; and thematized meaning, 143; and the past, 143–44; and recollection, 144; as innate, 144; and evolution, 144; and the pre-noetic, 145
cosmology, 123
critical enterprise: and naivete of its language, 160; as juridical, 160; as transcendental, 160; as vulnerable, 160
cultural identity, 230
cultural minus position, 230
culture, 120; as identity, 218; as subject, 218; as different with itself, 218; as not identical with itself, 218
Cyclops, 169–71; as monocular Western philosophical tradition, 168

Dasein, 123; ontological structure of 122; and ego, 122
death: as absence/break in presence, 81; of subjects through writing, 81; and writing, 84, 176, 181; as sheer presence, 178; and *différance*, 179; and signifiers, 179; as impending, 179–80; and text, 179; as answered in death, 181; as dissemination, 183; "no" of, 186; as going under, 186; as silence, 186; sensing of, 186;

and the body as nobody, 186; and birth as pre-personal horizon, 187; and openness of world, 187; and knowing, 187; and perception, 187; and sensation, 187; and hyper-reflection, 228
decentering: and meaning, 34
deception: and thinking, 40
deconstruction, xi, 32–33, 45, 97, 100, 118, 121, 220; and metaphysical presence, xiii; presupposing a subject, xiii; as reduction of meaning, 20; as grammatological reduction, 20; as undercutting primordial givenness, 20; as emancipation, 21; as liberation praxis in textual operation, 22; and phenomenology, 45; and presence, 45; as dead-end, 104; and truth, 105; error of, 105; and aporia, 106; and semiological reduction 106; as not a philosophy, 115–16; as parasitic strategy, 115; and skepticism, 115; as strategy, 116; strategies of, 117; and first philosophy, 122; and negative philosophy, 128; and time, 134; and conception of constitution, 137; of dualism, 170; and inability to think identity, 231
deferral: and *différance*, 63
dehiscence, 102, 128, 156; as presence, xii; and play of *différance*, 63; and rift, 67; and flesh, 126; and auto-affection, 154
delay, 156; as philosophical absolute, 161
democracy, 100, 230
destiny, 156
diachronic, xii
diachronic events, 47
diachronic linguistics, 224
diacritical language, 55
diacritical theoretics, 46
diacriticality, xii, 5; and presence, 10
diacritics, 86

ur-phenomenology, 121
origination, 10, 59; as *écart*, 11
other (Other), 125, 129–30; as
reduction to same, 22; as
infinitely other, 22–23; and
Stephen Dedalus, 174; and
Leopold Bloom, 174
outside: as "not," 172; as
redemptive, 179

painter, 36–37; and writer, 34; eye
of as inhabiting texture, 195
painting, 40, 52; as speaking, 38;
reversibility, 38; limit of, in
discourse, 40; discourse on, 41;
and writing, 41; self-reflection of
itself, 41; and language, 53; and
enigma of invisibility, 195; as
commemorating invisible of
visible, 201
particularity, 232
passage: as neither rest nor
movement, 180
passivity, 154
past, 104; and retention, 143; and
perception, 143; as extra-
intentional, 143; and corporeal
schema, 144; as pre-noetic, 144;
and present, 144; and *écart*,
144; as evolution, 145; as trace
effect, 145
path-breaking (*frayage*, *Bahnung*),
13
perceived, 129–30
perceived world: meaning of as
foundational, 5; as silent, 127;
as indeterminate, 222
perceiving, 129–30; and becoming,
170
perception, 4, 13, 23, 97–98, 124,
127, 140, 150, 153, 191, 221;
and presence of being, 4; and
différance, 5; and vision, 5; and
écart, 5, 7, 186; and chiasm, 7;
and reversibility, 7; *ek-stasis* of,
7; the *écart* of figure-ground
divergence, 10; as diacritical,
25; as inseparable from
consciousness, 31; as separation,
41; as diacritical, relative, and

oppositional system, 53; and
language, 53, 99, 101; and
fusion, 76; and partial
coincidence, 76; and experience,
99, 101; and sense, 113; and
mediation of senses as causal,
113; and the cogito, 129; and
binocular vision, 142; and
imperception, 143; and the past,
143; and the world, 151; and
cognition, 168; and relation to
reality, 175; and flesh, 182; as
groping never reaching closure,
186; and death, 187; as
phenomenological concept, 192;
as visual, and skepticism, 192;
as sacrificed, 195; as
commemorated in writing, 195;
and style, 198; and real world,
222; and perceived world, 222;
as determinate, 222; as
indeterminate, 222
perceptual competence, 122
perceptual consciousness, 113
perceptual experience; and
thinking, 114; and societal
cognizing practices, 114
perceptual faith, 74; forgetfulness
of, 77; and resistance to
mortality, 183
perceptual horizon, 5
perceptual presence, xi; as
decentered, xi; as denied, xi;
figure of as irreducibly complex,
9; and gestalt, 9
phallocentrism, 8
pharmakon, 177
phenomenality: as condition for
facticity and situatedness, 23
phenomenological consciousness,
57
phenomenological reflection, 145
phenomenological reduction, 12,
20, 24
phenomenological universality,
121
phenomenology, xiv, 12, 53, 95,
97–98, 100–101, 106, 114,
117–18, 122, 124, 126–27, 129,
137, 140–41, 143, 150, 153, 156,

écart, 142; as human, 155; primordial absolute of, 158
tenses: and subject, 103
text, 81, 138, 180, 238; as self, 102; as having nothing outside of, 116; as reality, 139; and time, 139; and trace, 172; and death, 179; and non-presence, 179; and writing, styling, 203; as event, 208; and flesh, 234
textualism, 96; and idealism, 139
textuality, 220; and the visual, 33; and the pre-noetic force of language, 146; and *différance*, 237
Thanatos, 183
thankfulness, 150
theology, 223
there is, xvi, 227; and *écart*, xvi, 228; and *différance*, xvi; of the world, 223; and play of difference, 225; and hyper-reflection, 118; as irreducible contingency, 231
thing(s), 23, 124; in itself as partial coincidence, 9; in itself, 46; as inter-sensory entity, 129; as ready-to-hand, 162; and abyss between it and representation, 197
thinker: as detached, 169
thinking, 68, 152; and being, 14; and deception, 40; and perceptual experience, 114; and societal cognizing practices, 114
thought, 3–4, 36, 127; and presence, 4; as vision, 41; ethics of, 59; as differentiation, 59; history of, 73; and reality, 95; and representation, 95; and universals, 119; dominating mode of, 121; domain of, 124; and immediacy, 160; thought of as writing, 177; thought of as thought, 179
time, ix, xiv, 171, 176, 238; and *écart*, xiv, 141, 143, 150, 241; and *différance*, xiv, 61, 134, 135, 138; as transcendent consciousness, xiv; as history,

xiv; metamorphosis of, 61; and subject, 64; and object, 64; and presence, 64; and consciousness, 134, 145; metaphysics of, 134; as produced by human consciousness, 134; and objective reality, 134; conception of, 134; reality or unreality of, 135; textuality of, 135; and language, 139; as independent of consciousness, 139; as not real, 139, 146; and writing, 139; as dependent on arche-writing, 140; as subject, 140; and embodiment, 143; as transcending consciousness, 144; and the pre-noetic, 144; and textuality, 145; ontological status of, 146; and *écart* with body, 146; flesh of, 146; as psychological, 146; as transcendental, 146; as unreflected, 146; as subject, 154; and being, 155; as human, 155; and ontology, 155; as not irreversible, 180; and capital, 241
time-consciousness, 120, 137, 140, 142; language as transcending, 139
totality, 62; as modern, 215
trace, 24, 41, 59, 103; and retention, 136; and living present, 136; and *différance*, 136; and transcendental phenomenology, 137; as retentional, 138; of signifier, 169; as originary, 171, 172; presence/absence of, 171; play of, 171; and text, 172; and erasure of self, as death, 183; of trait in drawing, 199; as unified movement, 226; infrastructure of, 226
trace$_1$ (erased trace), 5
trace$_2$ (trace of erased trace), 5
tradition: monovision of (as dualism), 169; and presence, 171; and eternity, 171
trait, as elusive, 194; as drawn,

Name Index